# ON THE SHORT WAVES, 1923–1945

# ON THE SHORT WAVES, 1923–1945

## Broadcast Listening in the Pioneer Days of Radio

*by* Jerome S. Berg

McFarland & Company, Inc., Publishers

*Jefferson, North Carolina, and London*

*This is a reprint of the illustrated casebound edition of*
On the Short Waves, 1923–1945:
Broadcast Listening in the Pioneer Days of Radio,
*first published in 1999 by McFarland.*

LIBRARY OF CONGRESS CATALOGUING-IN-PUBLICATION DATA

Berg, Jerome S., 1943–
On the short waves, 1923–1945 : broadcast listening in the
pioneer days of radio / by Jerome S. Berg.
p.    cm.
Includes bibliographical references and index.

ISBN-13: 978-0-7864-3029-1
(softcover : 50# alkaline paper) ∞

1. Shortwave radio—History.   2. International broadcasting—
History.   I. Title.
TK6547.B425   2007        384.54—dc21        98-44921

British Library cataloguing data are available

On the front cover: Detail from cover of *The Official Short Wave
Listener* magazine (February-March 1935)

Manufactured in the United States of America

*McFarland & Company, Inc., Publishers
Box 611, Jefferson, North Carolina 28640
www.mcfarlandpub.com*

*To Jack Jones*
who was there when it started
(and still remembers most of it)

and

*to P.V.*
who has always been there

# CONTENTS

# Abbreviations

ABSIE American Broadcasting Station in Europe
AFRS Armed Forces Radio Service
ARRL American Radio Relay League
AVC automatic volume control
BBCMS BBC Monitoring Service
BCB broadcast band
BCL broadcast listener
BFEBS British Far East Broadcasting Service
BFO beat frequency oscillator
CIAA Coordinator of Inter-American Affairs
COI Coordinator of Information
CPRV Committee to Preserve Radio Verifications
CQD Early SOS signal
DX long-distance reception; DXer, DXing
EIAR Ente Italiano Audizione Radiofoniche (station I2RO in Rome)
FBIS Foreign Broadcast Intelligence Service, Foreign Broadcast Information Service
FIS Foreign Information Service

FRENDX Bulletin of the North American Shortwave Association
IBC International Broadcasting Company
IDA International DXers Alliance
IF intermediate frequency
IIIS Interim International Information Service
ISWC International Short Wave Club
MW medium wave
NNRC Newark News Radio Club
NRC National Radio Club
OSS Office of Strategic Services
OSWL *Official Short Wave Listener*
OWI Office of War Information
QRM interference
QSL telegraph term to acknowledge receipt
RADEX *Radio Index*
RF radio frequency
RSSL Radio Signal Survey League
SW shortwave
SWBC shortwave broadcast
SWL shortwave listener
TRF tuned radio frequency
URDXC Universal Radio DX Club

# PREFACE

THE STORY OF AM BROADCASTING has been told many times, as has the story of amateur radio, where ham operators talk to each other over the airwaves. And while the tea leaves of history still prompt occasional debates over some of the finer points, both the general contours and the details of these subjects are now well established.

Much less well known is the history of shortwave broadcasting, which was, to varying degrees, the progeny of both AM broadcasting and ham radio. Shortwave broadcasting is the transmission of news and entertainment programs over shortwave frequencies that permit reception over great distances. To the extent that the shortwave broadcasting story has been told at all, it has been done in either very small pieces or with an emphasis unrelated to what should be its main focus—the listeners who actually tuned in. Shortwave broadcasting gave birth to a special aspect of the radio listening culture that survives to this day: a body of enthusiastic shortwave listeners—some who tune the bands to enjoy the programming, and others whose main interest is DX, or long-distance reception, pursued mainly for the thrill of the hunt. The purpose of this book is to relate the story of the rise of shortwave broadcasting and the listener community that was attracted to it.

For most present-day shortwave aficionados, shortwave history is whatever happened before *they* got into it. In my case that was 1958. I have been an active shortwave fan for most of the years since. However, my interest in shortwave broadcasting's *history* dates from 1986. In that year, the Association of North American Radio Clubs, an umbrella organization of shortwave listener clubs, sponsored a project called the Committee to Preserve Radio Verifications. The purpose of the CPRV was to preserve for future research and enjoyment the cards and letters that stations sent, and still send, to listeners as verification of their reception based on the listener's description of what he or she heard. These verifications are called QSLs, the telegraph term meaning to acknowledge receipt.

I was appointed chair of the committee, and consequently, oldtime radio listeners and their families started sending me QSLs from broadcasting stations of the 1930s and 1940s. Despite my familiarity with the shortwave scene, these QSLs were new to me. Here were important radio mementos from long ago, artifacts that captured both the fact and the flavor of early radio broadcasting. I began attending antique radio club meets as well as paper and ephemera shows, searching out old shortwave magazines and memorabilia. It was there that I began finding information on the stations, equipment, names, and events of shortwave broadcasting's past, all of which at last came together to form this book.

This concise history covers the period from shortwave's prehistory—the early 1900s—to approximately 1945, a more or less arbitrary point of demarcation between radio's early phase and the more modern post–World War II era. Except for chapters 1, 2, 10, and 11, the book concentrates on the 1930s, which was the heart of the medium's early development.

I have tried to make the book both accurate and comprehensive, though of course it cannot be an exhaustive study of the subject. While some professional sources have yielded valuable information, my research is based primarily on popular sources from shortwave's early era, sources that convey the romance and adventure that has always made the shortwave spectrum unique. The illustrations that accompany the text are an important part of the story. I wish I could have included many more.

Because shortwave broadcasting and shortwave broadcast DXing trace their origins to the early days of medium-wave broadcasting and amateur radio, the reader will find some treatment of these subjects (from an American perspective) when it is relevant to the discussion. A familiarity with the very early days of radio in general, and the growth of broadcast-band listening in particular, is necessary to a full understanding of shortwave broadcasting's early development.

In order to preserve a bit of the flavor of radio's early days, I have at times used conventions that were well known to early radio enthusiasts, and that will still be familiar to their modern-day counterparts who know something of long distance listening: for example, SWBC for shortwave broadcast, and BCB (broadcast band) or MW (medium wave) for the standard AM broadcast band. "Shortwave" usually appears as one word today, but early radio literature invariably had it as two, sometimes hyphenated, sometimes not. In the 1920s and 1930s, frequency ranges were spoken of in terms of wavelength (meters), not frequency (kilocycles). Wavelength decreases as frequency increases: the higher the frequency, the lower the wavelength. Thus, while the shortwave spectrum is today thought of as being "above" the standard AM broadcast band in frequency, in the 1920s and 1930s it was usually referred to as being "below" the lower BCB frequencies.

The reader will also note the use of "kilocycles" rather than the more modern "kilohertz" that replaced it in the mid–1960s. Kilohertz just doesn't seem appropriate to a discussion of shortwave history. I agree with medium-wave DXer Dick Cooper, who said, "[D]amn the college guy who changed [kilocycles] to kiloHertz! Some smart-aleck from MIT, I suppose. You had a good word there, and it's self-explanatory for guys like me; I can understand it. I know who Hertz was; he didn't deserve the honor any more than the rest of us."[1]

The history of shortwave broadcasting, particularly as viewed from the perspective of popular culture, is to be found mostly in the basements and attics of practitioners, not on library shelves. Much of the impetus for this book came from the many serious radio hobbyists who, over the last 13 years, donated their QSL collections to the CPRV, awakening in the author an interest in shortwave broadcasting history. Well-known shortwave DXers past and present like August Balbi, Ed Bellington, Anson Boice, Roger Legge, Al Niblack, and Ray LaRocque, and renowned medium-wavers like Eugene Allen, Frank DeMacedo, Art Hankins, John Tweedie, and Carroll Weyrich are thus the principal godfathers of this book. No less important are the many collectors and dealers from whom, over the years, I have been able to obtain the material upon which many of my observations are based.

At closer range, I would like to express thanks to John H. Bryant, Harold N. Cones and David M. Clark, longtime observers of and participants in the shortwave broadcasting scene. They are authors themselves, and, most importantly, they are friends of long standing. It was through their encouragement, and their advocacy for recording this largely unrecognized part of radio history, that this book came to be. Special thanks are also due to radio professionals Paul A. Karagianis and Lou Josephs, whose keen analytical talents (along with those of John Bryant) were applied to the text, reminding me that I wasn't as smart as I thought.

Because QSLs are among the few remaining direct mementos of early radio stations, and because they usually evince something of the station's character, the reader will find the text liberally illustrated with them. Most of them are from the collection of the CPRV. The other illustrations are from my personal collection of early radio memorabilia. I would like to thank Ziff-Davis Publishing Company and Gernsback Publications, Inc., for permission to reprint graphics from various early radio magazines, such as *All-Wave Radio, Official Short Wave Listener, Radio News, Radio Craft*, and *Short Wave Craft*, the ownership trails of which eventually lead to either Gernsback or Ziff-Davis.

The search for history is a continuing process. The author welcomes corrections of fact or interpretation, as well as comments and information, from those who share his interest in the subject.

*Part I*

# THE EARLY DAYS

## Chapter 1

# BROADCASTING ROOTS

EXPLORING SHORTWAVE BROADCASTING and the shortwave broadcast DXing of the 1930s and 1940s requires passing through broadcasting's earliest portals. Because things were so different then, a little stage setting is in order.

## Before 1912

Although we commonly think of broadcasting as starting with KDKA in 1920, the history of radio itself goes back much farther. The pre–1912 radio landscape was strewn with many now obscure devices, such as the spark gap transmitter, the coherer and the decoherer, the audion, and the variocoupler. It was typified as well by fierce personal and professional competition among their inventors. The development of the "Hertzian waves," as radio's emanations were first called, is a tale of entrepreneurship, corporate intrigue, and personal egos as well as technical advancements. The marketplace was a frontier. Companies came and went, along with patent battles, lawsuits, stock swindles, and publicity campaigns designed to convince a skeptical public that this or that person was the true inventor of a new and potentially profitable radio-related product, and thus deserving of a place in history.

The inventors and their wireless companies, such as Fessenden's National Electric Signalling Company, and the various Marconi and De Forest companies, were key players. In addition to vying for a competitive advantage, they were out to prove the usefulness and commercial viability of the new medium. Two other important participants in radio's early development were the U.S. Navy—the first major organization to integrate radio into its work (and a persistent and nearly successful force for government monopoly of the entire medium)—and the amateurs—or "experimenters"—who were in the game for the fun of it and to see how far they could push the technology involved.

While there are some other candidates, if anyone can justly claim the title "Father of Radio," it is Guglielmo Marconi. In some respects he was also the first DXer, since he was constantly trying to increase the range of his early transmissions. It was Marconi who, on December 12, 1901, bridged the Atlantic by wireless for the first time with the now famous "S" transmission from Cornwall, England, to St. Johns, Newfoundland, where he had rigged a receiver to an antenna held aloft by a kite.

Combining the confidence of a self-taught experimenter with the promotional skill of a successful entrepreneur, Marconi was more interested in the commercial possibilities of wireless than its theory. He formed his first company, the Wireless Telegraph and Signal Company, in England in 1897. Within a few years, European steamship companies were installing Marconi equipment for communication with Marconi shore stations. He gained fame in the United States by using his equipment to report the international yacht races in New York in October 1899, announcing the winners even before the ships had returned to port. The Marconi policy of leasing rather than selling equipment, supplying Marconi-paid operators aboard ships, and refusing to communicate with ships carrying competing equipment, is an example of technology's early purported need for a "systems" approach. Although these anticompetitive policies could not be sustained over the long run, Marconi's American company eventually became the cornerstone of the world's biggest radio monopoly, the Radio Corporation of America.

Another famous inventor was Canadian-born Reginald, A. Fessenden. A professor of engineering and former employee of both Thomas Edison and Marconi, Fessenden created the electrolytic detector. More importantly, he was an early proponent of continuous waves, as distinguished from the surging, intermittent "damped" waves of the spark gap transmitters of the day. Using a specially built General Electric alternator designed by Dr. Ernst F. W. Alexanderson and operating at ten times the speed of the fastest alternators theretofore in existence, he produced a current that oscillated much more rapidly than spark. This permitted the relatively efficient transmission of voice signals for the first time. Fessenden is usually credited with the first experimental voice program, transmitted on Christmas Eve in 1906. He was also probably the first to request and receive reception reports for voice transmissions. "Those listening [on Christmas Eve] were asked to write to R. A. Fessenden at Brant Rock, Massachusetts [the location of his station], and many seem to have done so."[1]

The problem with alternators was that they could not produce signals on frequencies above 50–80 kc. The use of higher frequency broadcasting necessary for long distance communication would require an entirely different concept of radio signal creation. Enter Dr. Lee De Forest and Edwin H. Armstrong. The enigmatic De Forest was both one of the greatest and the oddest of the radio pioneers. He was the creator in 1906 of the audion, or three-element (triode) vacuum tube, which added a grid mechanism that greatly increased the plate voltage in the tube. The resulting device served both as a better detector, and an amplifier, of signals (particularly when the tubes were connected in parallel), and was the key to producing the kind of continuous waves that were necessary for effective voice transmission. As much a publicist as a scientist, De Forest was often perceived—to put it charitably—as a borrower of others' ideas, which he then refashioned, improved upon, and called his own. It was Marconi's chief engineer, John Ambrose Fleming, who in 1904 had invented the Fleming valve, or two-element radio tube (diode), based in large part on Thomas Edison's discovery that a current would run between two filaments when each was lit. It is said that, having built on Fleming's work in developing the audion, De Forest did not know how or why it worked. He was repeatedly discredited through the financial frauds and stock swindles of his business partners, and generally gave the appearance of cashing in at others' expense.

A postcard view of the Fessenden wireless facility, Brant Rock, Massachusetts, from which the first experimental voice transmissions were made (postmark 1906).

Edwin H. Armstrong was an early radio inventor who never received the credit he deserved. It is to him that DXers owe the most. Despite Supreme Court cases giving the favorable decision to De Forest, Armstrong is universally credited with the discovery (at age 21) of the principle of regeneration, a revolutionary technique that multiplied the amplification of an electronic circuit many times over and generated oscillations that could make the radio tube into a transmitting as well as a receiving device. It permitted Fleming's and De Forest's inventions to achieve their full potential. Again, legal decisions to the contrary notwithstanding, Major Armstrong (so commissioned in World War I) is also widely acknowledged as the inventor of superheterodyne radio technology. The superhet was perhaps the most extraordinary advance in radio, and the one that has had the greatest longevity.[2] And if these accomplishments were not enough, Armstrong also invented FM broadcasting. His story is one of extraordinary highs and lows, and a life constantly embroiled in litigation (and finally ending in suicide).

**Columbia University**
**in the City of New York**

DEPARTMENT OF ELECTRICAL ENGINEERING

June 6, 1941.

Mr. Peter A. Clarius,
11 Marianne Street,
Port Richmond, Staten Island,
New York.

Dear Mr. Clarius:

        I am glad to confirm your
reception of W2XMN.

        At the present time the
station has no news period or commentators,
but will shortly.  The schedule is:

  Mondays thru Fridays- 11 am to 2 pm;
                     4 pm to 11 pm.

  Saturdays and Sundays- 11 am to 11 pm.

        Trusting this will answer your
question,

           Very sincerely yours,

*Edwin H. Armstrong*

           Edwin H. Armstrong.

eha:s

P.S.-  I think I can assure you that if you use
the proper kind of FM receiver you will have no
interference of any kind whatsoever.

The father of FM broadcasting, Major Armstrong would occasionally verify reception of his own FM station, W2XMN, personally. Armstrong was a graduate of, and had a long affiliation with, Columbia University (QSL, 1941).

From the radio operator's point of view, things were not regulated or controlled before 1912, especially among the transmitting amateurs, to whom belongs most of the credit for the later development of short-wave. These were the days before licenses and call signs. You chose a few letters of the alphabet (often your initials) and commenced operation, which usually meant sending code to other amateurs over varying distances from a few to 100 miles. The only sender available at first was the spark gap transmitter, a device that was used untuned until around 1904. An untuned spark transmitter sent out electrical waves in random patterns, the resulting wavelength being largely a matter of accident. The subsequent tuned sparks did a little better, but "choosing" a frequency on a spark transmitter was problematic at best.

It is hard to believe today that, until around 1920, virtually all transmitting, by everyone and for all purposes, both short range and long range, was in the frequencies *below* approximately 1500 kc., or the area that we think of today as the long- and medium-wave bands. This was partly the case because shorter waves were difficult to produce without tubes, which were still in their infancy. It was widely believed that these low frequencies were the only ones of value, and that higher-frequency channels, to the extent they could be reached at all, were either worthless for communication purposes or the lairs of technological dragons. As a result, huge generators, large antennas, and tremendous power were needed and utilized for long-distance communication on the lower frequencies. The belief that long distance required long wavelengths (that is, low frequencies) was one of the great scientific mistakes of radio's infancy.

## 1912–1919

The first major attempt to bring order to the radio spectrum was in 1912. Although there was still much argument over both the theory and usefulness of wireless, as a practical matter a high level of interference had developed, and it was getting worse. Huge transoceanic commercial stations carrying point-to-point messages had been erected in the United States, Europe, and elsewhere. There was much competition for the use of the airwaves between the amateurs and the commercial traffic stations, not all of it polite. To those who decry a perceived loss of personal civility in more contemporary times, it is worth noting that, in those supposedly better days, "[a]mateurs would send out fake orders to naval vessels, purporting to come from admirals; they broadcast false distress calls and had Coast Guard and other vessels running wildly about, trying to find the ship in distress…. There being no law to cover most of the amateurs' tricks, few or no police searches were made for them, and the names and locations of the worst offenders were unknown. When remonstrated with by air, these were apt to respond with curses and obscenity."[3]

Because shipboard safety was an important issue, ship-to-shore contact had become one of radio's major early uses. By 1904 the De Forest Company had marine stations in Buffalo, Cleveland, Detroit, and Chicago, and when they were taken over by United Wireless Telegraph Company in 1907 stations were added all along the Atlantic coast. Marconi had stations in Massachusetts and New York. The Wireless Ship Act of 1910 required every passenger vessel carrying 50 or more persons to have equipment that would transmit and receive over a distance of 100 miles. By 1912 over 250 ships had been equipped with radio apparatus. The number soon grew to 600. However, the cavalier attitude toward wireless on some vessels, including several that could have reduced the loss of life on the *Titanic*, plus the interference, rumors, and misleading messages from unknown sources that filled the air during that tragic event (the amateurs were suspected) engaged the public's interest and spurred the government to further action.

Despite antiregulatory lobbying by the wireless companies and the amateurs—both of whom were still relatively disorganized and ineffectual in terms of their influence on the government—Congress enacted the Radio Act of 1912. This

**Another postcard view, this one of the Marconi marine radio site in Wellfleet, Massachusetts (post-mark 1904).**

legislation was mainly maritime in nature, and did not even contemplate broadcasting as one of radio's uses. For the first time, wavelengths would be apportioned to particular services, a radical step at a time of minimalist government and free enterprise spirit. It required that stations and operators be licensed. From the standpoint of the later development of shortwave, its most important provision was to deny the amateurs the freedom to roam. In addition to having to obtain licenses—a constraint to which they adapted only slowly—the amateurs were, with some exceptions, restricted to the range below 200 meters (that is, above 1500 kc.), bands that were largely unexplored and thought to be of little value. The navy attributed most interference to the amateurs, and was happy to see them on the road to a hoped-for extinction. From the amateurs' point of view, their development of the shortwave spectrum began less as a love affair than a shotgun marriage. However, all that would change.

Between 1912 and 1920 the development of radio technology was monopolized by the military and the big corporations. There was huge growth in the amateur ranks as well, with the number of licensed amateurs growing from 322 in 1913 to over 10,000 in 1916. It was during these years that the first major radio amateur publishing efforts began. The American Marconi Company commenced publication of *Wireless Age* in 1913, and in 1915 the American Radio Relay League (ARRL)—a body organized to promote amateur radio—was formed and began publishing *QST* magazine. Not long before, the government and the ARRL had published the first amateur radio call books. These documents contained lists of licensed amateurs, revealing to the experimenters for the first time their actual numbers.

Although spark transmitters (and later arc senders) were the standard prior to World War I, they were fundamentally unsuitable for effective voice transmission. It was the development of transmitting tubes and amplitude modulation that permitted broadcasting as we know it. Of those amateurs who could obtain the necessary equipment, more and more were supplementing code with voice and occasional impromptu music broadcasting. The major radio interests considered such entertainment transmissions frivolous. This broadcasting persisted until April 6, 1917, when the amateur stations were closed down for the duration of World War I, not to reopen until September 1920 (the ban on amateur receiving was lifted a year earlier). Between 3,500 and 4,000 amateurs answered the wartime call for skilled radio operators.

## *1920 and After*

Spark gap and arc transmitters faded into history after the war, and the needs of the military transformed the radio business from a preserve of lone inventors to an industry dominated by large corporations. However, of greater importance to the development of shortwave were the amateurs. Those who were able to get their hands on the new (and expensive) transmitting tubes resumed talking over the air, occasionally playing a bit of music as well.

One of the most famous of the amateurs was Westinghouse engineer Frank Conrad, who had been an amateur operator before the war, having been assigned the call 8XK in 1916. Although the government suspended all amateur activities during the war, Westinghouse—as a result of its research work and the nation's wartime needs—was authorized to build and operate two special experimental stations, one at Conrad's home and the other at the Westinghouse plant. These were stations 2WM and 2WE respectively, and they permitted Conrad to continue his radio research during the war.

When Conrad resumed his amateur activities after the war, he would talk to other amateurs, play records, and even broadcast some live performances over his old 8XK station. Amateur stations were not assigned "W" and "K" prefixes until after the 1927 International Radiotelegraph Convention in Washington, DC. They were required to use the official W and K prefixes beginning on October 1, 1928. Before then, American hams sometimes used the informal prefix "U" for "USA" or "NU" for "North America–USA," followed by the district number and two or three letters.[4]

Frank Conrad, General Electric engineer and early shortwave experimenter (*Radio Craft*, June 1930).

In September 1920, in order to promote the sale of electronic gear, Pittsburgh's Joseph Horne department store ran an ad informing the public that radio sets capable of receiving Frank Conrad's programs were available. Westinghouse was the first to perceive a potential market in activities that went beyond merely the technically inclined customer. They authorized Conrad to build a more powerful transmitting station right at the Westinghouse plant. This was KDKA. Notwithstanding some earlier experimental broadcast programming by others (De Forest himself had operated an experimental broadcasting station in the Bronx in 1916), KDKA is generally acknowledged to be the oldest nonexperimental broadcaster, that is, the first station, still on the air, whose signal was intended for widespread reception by a nontechnical, general listening public, and it was promoted as such.[5] On November 2, 1920, KDKA made history by being the first radio station to carry the results of a presidential election (that of Warren G. Harding). The power at the time was 100 watts, which was soon to be increased to 500. It is estimated that about 50 people heard the broadcast.

Only nine additional stations were licensed between November 2, 1920, and December 31, 1921, but then the general public became enamored of the new medium and the radio business exploded. A new word was needed to describe what some thought would be just a fad. The familiar "wireless" and "radiotelephony" conjured up images of the telegraph and telephone, which were point-to-point media. So a term was borrowed from agriculture: "broadcasting," meaning to cast seeds widely.

By March 23, 1922, there were 98 licensed broadcasting stations. By August the number had grown to 253,[6] and by October 502.[7] Radio receivers sold as fast as they could be made. Receiver manufacturers recognized that a strong broadcasting industry was essential if receivers were to be sold, and so they became a major force in the development of broadcasting. Although a receiver industry shakeout followed, growth in the number of broadcasters was just beginning. The Department of Commerce, which was in charge of licensing, was receiving three or four license appli-

*Opposite:* KDKA, Pittsburgh, popularly regarded as the first American AM radio station, was first in American shortwave as well (QSL, 1923).

# [ K D K A ]

*"The Pioneer Radio Broadcasting Station of the World"*

EAST PITTSBURGH, PA.

May 15, 1923.

Mr. Samuel J. Murphy,
4640 Wyoming Avenue,
Frankford, Philadelphia, Pa.

Dear Radio Friend:

      In answer to your recent communi-
cation, we are glad to inform you that the
features which you heard were broadcasted
from KDKA - the Pioneer Radio Broadcasting
Station of the World, on the evening of
April 25th.

      Yours very truly,

*M. A. Hancock,*

H:IC           Westinghouse Station KDKA.

WESTINGHOUSE ELECTRIC AND MANUFACTURING COMPANY

**9WS**  **WBBZ**

**233 IOWA STREET** • • **INDIANAPOLIS, IND.**

An example of a station that operated sometimes as an amateur station (9WS) and sometimes as a broadcast station (WBBZ) (QSL, 1924).

cations a day, many from amateurs wishing to go from experimenter to regular broadcaster. Among the early station owners were radio and electrical manufacturers and dealers, newspapers, churches, department stores, municipalities, retailers, colleges, and the YMCA.[8]

In 1922 station WWJ in Detroit, the first station owned and operated by a newspaper (the *Detroit News*), described what had happened as follows:

> The dream of actual vocal contact between points far distant and without any tangible physical union had come true on an astonishingly large scale. The public of Detroit and its environs was on that date [August 31, 1920, the WWJ start-up date] made to realize that what had been a laboratory curiosity was to become a commonplace of everyday life, and that the future held extraordinary developments which would affect all society.... Soon reports commenced coming in from outlying communities that the concerts were being successfully received and enthusiastically enjoyed. The radio has become such a familiar affair in so short a space of time that it seems odd to consider how remarkable this was regarded at the time. The thing from the first held the element of magic. The local receiving set became the center of wondering interest in the little suburban towns.[9]

The programming of the time was pretty basic:

**360 Metres**
Illustrations Show Operating and Dynamo Rooms

**500 Watt**
**Western Electric Equipment**

## Program Schedule—Station W-J-A-R

| | 10-11 a. m. | 1.05-2.15 p. m. | 7-8 p. m. | 8.15 p. m. | 10.30-12 p. m. |
|---|---|---|---|---|---|
| SUNDAY | | | SPECIAL CONCERT 7.20 to 10.20 | | |
| MONDAY | Housewives Radio Exchange Music | Weather Report Music | Weather | | |
| TUESDAY | | Weather Report Music | Weather Musical Program | | |
| WEDNESDAY | Housewives Radio Exchange Music | Weather Report Music | Weather Musical Program | Special Concert | |
| THURSDAY | | Weather Report Music | Weather Musical Program | | |
| FRIDAY | Housewives Radio Exchange Music | Weather Report Music | Weather Musical Program | Special Concert | |
| SATURDAY | | Weather Report Music | Weather | | Musical Program |

This station acknowledges your correspondence and
trusts you will be a continued listener to our programs.

Very truly yours,    Station W-J-A-R,

"The Gateway to Southern New England"

PROVIDENCE, R. I.

This 1923 QSL from WJAR in Providence, Rhode Island, provided interior photos of the station as well as a program schedule.

[P]rograms consisted of anything at all to fill in time. Phonograph records were played and re-played. Poetry was recited, column upon column was read from the daily papers, then more records, perhaps a pianola roll for a change. On rare occasions a harmonica solo, then singing, comments on reception, new circuits, personal messages to other broadcasters who might be listening in, records again, more

You might get London, England
Havana or Peru,
But none will ring more clearly
Than my good wish for you!
Birthday Congratulations!

A Merry Christmas
You're in my Christmas circuit
And on the waves of thought
A Happy Christmas and New Year
To you is gladly brought.

The miracle of wireless communication led many to express their thoughts in rhyme, and use radio as part of a friendly greeting (postcards, undated).

From my very own
radio station
I am sending
a message to say
Good morning to you and how do you do?
Much better, I hope, to-day.
And isn't it fine to think
That regardless of pen or ink
A message straight to your heart from mine
Can go like a flash on our own private line?

Greetings for a Happy New Year

newspapers, poetry, a new pianola roll, finally the call letters, then the grind once more. Those were the amateur days of radio.[10]

Dial accuracy wasn't very important because all broadcasting was done on only *two* wavelengths. The main channel, 360 meters (833 kc.), was used for news, lectures, and entertainment. A second channel, 485 meters (619 kc.), was used for government-sponsored market and weather reports. Some stations used both frequencies. Channels were referred to by their wavelength, that is, in meters, not kilocycles.

As power increased from the initial levels of 10–50 watts in most cases, so did

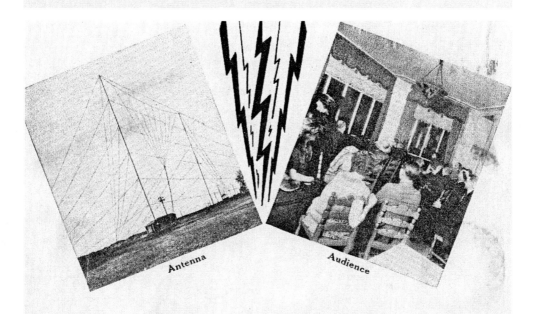

Antenna

Audience

STRUCTURAL DATA — STATION WJAZ

Height of Towers — 175 feet...........................................

Generator Power — 10 kilowatts at 4,000 volts....................

Type of Antenna — 8 wire vertical fan with cage lead in..........

Antenna Insulation— Porcelain throughout........................

Type of Ground — Insulated counterpoise........................

Microphones — Special Zenith design stretched diaphragm type.

Wave Length — 448 meters ...............................

**ZENITH**

**EDGEWATER BEACH HOTEL**
RADIO BROADCASTING STATION

**WJAZ**

ON THE LAKE 5349 SHERIDAN ROAD
CHICAGO, ILLINOIS

The Zenith station, WJAZ, Chicago, Illinois (QSL, 1923). This is the last page of a 5-page brochure describing the station ("not only the most powerful, but also the finest and most elaborate broadcasting station in the world").

The QSL from WJAZ included this shot of the station's Crystal Studio, a glass-encased facility that allowed the public to "witness and enjoy the broadcasting as it is actually being done in plain view."

interference ("QRM" as the telegraphers put it). A listener described reception on 360 meters this way: "In regard to the broadcasting wavelengths, cannot something be done? Monday night, April 3 [1922], I invited a few friends to listen to KDKA.... I just got him nicely tuned in, and in came WWJ, and in a few minutes along came KYW, and I could not tune them out because they were all on 360 meters.... Why can't the different broadcasting stations split up on a five meter difference?"[11]

The problem was partially addressed in August 1922 when a special "Class B" license was authorized for "super" broadcasters, the larger, well-established stations that could meet more stringent technical requirements and that featured high-class entertainment ("mechanical music" was forbidden).[12] Class B stations operated on 400 meters (750 kc.) with a required power of 500–1,000 watts.

However, the interference wasn't eliminated. Within a few months congestion had developed on 400 meters in the large population centers. Voluntary time sharing was instituted, but with limited results. Some stations changed their frequency at will (if their primitive equipment could be made to stay on frequency at all). In May 1923, after the navy agreed to release some of its frequencies, a broadcast band extending from 550 to 1350 (soon 1500) kc. was established, with stations classified according to power, frequency, and type of programming.

In 1926 the authority of the secretary of commerce to allocate frequencies was successfully challenged in court by Zenith station WJAZ. This was a discretionary power that the secretary had exercised since 1912 in conjunction with a series of national radio conferences attended by representatives of various branches of the radio industry. WJAZ wanted to use a frequency that had been allocated to Canadian stations (910 kc.), instead of accepting what it viewed as an inequitable time-sharing arrangement on 930 kc. The courts held that the Radio Act of 1912 contained no express grant of regulatory power to the secretary of commerce, and that he was *required* to issue licenses subject only to whatever specific provisions were contained within the act itself. He could not, for example, specify wavelengths or limit power.

The decision resulted in a temporary moratorium of station licensing, and a general free-for-all. Stations took to the air without benefit of license and changed frequency at will (the first broadcast pirates). It soon became impossible to obtain consistent reception in most areas.

The chaos was brought to an end with the passage of the Radio Act of 1927. Among other things, it established a Federal Radio Commission (replaced by the Federal Communications Commission in 1934).[13] The commission could classify stations, prescribe the nature of their service, determine wavelength, power, and hours of operation, regulate equipment, make regulations to prevent interference, and take other steps that would make the radio spectrum a more orderly place. The act came none to soon, for by this time there were over 700 broadcasting stations in operation, with another 200 under construction.

*Chapter 2*

# DISTANCE

WHAT WERE THINGS LIKE during radio's early days? A retrospective prepared by the Newark News Radio Club (NNRC), one of the earliest and largest listening clubs in the country, described 1927 this way:

> [T]he women wore tube-shaped dresses ending just below the knees, with the waistline in the middle of the hips. The latest Tom Swift book was *Tom Swift and His Air Glider*. A best-seller was Gena Stratton Porter's *The Magic Garden*. Roll-top desks remained in vogue; the Sears catalog devoted a dozen pages to buggies, harnesses, horse blankets, etc. A one-carat diamond ring cost $488.50. The Model T Ford remained an important mode of personal transportation. Wood-burning cook stoves still were an important item; many still heated their home with soft-coal heaters. The hi-fi sets were hand-wound victrolas with mechanically reproduced sound. Player pianos were a big item, with rolls featuring tunes like "It Made You Happy When You Made Me Cry."[1]

In assessing how long-distance (DX) shortwave listening (SWL) developed over the years, it is necessary to understand the early *broadcast band* activity, because the roots of shortwave DXing are firmly planted in the realm of the broadcast band. Shortwave DXing developed from broadcast band DXing as the properties of the shortwave spectrum were discovered.

Indeed, before anyone had thought of the term SWL, another acronym, BCL (broadcast listener), was in wide use. It is important to remember that, at first, the use of radio for *broadcasting*—transmitting news, entertainment, and the like—was considered a novelty. Until the advent of KDKA, radio was thought of mainly as a *point-to-point* medium: a particular transmitter sending to a particular receiver for a specific purpose (for example, a message from a ship's passenger to a person on shore). That someone might want to transmit into the ether generally for whoever

By 1923 the broadcast listener had been identified as a new category of radio enthusiast (*Radio News*, June 1923).

might be listening was a concept that developed only after 1920. De Forest had seen this potential use of radio years before, but he could neither capitalize on it himself nor convince others of its value.

Broadcasting was not without its critics. Authors, publishers, and other copyright holders, concerned that the new medium was using their property without compensation (which it was), sought royalties for the playing of their music over the air. The result was the formation by the stations of the National Association of Broadcasters, the first president of which was Commander Eugene F. McDonald, Jr., the leading figure at Zenith Radio Corporation and the godfather of the Zenith Trans-oceanic receiver. Phonograph and theater interests were vigorous opponents of entertainment broadcasting, fearful that their share of the market would be displaced (just as AM radio interests frustrated the early growth of FM, and, more recently, the entertainment industry opposed home digital recording).[2]

On the other side of the ledger, David Sarnoff had long been promoting the development of radio music boxes, home devices for the reception of entertainment and information. He eventually made the development of consumer radio receivers—RCA called them "radiolas"—one of RCA's cornerstone businesses (although not as a public service, which was his original concept of broadcasting).

Radio was not easily accepted everywhere. In Poland in 1927 farmers near Vilna attacked a district school teacher, blaming his radio for the torrential rains that destroyed their crops. Only the devil's voice could emanate from such a machine, they thought (as would parents down through the years). A report in the *New York Times* stated: "After beating the teacher they smashed his radio set to bits. The discouraged pedagogue predicts that this part of Poland will develop to the point of having a court action over the Darwinian theory in about the year 2127."[3]

Until the creation of networks and the ability to receive the same program in different parts of the country, many ordinary people spent a lot of time tuning the standard broadcast band, seeing how far their receivers would pick up. The 1920s probably boasted the highest percentage of long-distance radio enthusiasts. According to the late Carleton Lord, a widely known DXer of the day, "[it] was a time when every radio owner was a DXer for a while. He was interested in the new gadget he had at home, and with it he could hear farther than just across the street. It was fairly common each morning on the way to school or work to hear someone say: 'Well! I picked up Schenectady ... or Pittsburg ... or someplace last night.'"[4] Comparing the situation with that in England, the chief engineer of the BBC said in 1924: "In England, the program is of supreme importance.... American listeners are interested chiefly in distance. It is still a hobby with 90 per cent of them. In England, only about 10 per cent of the listeners are interested in distance. The majority prefer to tune in local programs."[5]

But some on the other side of the Atlantic were listening as enthusiastically as

Americans were. In the early 1930s an English author reported that "medium-wave stations in the United States and sometimes one or two of those in Canada are by no means difficult to receive in [England] with a reasonably efficient set.... When conditions are favourable almost any set will receive American stations."[6] Another report in the *New York Times* in November 1926 stated:

> A letter from a British radio fan this week reports that American broadcasting stations are now reaching England frequently as Winter approaches. He said that he was able with little difficulty to hear WBZ, WGY and WJZ, but that WPG, Atlantic City, was received with the most volume, using a three-tube set....
>
> When tuning for the Bound Brook waves the British auditors tune in Leipzig on 452 meters and WJZ's wave is very close on the dials. WGY is a shade above Manchester; WBZ near Liverpool's wave, or a trifle below PTT, Paris, and WPG is a little above the settings required to bring in Hanover.[7]

Regular listeners were called, somewhat awkwardly, "listeners in," and DXers were referred to quaintly as "fans." Serious DXers were "DX hounds" or "DX fiends."

> He was a distance fiend,
>      A loather of anything near.
> Though WOOF had a singer of opera fame,
>      And WOW a soprano of national name,
> He passed them both up for a Kansas quartet
>      A thousand miles off and hence "harder to get."
> New York was too easy to hear.
>      He was a distance fiend.
>
> He was a distance fiend,
>      His radio ruling his life.
> When he and his family went to the play,
>      He'd take them to Yonkers instead of Broadway.
> The show being over, he'd blow to a bite
>      In far Staten Island, that very same night.
> God pities his daughter and wife.
>      He was a distance fiend.
>
> He was a distance fiend.
>      Alas, but he died one day.
> Saint Peter obligingly asked would he tell
>      His choice of a residence—Heaven or Hell?
> He replied, with a show of consistency fine:
>      "Good sir, you have hit on a hobby of mine.
> Which place is the farthest away?"
>      He was a distance fiend.[8]

The activities of long-distance radio enthusiasts were not always appreciated

Late nights at the radio produced long distance, or "DX," signals (*Radio News*, January 1926).

by others in the family. Radio magazine covers sometimes depicted wives and mothers angry over the men's radio antics. Early medium-wave DXer Dick Cooper declared, "[T]here was a phrase crept into the language; you've heard it in your household, probably; being a DX man I'm sure you have. I heard it in mine many a time. That phrase was: 'Turn that damn thing off!'"[9]

As a letter to station WEAF attests, both sexes were susceptible to the DX bug.

December 1922

> It is 5:25 P.M.—you have just finished broadcasting; you have also practically finished breaking up a happy home. Our set was installed last evening. Today, my wife has not left her chair, listening in all day. Our apartment has not been cleaned—the beds not made—the baby bathed—and no dinner ready for me, her husband, and the former boss. Now, she is in love with the beautiful voice of the gentleman who announced your different soloists, etc. this afternoon, and has ordered my trunk brought up from the cellar and visaed my passport to leave tomorrow A.M. She enjoyed her day immensely and hopes it will continue forever. Hereafter, I shall sleep in the park. Merry Xmas.[10]

Radio often entered the home at the urging of a younger member of the family. "Kermit Geary of Walnutport, PA, talked his family into buying their first receiver in December 1925. The dealer came to install it, but was unable to bring in a single station. After nearly a half hour of fiddling, with the family about ready to send the set back to the store, they finally brought in WIOD [Miami Beach] loud and clear. It seems there had been a maritime SOS call, all stations had gone off the air, and WIOD was one of the first to resume transmission. Thus the first station heard by Kermit was a real DX catch, and he was hooked on the hobby."[11]

Indeed, radio was thought a worthy pastime for the young. In 1927, Charlotte Geer, radio columnist for the *Newark Evening News*, described in verse how to win a young convert. One stanza read,

> You must lead him and prod him by turns,
>     He'll yawn and seem bored and forlorn
> Till he hears that first call from the coast—
>     And behold a DXer is born.[12]

Long-distance reception was news even in the nonradio press. A writer in *Scribner's* magazine observed in 1923: "One of our visitors remarked that it is about as much fun hearing the announcements, and thereby finding where you are among the red spots on the map as it is listening programmes. And it is even so. This fishing in the far away with the radio hook and line is rare sport. The line is long, the fishing

THIS IS WHAT WE GOT LAST NIGHT ON OUR SET !

HOW MANY TIMES HAVE I TOLD MARTHA NOT TO SING WHEN I'M LISTENING IN?

FANCY ME TRYING TO LISTEN TO THE WORLD'S PRIMA DONNA WITH HER HUSBAND'S DIRTY OLD TOGS ON MY AERIAL

is getting better all the time, and it usually does not take many minutes to find out what you have on the hook."[13]

The distinction between program listening and DXing was already being drawn. As one early commentator put it, "Some day, perhaps, I shall take an interest in radio programs. But at my present stage they are merely the tedium between call letters."[14]

> Radio fans wanted distance, not programs. They were satisfied with the mere thrill of snatching sounds out of the air. If they were to have had their way there would have been no programs at all. Every station would have gone on the air to do nothing but repeat its call letters. That was all that mattered. Get a station. Wait until its call letters were announced so that the listener might feel the thrill of getting Chicago, or Davenport, Iowa, then on to another station. The wait for announcements was delay, programs were but excuses for the broadcasting stations to go on the air that they might fulfil their true destiny, which was to announce their call letters.[15]

It was also the time of the beginning of interference from amateur radio operators. In the early days, the term amateur was used in a broad sense to include all radio aficionados, that is, the listening amateurs who listened to voice (or "radiophone" as it was then sometimes called), as well as those with transmitters. In December 1921 *QST* even began a column, "With the Radio Phone Folks," later renamed "With Our Radio Phone Listeners."

According to an account by the ARRL,

> The two groups started drifting apart in early 1922. Many radio magazines which had catered to the transmitting amateur swung away from him, one even so far as to run an editorial attacking the "selfish amateur" for "causing interference," another prophesying the end of amateur radio.... [I]n June 1922 [the ARRL] announced that *QST* would not "go popular." The [word] "Citizen" on the cover ["Devoted Entirely to Citizen Wireless"] was quietly changed back to "Amateur," the name of the phone column was changed to "The Junior Operator," and its emphasis shifted accordingly. Phone people became "novices" or "BCLs," and an editorial declared that "novices were *not* amateurs, as the press seems to think."[16]

Until the arrival of broadcasting stations and broadcast listeners, transmitting amateurs were basically a self-contained population whose peccadilloes impacted mainly commercial stations or others who were technically inclined. Now the BCLs, with their usually modest equipment and nontechnical orientation toward *listening*

*Opposite:* Radio humor was everywhere, as evidenced by these early radio postcards (undated).

# A Guess Evermore
### (As Poe might have written it.)
## By WARREN W. SCHULTZ

ONCE upon a midnight dreary, while I
pondered weak and weary;
Before the dials which I had purchased
lately from a Radio store;
Suddenly there came a tapping, as of some-
one gently rapping.
Rapping at the speaker's core.
'Tis some static then I muttered rapping
at the speaker's core,
Only this and nothing more.

It could not be I had blundered, yet the
good loud speaker thundered,
For the tapping, growing tapping, moved
the dog outside the door.
Quickly out the door he lumbered, and he
neither slept nor slumbered,
While the good loud speaker thundered,
thundered at its very core;
But he joined the mellee howling, sometimes barking, sometimes growling

As he'd never done before.
Only this and nothing more.

Now this roaring set me thinking, for I
know I'd not been drinking,
Thinking evil thoughts about the man in
our own Radio store.
Then I wanted to start cussing, just like
married people fussing,
But I dared not do a thing that I had
never done before.
Instead within me I conspire, that all Radio
men are liars,
That the fools of course are buyers, and
it made me very sore;
And that next day I'd consult him, use the
noose and big tree on him,
Or knock him down upon the floor.
Only this and nothing more.

Quiet, quiet, awful quiet, as in some great
Chinese diet;
For the tubes which glowed so brightly
now were silent evermore.
All the air rushed from my sails, and not
as slow as gait of snails;
So I stayed inside the door.
Still on the rack reclines my hat, for I
mistook "B" for "A" bat.
Which I shall do nevermore.
Only this and nothing more.

MORAL

If you blame anyone for anything, first
be sure you are not to blame yourself.

The joys of listening (with apologies to Edgar Allan Poe; *Radio News*, December 1924).

to stations, started complaining about amateur interference. What had been occasional technical conflicts among hobbyists now became fights between neighbors, especially in the case of spark transmitters, which were prone to producing interference in the standard broadcast band, the high end of which—1350 kc.—was only 150 kc. away from 200 meters, where the amateurs were active.

In some places this resulted in the establishment of "voluntary" quiet hours between 8:00 and 10:30 P.M., during which amateurs were supposed to refrain from transmitting so that broadcast supporters could enjoy their listening. So began the many years of intermittent conflict between amateur radio operators and their neighbors. It all hastened the coming of continuous wave technology, which was less prone to producing interference.

Quiet hours were later mandated by the Department of Commerce due to the widespread failure to observe them voluntarily, but they were dropped in 1923 for those amateur frequencies that were far away from the broadcast band. A similar practice of quiet periods existed among the broadcasters themselves. In the fall of 1922 stations in many cities adopted a "silent night:" a several-hour period on a particular night when the stations would close down in order to permit their listeners to hear stations in other cities on the same wavelength. Questions over the desirability of the practice led one commentator to wonder what radio reception was really all about. "If radio is really entertainment," he observed, "then the program is the important thing. If that is true, the source matters less than, in a manner of speaking, the bone and sinew of the program itself [and thus silent hours should be dropped]. But on the other hand, if radio reception is a kind of elaborate animated geography lesson, then every effort ought to be bent to give those devotees the chance to hear distant names whisked through the microphone."[17] The decision was ultimately an economic one. As broadcasting matured, silent nights were abandoned because of their negative impact on station revenues.

There were some amazing demonstrations of long-distance medium-wave listening in the 1920s. One was by New Zealander E. H. Scott, founder of the world-famous American receiver line that would bear his name. Scott's success in using his homemade "World's Record Super 9" superhet receiver to hear North American medium-wave stations from New Zealand in 1925—including some with whom he had arranged special tests—was the impetus for starting the company. Ten years later, Roy W. Arthur, an NNRC member in Australia, reported that KFI, Los Angeles, "romps in with great effect ... being quite on a par with local reception on most occasions. KPO's [San Francisco] organ recitals have boomed in on the speaker from 5:30 to 6:00 P.M., East, literally compelling the old Stromberg to walk around the room."

Around the same time Jack Moskovita of San Pedro, California, had confirmed loggings of 287 stations, 66 of them outside the United States. His best reception was a 140 watt Australian, and he had regular reception from that country as well as from Japan. In 1936 an NNRCer in Lynn, Massachusetts, wrote that after WRC and KMBC signed off 950 kc. at 1:00 A.M., Radio Belgrano, Argentina, was among the stations that came through very well. "In fact, you can roll back the rug and dance if you wish as they come in so well."

Ollie Ross of Vallejo, California, was surely the world's champion broadcast-band DXer in 1931, with 1,309 stations logged, many of them in foreign countries. He claimed to have tuned the bands over four years from 36 states, sometimes listening 22 hours a day. Commenting on the questioning of his feats by some readers, a *RADEX* (*Radio Index*) editor observed: "At first I, too, felt some skepticism about the Vallejo log, as I could not find enough stations to accord with it, but the great mass of verification reports convinced me.... Mr. Ross has just forwarded to me another large consignment of astonishing, even bewildering, verification reports. They are in all sorts of foreign languages."[18]

Doubting other people's claims of reception was fairly common on the early BCB scene, and people went to great lengths to prove or disprove reception. A case in point began with a letter from one George Lilley of West Chester, Pennsylvania, which appeared in the August 1932 issue of *Radio News*. Lilley claimed that, using a two-tube receiver, he had heard medium-wave stations in Japan, Italy, Argentina, Uruguay, Hawaii, Australia, New Zealand, El Salvador, and other faraway places.

He attributed his success to his antenna and ground, and to his knowledge of the right season and the right time of day to listen. He gave his address and offered to respond to queries.

Other readers called Lilley's reports grossly exaggerated and even impossible, so *Radio News* arranged a demonstration at Lilley's home on October 29, 1932, from midnight to daylight, with A. H. Brackbill, a Lilley critic from a neighboring town, sitting in.[19]

The results: Brackbill heard 600-watt Queensland station 4BH on 1380 kc., Sydney station 2BL, 5,000 watts on 855 kc., and Brisbane's 4QC, 5,000 watts, on 760 kc., along with 100 watt KERN in Bakersfield, California and several other West-coast stations. The men did not agree on everything, but Brackbill did report as follows:

> I am of the firm opinion that they were Australians beyond a doubt. I believe now that he (Lilley) can get them, and I believe he can get them better than he did yesterday morning, because while the weather was perfect, it was a bit too cool. There was a little static at first, but by the time the Australians came in the weather was okay all around....
>
> I am fully satisfied with the results and Lilley was perfectly honest in every way. I have no more to say on the subject except that he is honest in his claims of Australians and was perfectly willing to give the demonstrations.[20]

The George Lilley story is an example of what serious long-distance radio listeners have always known, namely, that the ability to hear DX stations is more the product of technique and experience than equipment and propagation. This is sometimes difficult for the more casual listener to understand. Knowing what to listen for, and when, understanding how signal qualities vary from different parts of the world at different times of the day, being familiar with the languages and programming styles of different countries, and being able to discern program details from what appears to be just noise or a jumble of stations, are all capabilities that come mainly with experience. It is not to say that such experience is essential to positively hearing weak, long-distance signals, only that those without such experience may not appreciate what is possible.

Examples showing how different broadcasting was in the 1920s are illustrated in events that are beyond comprehension today: the international radio broadcast tests, held annually from 1923 through 1926. During these tests, nearly all but certain selected North American and European BCB stations closed down at agreed hours each night for a week in order to give listeners on one continent a better chance to log medium-wave stations from the other. Although actual results did not match the level of pretest promotion, that nearly the entire broadcasting industry would cooperate in such a venture is a measure of the seriousness that was attached to

OFFICIAL CERTIFICATE OF VERIFIED INTERNATIONAL RECEPTION
Issued by

# Radio Digest
PROGRAMS
Illustrated
REG. U. S. PAT. OFF. & DOM. OF CAN.

*THIS CERTIFIES that:*

Eugene S. Allen,

*of* Doniphan, Kans.

has submitted to RADIO DIGEST for official verification, evidence of international reception during International Radio Week, January 24 to 30, 1926.

*AND, this further certifies* that RADIO DIGEST has verified the evidence submitted by comparing with official confidential data on programs broadcast by foreign stations cooperating in International Radio Week.

Given under our hand and seal this *tenth* day of *February* 1926.

Foreign Tests Editor.

Magazines, such as *Radio Digest*, would issue certificates to listeners who submitted the results of their listening during "Radio Week" (1926).

long-distance radio reception.[21] Other special international medium-wave tests were arranged as well, including in 1936 several sponsored by the U.S. Department of Commerce over stations in Argentina and Uruguay and several European countries. The purpose of these tests was to determine the relative absorption of radio waves at different latitudes.

The equipment environment for the BCL was, of course, very different from what we know today. The first popular radios were of the regenerative type, manufactured under license by Edwin H. Armstrong. They utilized Armstrong's regenerative detector, which fed some of the output of the RF (radio frequency) amplifier back through the antenna input circuit. Called "bloopers," regenerative receivers were temperamental to operate and often generated oscillations loud enough to interfere with reception on other receivers in the neighborhood, in essence turning receivers into miniature transmitters. It was reported that when American hams made transatlantic tests in 1921, "[s]o large was the number of English listeners on the 200 meter wavelength, all using regenerative or self-radiating receivers, that they jammed each other by emanations from their own receivers!"[22] Automatic volume control had not yet been invented, so receivers also tended to blast the ears as they were tuned from one station to another. An ode appearing in 1927 in the Australian magazine *Wireless Weekly*, told the following tale of an Aussie listener's search, with a self-oscillating, regenerative receiver, for KGO, Oakland, California, which occasionally made it across the Pacific.

> When Jenkins hunts for KGO,
> For miles around the listeners know
> Who twists and twirls his radio—
> > "That's Jenkins."
>
> With whoops and howls the heavens abound,
> The local stations fade from sound,
> And fiercest static goes to ground,
> > For Jenkins.
>
> But Jenkins with his one-tube set
> Has never logged that station yet,
> No KGO can Jenkins get—
> > Not Jenkins.
>
> Yet always have I yearned to know
> If, in their Oakland studio,
> Our Yankee friends of KGO—
> > Get Jenkins.[23]

As unstable as they were, regeneratives were a huge improvement over the earlier, makeshift receiving apparatus that had been in wide use. They were followed by the relatively inexpensive tuned radio frequency (TRF) set, with one or more stages of RF (radio frequency) amplification before the detector stage and all tuned circuits adjusted to the same frequency; the more stable, oscillation-reducing neutrodyne receiver (which made dial settings mean something for the first time); and finally, in the mid to late 1920s, the more reliable and less complicated superheterodyne.

The most popular antennas were the long wire, which is still the most popular long-distance receiving antenna, and the box loop. But various oddball alternatives were available as well, like the Dubilier Light Socket Aerial ("the static is about gone, interference is reduced, and you've done away entirely with sooty aerials, lead-in wires, ground switches, and lightning arresters"), the Yahr-Lange "Super Ball" Antenna ("greater selectivity, volume and distance due to its conductive surface of 364 sq. inches"), and the Rogers Underground Antenna ("dig a small hole in the ground outside a window near your set, drop the Rogers Underground Antenna in the hole, cover it over with dirt ... and tune in on loud, clear, steady reception").

Proper grounding was also considered important. Carleton Lord offered the following tongue-in-cheek comments on the subject:

There was little magic in the common cold water pipe, but consider what you could do with a 6 foot copper-plated stainless steel rod, an old auto radiator, or a 40 gallon water tank. Burying such contraptions was not enough; you were supposed to dig a full-sized grave away from the light of the full moon, drop a tea kettle to the bottom, fill the pit with a proper mixture of gravel, rock salt, peat moss, Vigoro and top soil, and then hook up an automatic sprinkler system to moisten the filled pit for three hours before you turned a dial. Then you also had the U.S. Standard Ground, the Ollie Ross Ground, the inverse counterpoise and many others. One DXer buried 100 feet of trolley wire in a 3 foot deep trench that circled a spring, and another night owl tossed 500 feet of wire into the Pacific Ocean.[24]

Encouraged by the BCL market, it was in receivers rather than transmitters that companies made many of the early advances in radio technology. The high cost of ready-made receivers led many early radio fans to build their own, either from a magazine circuit diagram, using parts bought separately, or from one of the plethora of kits that were available. Reported one hobbyist: "It is possible … to go into any reputable radio store … and … be handed an attractive cardboard box containing the complete set of parts according to the author's specifications."[25] These sets were usually battery operated, and built on a wooden base, hence the term "breadboard."

There was a fascination with circuitry. At one time over 100 periodicals for the radio-set builder were available. They were filled with endless versions of receiver hookups bearing colorful names: the Globe Trotter, the Pentode Four (four being the number of tubes), the Explorer Eight, the Universal Two, the Professional Nine, the DX Super, the Candy Box Special, and so on. "The public began to consider radio technique about as stable as oil stocks." Even when store-built sets took over, "[s]ets were bought with great hesitation, for fear the next day would find them obsolete. Manufacturers made sets with great caution, preferring to employ skilled radio men to assemble the sets and wire them one by one, rather than rush into mass production, because of the uncertainty of the technique."[26]

Newspapers carried technical articles and circuit diagrams. The number of newspaper radio sections increased from 10 in 1922 to 600 in 1923.[27] Carleton Lord made the following comment:

> In those days, the *Philadelphia Evening Bulletin* would devote three or four pages on Friday night to radio. Much of the space was devoted to reports on new circuits and receivers, and the balance contained ads by radio stores telling you where to buy radio parts or complete kits for these advanced circuits. You would read up on the goodies Friday night, and Saturday morning you would go down to "Radio Row" on Market Street in Philadelphia to look and sometimes to buy. Between 1924 and 1930, my Dad and I must have built eight or ten receivers, all of them battery powered. The last, and probably the

With the aid of a few spare parts from a nearby garage, and a few borrowed tools, anyone, with a little engineering ingenuity and a hack-saw, can construct a very simple Micro-tuner. When carefully adjusted, this condenser control has produced remarkable results, bringing in distant stations in regular alphabetical order. The steering wheel control makes the coarse adjustment on the dial by means of the tiregear and left-handed monkey-wrench. A finer setting results from the step-down gearing from left-hand large dial, and vernier rod on the knob. Having reached the zero beat between the squeals, gently press the left foot working the crank control of the kerosene lamp flame. This regulates the heat that melts the ice. The drops of water move the fan delicately. The fan motion is reversed by the puffs of air from the tire pump as the dog moves back and forth, agitated by the cat on the kiddie car. Avoid boot-leg kiddie cars for best results.

**Homemade receivers were neither as easy to build nor as good performers as people were sometimes led to believe (*Radio News*, September 1924).**

best, was the Bremer-Tully "Nameless" circuits, which we modified several times.[28]

Although each receiver variation was heralded as important for one reason or another, the search for the little things that made a difference was more illusory than real. It was encouraged by radio parts manufacturers, some of whom paid to have their parts named in construction articles that implied that use of their parts was essential to the success of a particular design. But as one magazine commentator put it,

> [c]laims to the contrary notwithstanding, practically every popular circuit used in receiving sets [in 1924] is but an improvement or a modification of some long-established, universally accepted method of reception which has been recorded in the Patent Office for years.
>
> It has been the degree or the scope of these improvements that has kept the fires of interest alive and made each slight change in these fundamental circuits appear as some new and revolutionary method of bringing in signals destined to consign all the old principles to the scrap heap.
>
> There has been nothing fundamentally new. Names have been changed, the trimmings have changed, some of the units have

changed, but whether the set possesses one tube or twenty, the process of detection and amplification is still accomplished by one of the several tried and proven methods.[29]

During the radio boom, there were 3,000 radio parts manufacturers in the United States. During the 1920s, radio magazines—*Radio News* in particular—were thick with advertisements for radio parts companies, each promising more than its competitors. There were Dubilier, Hammarlund, and Coto-Coil condensers; batteries by Exide, Valley, Burgess, Willard, and Westinghouse; Tungar battery chargers; Cunningham radio tubes; Murdock and Brandes headphones; Tower, Herald, and Dictograph loudspeakers (originally called "loud talkers"); Bradleystat potentiometers; Frost-Radio and Pacent plugs and jacks; Federal transformers; Chelsea dials; Radion sockets; Acme amplifiers; and Formica, Celoron, and Bakelite panels.

The electronic parts store came into existence, with both walk-in and mail-order service. Among those who advertised in the popular radio magazines of the day were Atlantic Radio Company in Boston, Barawik of Chicago, Newman-Stern in Cleveland, and the Radio Specialty Company of New York.[30] In addition to the manufacturers, there were 30,000 dealers handling radio equipment.[31] In the early 1920s it seemed that everyone had a franchise. You could buy radios from florists, grocers, plumbers, and undertakers. Manufacturers could sell anything and everything, and they did.

As ready-made sets came into vogue, there were countless names to choose from, including Bosch, Grebe, Clapp-Eastham, Magnavox, Atwater Kent, Crosley, Zenith, Phenix, Paragon, Mu-Rad, DeForest, and Radiola (RCA).[32] Ready-built sets were expensive at first, with most table models selling in the $60–180 price range, some even more (and consoles *much* more). Although their engineering far surpassed that of homemade sets, as circuits became standardized and tubes mass produced, prices dropped.

Some companies that would become major shortwave receiver producers in later years, along with others that would quickly disappear, got their start in the 1920s with the introduction of presuperhet radios. The Hammarlund-Roberts series of "Hi-Q" broadcast band receiver kits and ready-made sets made their debut in 1925. National's first shortwave receiver—the two-tube, regenerative SW-2—appeared in 1927 and sold for $35 in kit form, $45 ready-made. It was followed by other models of the National "Thrill Box" line—the SW-4, the SW-5 (one of the first sets designed for AC operation), and the highly regarded SW-3—plus the SW-58, a five-tube regenerative that sold in 1932 for $90.[33] In the late 1920s E. H. Scott Radio Laboratories introduced a line of respected DX receiver kits, starting with the World's Record Super 9, then the "10" and the "8" models, and the Shield Grid World's Record Super 9 and 10. A kit of parts for the Shield Grid 9 cost $138, plus $83 for the power supply and amplifier, a princely sum in those days.

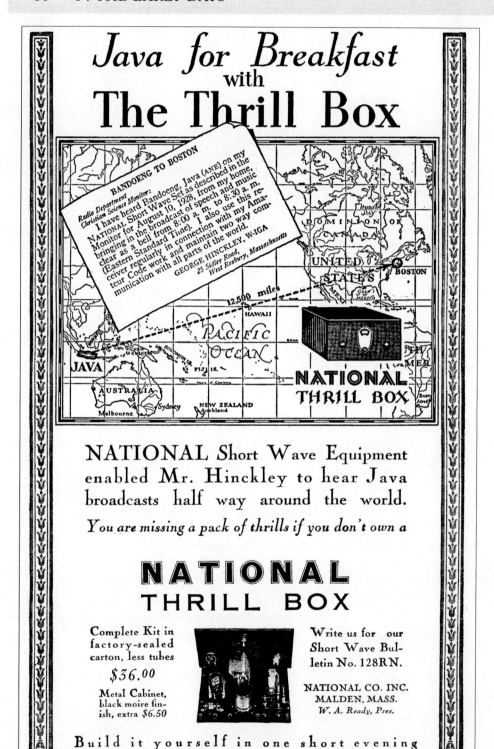

National was one of the major names in early shortwave receivers, and the "Thrill Box" one of its most enticing models (*Radio News*, January 1929).

## ATWATER KENT RADIO

### SCREEN-GRID

### SO REAL
#### *she stole away on tiptoe*

JUST the other day we heard of a woman who stopped at a friend's to call. She was about to ring the door bell when she heard unfamiliar voices within. After listening a moment she tiptoed away, saying to herself: "They have guests; I'll call some other time." Guests? Yes, indeed—*but they were in a broadcasting studio far away.* Such is the reality —the *un*-mechanical perfection of true-to-life Atwater Kent tone!

On the Air: Atwater Kent Radio Hour, Sunday Evenings, 9:15 (Eastern Time), WEAF network of N.B.C. Atwater Kent Mid-Week Program, Thursday Evenings, 10:00 (Eastern Time), WJZ network of N.B.C.

## ATWATER KENT RADIO

### SCREEN-GRID

### SO MUCH BETTER
#### *there's just no room for argument*

IT'S not merely the wonderful Screen-Grid tubes. It's the way the new tubes are *completely used* to make radio so much more enjoyable that there is just no room for argument. You get more stations and more distant stations, and separate them with needle-point precision. You get clearer, richer, Electro-Dynamic tone. You get more volume than you can use, controllable at will. And you *don't* get any *hum.*

*Write for illustrated booklet of Atwater Kent Radio*

## ATWATER KENT RADIO

### SCREEN-GRID

### SO BEAUTIFUL
#### *with your choice of cabinets*

NOW you can have a cabinet just like your neighbors'—or as unlike it as your home differs from theirs. With Atwater Kent Screen-Grid Radio you make your own selection instead of being restricted to one or two designs. Highboy or lowboy, simple or elaborate, sliding doors or swinging doors, or without doors, for a large room or a small room—now *you* do the choosing, just as you choose other furniture for your home.

ATWATER KENT MFG. CO.
*A. Atwater Kent, President*
4822 Wissahickon Ave.
Philadelphia, Pa.

Atwater Kent promised that Screen-Grid would add a new dimension to early radio listening.

component sculpted in gleaming Bakelite with brass trim and mounted on a rich mahogany board. An Atwater Kent radio possessed an elegance that made it more pleasing to the eye than to the ear.[35]

Companies tried to distinguish themselves in their advertising. The ads of A. H. Grebe featured segments of oriental wisdom from "Dr. Mu," symbol of the Grebe line. Examples of these are as follows: Confucius: "The coming of a friend from a far-off land—is this not true joy?" Dr. Mu: "Your friends of radio come to you each night through the Grebe Broadcast Receiver." And Lao Tzu: "Live in harmony with your age." Dr. Mu: "To be in harmony with the present age, you must own a Grebe Broadcast Receiver."

Atwater Kent ran a series of ads showing pictures of A-K sets in the homes of famous people of the day, like adventure author Rex Beach, journalist and writer Wallace Irwin, and author and dramatist Booth Tarkington. Scott boasted multipage ads featuring letters from satisfied customers attesting to their long-distance reception. Browning-Drake's 1925 advertising pointed out that "during the transatlantic tests made earlier in the year the Browning-Drake Receiver received Madrid, Spain. Owners of Browning-Drake Receivers living in the East have verified reception from KGO, Oakland, California, KFI, Los Angeles, California, Mexico City and Calgary, Canada."[36] In the 1930s, American-Bosch promoted the American-Bosch Radio Explorers Club, and its commander and master mariner, James P. Barker. Many other advertisements featured letters from proud owners attesting to their DX feats while using a particular receiver.

When it came to radio, young people were especially important customers. The editor of *Electrical World* reported in 1922 that

> [a] large portion of [customers] are youths ranging from ten to twenty-one. They are not technically trained, and yet even the youngest of them can talk inductance, capacity, impedance, resistance and the other technical terms with a pretty thorough grasp on their meaning and a good appreciation of their application in radio work.... Fad though the movement may be styled at the present, the education that these young people are getting is of untold value. It may well prove to be one of the most effective aids in dispelling the mystery that has enveloped the electrical industry in the public mind. At the very least it is taking the minds of the younger generation from amusements that may be questionable and giving them something that will be of tremendous use in the future.[37]

Partly as a result of this youthful tinkering and set building, radio became the preserve of the youth heroes of the day, both real and fictional. Among the real radio heroes were people like Jack Binns, the wireless operator on the White Star liner

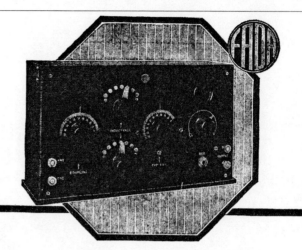

This Fada receiver meets the demand for dependable radio sets within the price range of everyone. Fada prices make it possible for "a radio receiver in every home"

**$35.00**

Interior of Fada Receiver

"Hook on a Fada Amplifier- Increase *Your* receiving range"

# A Fascinating Recreation— Build Your Own Radio Set

THAT inherent instinct, within us all, to experiment, create and construct, influences many to build their own radio sets.

Fada equipment is so designed to give you the greatest possible reward for your creative efforts. All instruments and parts are definitely simple in construction and unusually easy to assemble into neat, dependable radio sets. Anyone, with the aid of the Fada handbook, can assemble Fada parts with greatest ease and assurance.

Fada detectors, mounted in cabinets with both one and two stage amplifiers, hook up with any set, and increase your receiving range. The addition of Fada amplifiers in no way necessitates any change in your original construction.

Fada rheostats, variable condensers, switches, variocouplers, dials, etc., can be used with other equipment to make even a better radio set. Fada parts, if used exclusively in your assembly work, will give you a finished instrument of good appearance and highly satisfactory.

After you once use Fada equipment, you will take great pride in having Fada imprinted on every radio part you use.

## Frank A. D. Andrea
**1581-B JEROME AVE.**  NEW YORK CITY

Now $2.00        Now $ .75        $4.00

*Above and opposite page:* The FADA line, named after company founder Frank A. D. Andrea, was one of the best known (*Radio News*, November 1922).

The Fada receiver, detector and two-stage amplifier represents the highest type of cabinet construction. A fitting instrument for the finest home and instantly responsive to various receiving ranges

$$80.^{00}$$

## An Ideal Home Entertainer

THE Fada receiver, a result of the same perfection in design and construction that distinguishes all Fada products, is gaining popularity as an ideal home entertainer.

When it's radio time in your home, you can sit back in your favorite chair, among the family circle and command at your fingers' touch, the talent of such noted artists as May Peterson, Percy Grainger, Mme. Margaret Namara, or Lydia Lipkowska— Russian coloratura soprano of the Imperial Opera of Petrograd.

You marvel that their voices can come into your home with such depth of emotion and true personality. Music is an inspiration to everyone, it goes to the very soul of things and brings joy and happiness to all.

With a Fada radio receiver, music can be made part of your daily recreation. And after the musical program there is broadcasted a digest of important world events. You can, with a Fada receiver, literally keep a jump ahead of the headlines in tomorrow's newspapers.

Interior of Fada Receiver, Detector and Two-stage Amplifier

*The new Fada handbook will be sent to you upon receipt of 5c to cover postage. It's a How-To-Do-It book and you should have it.*

### Frank A. D. Andrea

**1581-B JEROME AVE.**          **NEW YORK CITY**

"Let me send you this Fada Handbook."

$2.00          $ .50

$2.70                    $1.20

# What the Broadcasters are Doing

ON THE AIR—OFF THE STREETS

Radio made for busy hands and strong minds (*Radio Age*, May 1924).

*Republic*, whose SOS calls (actually CQD in those days) brought rescue ships that saved all but a few of the crew and passengers in the liner's 1909 collision with another ship. Lionized by the press, Binns became a national hero, and the event helped ensure the necessity of wireless in maritime communication.

Edwin H. Armstrong would also have to be considered among the early radio youth heroes. He was 21 years old when he discovered the principle of regeneration. Perhaps the greatest radio youth hero of them all, however, was David Sarnoff. Sarnoff arrived in the United States from Russia, penniless and speaking no English. He spent much of his career with the Marconi Company of America. Years

Dr. Mu often related the performance of Grebe Radio products to the wisdom of the ancient Chinese sages (*Radio News*, August 1923).

after 1912 he would be repeatedly depicted in both the popular and the scholarly press as the boy who stayed at his key during the *Titanic* disaster, relaying the names of survivors and serving as the world's link to the tragic event. Although he appears to have contributed to the mythology that has developed around what was in fact a very small part in the ocean drama, Sarnoff's ability more than compensated for his immodesty. Starting as an office boy, he moved up through the company with a skill reflecting his leadership and management ability, eventually becoming president of the Marconi successor firm, the Radio Corporation of America.[38]

The excitement and mystique surrounding early radio and electronics turned the science of the day into an adventure for millions, inspiring youngsters to learn the lessons of radio and reminding parents to encourage them and thus help shield them from the evils of idle minds and hands. This attitude was reflected in the popular literature of the time. There were the *Radio Boys* (and *Radio Girls*) series of youth novels, with titles like *The Radio Boys' First Wireless, The Radio Boys on Signal Island,* and *The Radio Boys in Darkest Africa,* plus radio-related volumes in other youth series and individual novels. The early *Radio Boys* books carried an inspirational foreword by Jack Binns.[39] The *Boy Scout Manual* had a section on radio, and urged boys to try their hand at making their own sets (a crystal set could be made for about $2, plus $4 for the headphones). In a 1923 survey of subscribers to *Boy's Life* magazine, 94 percent of the respondents indicated an interest in radio, while 75 percent owned a radio, and 66 percent had built one themselves.[40] Publisher Hugo Gernsback regularly incorporated in his radio magazines short stories wherein radio played the decisive role in saving a damsel in distress, averting a natural disaster, or bringing a scoundrel to justice.

There would be many, many more chapters in the story of broadcasting, including the tortuous debate over the place of advertising on radio (it was widely opposed at first),[41] the development of various types of programming and program production techniques, and the growth of networks. Most of this activity would take place on the standard broadcast band that had become familiar to the general listening public.

On the DX side, however, broadcast band DXing was becoming more difficult as increasing numbers of all-night stations occupied the channels, blocking the reception of the smaller, more distant targets. In addition, some enthusiasts had discovered another corner of the broadcasting world that offered unparalleled possibilities for long-distance reception and armchair traveling: the short waves.

## Chapter 3

# THE ARRIVAL OF SHORTWAVE

MARCONI HAD EXPERIMENTED with shortwave spark transmitters as early as 1901. His transmitters operated around 2.5 mc.—considered a high frequency at the time—and were intended only as an alternative means of short-range transmission. The distance potential of the higher shortwave frequencies was not suspected until after 1920. As illustrated by a Westinghouse publication of that year entitled "Radio Receiving Apparatus for Short-wave Telegraphy and Telephony," shortwave receivers of the day covered the wavelengths of 180–700 meters, or roughly 400 kc.–1.7 mc., a range that today we would consider below the usual shortwave frequency range of 3–30 mc. It took several years before experimenters ventured above 2–3 mc. and started to understand such things as shortwave propagation and directionality. The short waves, as they were called, were surrounded with mystery. Said one observer in 1925:

> Adventuring into the radio region below about 1500 kilocycles (200 meters) is like exploring unknown territory. It is impossible to say what will be found there and no guess is too wild. From this frequency, 1499 kilocycles to be exact, down to goodness-knows where, is a region so vast that all existing stations could be placed in it without crowding. "DX" exists there that is undreamed of on the longer waves, and it is a territory into which any one may venture with the certainty that he will discover interesting things....
> It is an adventure into unknown fields.[1]

Interest among amateurs in a comprehensive exploration of the shortwave bands took a leap after the first transatlantic amateur contacts on 100 meters (3 mc.) in 1923. The British Marconi Company continued its exploration of the shortwave region during the mid–1920s as part of the development of the first major point-to-point service between Great Britain and the various outposts of the empire.

Although it would be many years before the United States would become a major international shortwave broadcaster, it was in fact the pioneer of the medium. Just as KDKA was first on the broadcast band, so was it first in shortwave broadcasting. In 1920 Westinghouse engineer Frank Conrad began experimenting with shortwave from his Pittsburgh ham station, 8XK. These transmissions were in the 2–3 mc. range with a power of 75–100 watts. Although not intended as a broadcast service, Conrad started keeping a more or less regular schedule, relaying the KDKA signal (which was fed to his home via a telephone line) on wavelengths as high as 60 meters (5 mc.). These relays occurred during 1921 and 1922.

In August 1922 a special shortwave transmitter with the call letters 8XS was installed at the KDKA facility and tests continued. A year later 8XS started relaying the evening programs of KDKA on a regular basis. This led to the rebroadcast of KDKA shortwave signals by station KDPM, located at the Westinghouse plant in Cleveland, and in 1923 the construction of Westinghouse station KFKX in Hastings, Nebraska. The purpose of KFKX was to pick up the KDKA shortwave signal transmitted by 8XS and relay it on medium wave for local use and on shortwave for rebroadcast by West coast medium-wave station KGO. KFKX started operation in 1923, marking another chapter in the on again, off again story of national broadcasting in the United States.[2]

The KDKA shortwave signals were also picked up and rebroadcast by medium-wave stations in other countries. A special program was transmitted to England on New Year's Eve, 1923. It was rebroadcast by Metropolitan-Vickers Electrical Company station 2AC in Manchester, which was soon carrying KDKA programs for up to 18 hours weekly.[3] In late 1924 KDKA programs were picked up in South Africa and retransmitted by the *Johannesburg Star* radio station. A similar rebroadcast was conducted in Australia in January 1925.

These programs prompted some interesting letters. In November 1924 a listener to the South African relay wrote as follows: "We are out on the lonely Wild Bush Prairie, away among so many lions, elephants, etc. that you would think that you were near the zoo, and to pick you up amongst such surroundings seems like a wild dream.... [T]he ... man [who] three decades ago ... would have forecasted such a wonder would have been put in a lunatic asylum—it was truly eerie and uncanny.... We were only using a 10-foot Brownie wireless receiver crystal set, and the JB [Johannesburg] broadcasting station broadcasted you."[4]

The 8XS call sign was eventually returned to the government, and Frank Conrad transferred his historic amateur call, 8XK, to Westinghouse. In 1929, 8XK became Westinghouse shortwave broadcasting station W8XK, which was widely heard around the world.

## WESTINGHOUSE EXPERIMENTAL STATION KFKX HASTINGS, NEBRASKA

### THE FIRST RE-BROADCASTING STATION IN THE WORLD.

Wave Length—286 Meters        Power—Variable

### LOCAL PROGRAMS EVERY MONDAY and THURSDAY

Re-broadcasting programs from KDKA at East Pittsburgh

Schedule not definitely determined.

Broadcasting from the studio of the Gaston Music & Furniture Co., at Hastings, Nebraska.

Dear Friend:—

We regret that we are unable to answer your kind communication in more personal form. That, however, is impossible because of the number of letters received  We wish, never-the-less, to express our appreciation for the time and trouble you have taken to commend our programs and assure you that your support will help us in planning better programs for the future.

Trusting to receive further suggestions and encouragement from time to time,

Gratefully yours,

THE WESTINGHOUSE ELEC & MFG. CO.

STATION KFKX

### THE STATION

The sending apparatus of KFKX is contained in a frame building twenty-five by forty feet. Briefly it consists of four panels; a rectifier, modulator, and two oscillator panels.

The antennae used consist of two eight-wire cages, each 100 feet long on poles 75 feet high, together with a fan counterpoise 100 feet long and 100 feet wide. For short wave transmission special antennas are used. On account of the very high frequency necessary for short wave length transmission, extraordinary rigidity is maintained.

The station is connected by telephone cables with the studios located in the Hotel Clarke and at Hastings Chamber of Commerce headquarters. Programs given in the studios pass through these cables and are put "on the air" at the station.

*Page Three*

For rebroadcasting, short wave signals from KDKA at East Pittsburgh are received on a special short wave set near Hastings, located about two miles from the station, amplified and sent to the station by telephone line and then out "on the air" again.

Illustration shows interior of Station KFKX at Hastings

KFKX was the First Radio Repeating Station in the world. Radio repeating is the receiving of programs from one station on short waves, and their transmission on standard waves. KFKX repeats on both long and short waves.

KFKX holds the record for mail received in first week of operation. Has received acknowledgement from every state in the Union, every province in Canada, Sweden, England, from Mexico, Costa Rica, Island of Cuba, Guatemala, Brazil, Guinea, Alaska, Hawaii, China, Holland, Uruguay, Island of Samoa, Australia, New Zealand, France, South Africa, Arctic Circle, and from many ships at sea.

*Page Four*

*Above and next page:* KFKX, Hastings, Nebraska, was the first shortwave relay station in the United States (QSL, 1923).

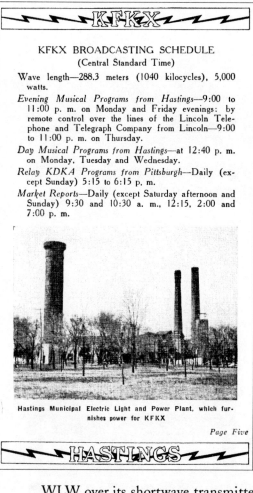

KFKX

KFKX BROADCASTING SCHEDULE
(Central Standard Time)

Wave length—288.3 meters (1040 kilocycles), 5,000 watts.

*Evening Musical Programs from Hastings*—9:00 to 11:00 p. m. on Monday and Friday evenings: by remote control over the lines of the Lincoln Telephone and Telegraph Company from Lincoln—9:00 to 11:00 p. m. on Thursday.

*Day Musical Programs from Hastings*—at 12:40 p. m. on Monday, Tuesday and Wednesday.

*Relay KDKA Programs from Pittsburgh*—Daily (except Sunday) 5:15 to 6:15 p. m.

*Market Reports*—Daily (except Saturday afternoon and Sunday) 9:30 and 10:30 a. m., 12:15, 2:00 and 7:00 p. m.

Hastings Municipal Electric Light and Power Plant, which furnishes power for KFKX

*Page Five*

HASTINGS

It was also Frank Conrad who gave David Sarnoff a real-world exposure to shortwave. At a 1924 London conference attended by both, Conrad showed Sarnoff how a one-tube shortwave set that he had brought with him, coupled to a hotel room curtain rod for an antenna, could receive the baseball scores from KDKA shortwave. Earlier, in 1922, the initial success of shortwave had caused David Sarnoff to predict that "it would not surprise me if in the next few years we find that a radio signal sent out on 100 meters with 100 or 200 kw. of power will travel around the world and be received through the highly sensitive and delicate receiving instruments which are rapidly projecting themselves into the radio art."[5]

The KDKA shortwave experiments were followed by additional American shortwave activity. In 1924 General Electric began shortwave relays of WGY by way of shortwave transmitters W2XAF and W2XAD at their Schenectady, New York, plant. That same year the Crosley Corporation obtained a license to relay the broadcast-band programming of WLW over its shortwave transmitter, W8XAL (later WLWO). In 1925 RCA and NBC joined forces to relay WJZ with a 50 kw. shortwave transmitter in Bound Brook, New Jersey. CBS carried WABC programming over shortwave station W2XE in Wayne, New Jersey, beginning in 1928. Also in 1928 *Radio News* publisher Hugo Gernsback began shortwave broadcasting on 9700 kc. from his station, WRNY, New York, using the call W2XAL. "A reader in New South Wales, Australia," reported Gernsback, "writes us that while he was writing his letter he was listening to WRNY's short-wave transmitter, 2XAL, on a three-tube set; and had to turn down the volume, otherwise he would wake up his family. All this at a distance of some 10,000 miles! Yet 2XAL … uses less than 500 watts; a quite negligible amount of power."[6]

Not everyone was in favor of allowing broadcasting on shortwave. Some felt there were too many broadcasters on medium wave already, and that many broadcasters had nothing worthwhile to put out over the air. It was also felt that amateurs, commercial interests, and other legitimate users would be pushed out, that

RADIO
BROADCASTING
STATION

**WGY**

SCHEDULE
FOR
JANUARY & FEBRUARY

MUSICAL PROGRAMS ¦.ℓ Meters
Every Monday, Tuesday, Thursday and Friday afternoon 2:00 to 2:30; evening 7:45
Special late program Friday evenings at 10:30.

**SUNDAY PROGRAMS**
10:30 a.m. and 4:30 p.m.

**CHILDREN'S STORIES**
Every Friday evening at 6:30

**WEEKLY HEALTH TALKS**
Every Friday evening at 7:40

**NEWS BULLETINS**
Daily, except Saturday and
Sunday, 6:15 p.m.

**N. Y. STOCK EXCHANGE
REPORTS**
Daily, 12:30 p.m. except Sunday.
Daily, 6:00 p.m., except Saturday
and Sunday

General Electric Company
Band

**U. S. NAVAL OBSERVATORY
TIME SIGNALS**
Daily, 11:55 a.m. and 9:55 p.m.
Wednesday and Saturday, 11:55
a.m. only. No time signals Sunday

**OFFICIAL WEATHER
FORECAST**
Daily, except Sunday, 12:45 p.m.,
on 485 meters

**TIME REFERENCE**
Eastern Standard. Changes in
schedule announced by Radiophone

**N. Y. PRODUCE MARKET
REPORTS**
Daily, except Saturday and Sun-
day, 12:30 and 6:00 p.m.

**GENERAL ELECTRIC COMPANY, Schenectady, N. Y., U. S. A.**

January, 1923

PC-244-10th Edition

From the late 1920s WGY, Schenectady, New York, provided the programming for General Electric's early shortwave stations W2XAD and W2XAF (QSL, 1923).

BCLs would need new receivers that would be complicated, inefficient, and suitable only for the technically inclined, and that fading and reception that was generally uneven would become the rule.[7] In the end, however, the exploration of the shortwave spectrum for broadcasting purposes could not be restrained.

As with medium wave, and unlike the governmental radio monopolies that existed in most other countries, the development of U.S. shortwave broadcasting was entirely in private hands. The regulations promulgated under the Radio Act of 1927 lumped international shortwave broadcasting in with other experimental services. License renewal depended on at least nominal proof of research that contributed to a better understanding of shortwave propagation. This was appropriate enough because, at the time, shortwave broadcasting was essentially experimental and not audience driven. It would continue so throughout the 1930s. Shortwave broadcasting developed out of a need for research in the shortwave medium and as a means to facilitate international program exchange (primarily, it was thought, from other countries to the United States, as a means of enriching American programming).

On a more practical level, the leading broadcasters also wanted to reduce reliance on cables for network connections among regular AM broadcasting stations, and eliminate the dominance of the national cable operator, American Telephone and Telegraph, which did not wish to lease telephone lines to stations. AT&T was the owner and operator of station WEAF, and thus a competitor of other broadcasters. The company was also in conflict with American radio companies on other issues concerning who would control U.S. broadcasting. With the settlement of these disputes in 1926, the resulting retirement of AT&T as a broadcaster, and its agreement to lease long-distance telephone lines to the radio companies for networking purposes, one of the early commercial rationales for the development of shortwave disappeared.

Overseas, the start-up year for shortwave broadcasting was 1927, with both PCJ (Eindhoven, Netherlands) and 5SW (Chelmsford, England) coming on the air on the still-familiar frequencies of 9590 and 11750 kc., respectively. TI4NRH in Costa Rica began broadcasting the following year.[8] In July 1928 increased interest in shortwave led *Radio News* to begin "On the Short Waves," one of the first—perhaps *the* first—shortwave broadcast column in a mass circulation publication. It lasted about a year.

Shortwave broadcasting remained experimental partly because there were few shortwave receivers available. The first AC (alternating current) radios appeared in the late 1920s, and, while this made radio listening much more convenient, the AC sets usually covered only the regular broadcast band, not shortwave. Alternating current receivers were much more sensitive than battery-powered units, but the early AC sets were also vulnerable to heavy line noise, especially on shortwave frequencies. Thus, early shortwave fans usually had to content themselves with battery operation.

Shortwave reception first became available to the general public by way of converters that permitted shortwave reception on regular broadcast-band sets. These were not satisfactory, however, and special shortwave receivers soon began appearing. A 1931 article in the Pilot Radio and Tube Corporation house journal, *Radio Design*, explained the problems of shortwave receiver development in those days.

> Short-wave broadcasting, as distinctly distinguished from amateur short-wave telegraphy, began attracting the interest of radio experimenters about two years ago, and quickly developed into an indoor sport of considerable proportions. It lured back to the radio fold many former DX fans of the 1920–1925 period who had dropped out of the "game" because chain broadcasting and high power had robbed it of its early glamor. The mere possibility of hearing voice and music from Europe and the Antipodes revived the old fever, and soon thousands were hanging breathlessly on vernier dials, swearing at the fading and the interference, and enjoying themselves thoroughly.
>
> At first these people were satisfied with "junk box" receivers operating on batteries and possessing hand capacity and many of the other troubles associated with elementary regenerative sets. However, they had been spoiled by the efficient all-electric broadcast receivers already on the market, and they began to demand comfort with their thrills. In an effort to fill their needs, radio engineers spent some effort on the receiver problem, and in quick succession there appeared a

series of improved sets. First, the simple regenerative tuner took on an untuned screen-grid R.F. stage and a little shielding. Then a *tuned* screen-grid job with double shielding made its commercial appearance. Batteries still remained a nuisance to those people who had outgrown the spilling-acid-on-the-rug stage, but A.C. short-wave operation, when successful at all, was usually a laboratory accomplishment and therefore unfit for the public. Finally David Grimes and John Geloso, Pilot engineers, discovered the source of the mysterious tunable hums that caused so much trouble, wiped them out with a few simple expedients, and produced the A.C. Super-Wasp, the first completely A.C. operated shortwave receiver on the market. Brought out in September, 1929, this set has enjoyed a phenomenal sale throughout the world, its popularity strengthening its sponsor's conviction that the short-wave fan was maturing and that his ranks were being increased by new converts who were never fans before but who were adopting the short-wave hobby because it was interesting.

There was still one feature of short-wave operation that caused concern, and that was the matter of plug-in coils. The early receivers used a maximum of three coils, which could be inserted and removed without much trouble because the sets were wide open. However, as the benefits of shielding became evident and the number of coils per set rose to as high as ten (five pairs to cover a range from 15 to 500 meters), the coils themselves became a nuisance. Getting them in and out of necessarily tight shield cans was an operation that tested the temper and bruised the knuckles, and left the set owner in no mood to make delicate adjustments on hair-trigger dials.[9]

The article went on to explain how these problems had been solved with Pilot's new Universal Super-Wasp AC shortwave receiver. The Wasp series was among the first lines of commercial shortwave sets on the market.

Shortwave got an important boost in the early 1930s with the introduction of "all wave" AC sets. These receivers permitted tuning either the regular broadcast band or the shortwave ranges without changing coils, and were a major technological breakthrough. Today, with shortwave broadcasting largely unfamiliar to the general public, it is hard to believe that Gernsback was correct in 1938 when he said that "practically all radio sets that you may purchase in the open market are built for broadcast and short wave reception."[10] The rationale for the Department of Commerce's 1935 publication of a list of shortwave stations, "World Short-Wave Radiophone Transmitters," was "[t]he acceptance of the all-wave receiver by the listening public as the standard of radio value."

From the start, shortwave reception had been a natural byproduct of the exploration of the new wavelengths below 200 meters. Those who engaged in it were experimenters at heart, and it was they who sustained the early development of shortwave radio reception. However, with the rapid advances in receiver design of the 1930s—improved selectivity, better sensitivity, easier tuning, and enhanced

fidelity—shortwave reception became less an experimental marvel and more just a technological fact of life.

The potential for shortwave as an information and entertainment medium was widely touted, and the public's interest in it grew. Shortwaves were the "thrill bands." Some magazines devoted exclusively to shortwave listening could be found on newsstands, with others offering shortwave news in smaller doses. New York's "Radio Row," Cortlandt Street—the most famous radio shopping center in the world (now the site of the World Trade Center)—went shortwave. *Short Wave Radio* magazine reported that "[t]he windows are full of the latest short-wave and all-wave receivers and the sidewalks during lunch hour and on Saturday afternoons are again crowded with little knots of fans who discuss their international DX accomplishments and swap circuit 'dope,' station verifications, etc."[11]

As early as 1928 Gernsback was predicting that shortwave would completely replace regular BCB broadcasting. In 1933 he spoke of a DX renaissance:

> When people were building their own sets, in the early '20s, the favorite pastime was a one-tube set with which you could listen to stations hundreds of miles away. People used to sit up all night trying to get the distant stations. Then, at the end of the '20s, the DX interest lagged somewhat, and by 1930 it seemed to have completely died down, except for a few professionals who kept at it with unabated vigor....
>
> [O]nce again editors of radio publications are beginning to be flooded with DX accomplishments which, this time, are of no mean order. A few hundred paltry miles are no longer of any interest. Your present DX listeners, and I am now speaking of broadcast listeners only, are going out for REAL distance. Listening from one end of the country to the other means nothing....
>
> On the short waves, DX listening is, of course, commonplace; because a good two-tube set will bring in stations from the maximum distance on this planet, i.e., 12,500 miles; and these records are so common that every schoolboy in the United States today who owns a short-wave set thinks nothing of listening to stations in Australia and other parts of the world.[12]

Despite the initial enthusiasm, however, widespread interest in shortwave as a popular radio medium could not be sustained. Among the nontechnical general public it fell victim to the massive growth of high power, high quality BCB broadcasting. Who could be bothered with shortwave reception that could not provide the reliability, fidelity, and ease of tuning that people were demanding and getting on the regular broadcast band? American ethnocentrism in matters of news and information probably played a part too. Who really cared what was going on in all those foreign places anyway? Shortwave broadcasting seemed like a solution looking for a problem.

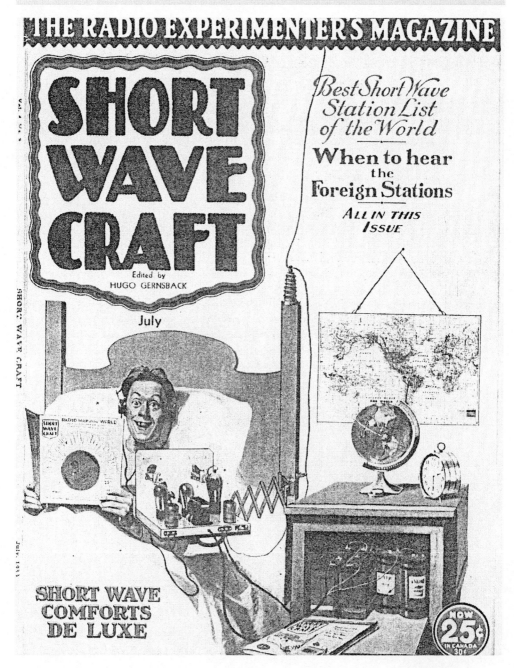

The enthusiasm of a youthful shortwave fan (*Short Wave Craft*, July 1933).

In addition, U.S. shortwave stations were discovering what some of their modern counterparts are rediscovering today, namely, that it isn't easy to make shortwave pay. This was particularly true in the early days when, because shortwave broadcasting was considered experimental, the government restricted commercial advertising on the shortwave bands. It was not necessary to excise commercials from a shortwave simulcast of a parent BCB station's programming, but neither was the station allowed to sell commercials exclusively for the shortwave audience, nor even tell local broadcast band advertisers that there *was* a shortwave audience. These policies were one element that prevented shortwave broadcasting from becoming a moneymaker for station operators.

The no commercials rule was reversed in 1939, largely as a concession to the broadcasters when the government increased the minimum acceptable power on shortwave to 50 kw. and required directional antennas. NBC became the most aggressive in seeking advertising, and landed contracts with United Fruit Company, RCA, Standard Oil, the Waldorf-Astoria and Astor hotels, Esterbrook Pen, Johnson Wax, Camel Cigarettes, and Adams Hat Stores. Crosley had paid advertising from Carter's Little Liver Pills, Kleenex, Firestone, Alka Seltzer, and Lockheed Aircraft, plus some foreign language spots. A Crosley employee "recall[ed] very well the Pepsi-Cola jingles and Planters Peanuts commercials in Spanish."[13] General Electric followed a different approach, offering paid advertising to companies that would produce programs for broadcast to Latin American audiences. Among those who took advantage of the offer were Vogue, Gillette, Royal Baking Powder, Mohawk Carpets, and American Express.[14]

Within the domestic shortwave listening community, not everyone approved of commercials, at least local commercials, on shortwave. Presaging an argument that would be heard many years later in favor of cable television, an *All-Wave Radio* magazine commentator observed that the absence of commercials on shortwave

> is the best sales argument for all-wave receivers.... The megacycle region is contaminated by the short-wave replicas of the very programs from which one has fled downward [in meters]!...
>
> There seems to us no adequate reason why commercial programs should be radiated in the short-wave channels unless the sponsor has paid for all-wave coverage. At the same time, the facilities of short-wave broadcasting should be denied any advertiser whose product is not internationally distributed. Aside from inflicting on short-wave enthusiasts a wholly undesired type of fare (they can listen to it on the long waves [broadcast band] if they want to), there is absolutely no sense in internationally advertising a soap powder or tooth paste that can be purchased only in the U.S.A.... We can hardly see justification for W2XAD (one of the s-w outlets of WGY, Schenectady, N.Y.) exhorting the citizens of a dozen different nations to buy furniture from Breslau Brothers (no down payment and a free refrigerator in exchange for your old ice box) when distribution is limited to within a few miles of Schenectady. There also exists an esthetic consideration. Typical of most spot programs, the Breslau Brothers opus is on an artistic level that couldn't be reached with a ten mile shaft. To put it mildly, the program is rank, and is hardly the sort of material to be chosen for international representation.[15]

# WORLD WIDE BROADCASTING FOUNDATION
### Educational Programs over W1XAL

TRANSMITTER
BOSTON, MASS.

* 6 0 4 0 K C
1 1 7 9 0 K C
1 5 2 5 0 K C
2 1 4 6 0 K C

Address Replies to

Station W1XAL
University Club
Boston - Mass
U.   S.   A.

Dear Listener:

We are very glad indeed to have you write us, as the engineering staff are always interested in knowing how and where the broadcasts are being heard.  We hope you will have many opportunities to listen in, and that conditions for reception will be satisfactory.

You may perhaps be glad to have the enclosed copy of the printed schedule of broadcasts over W 1 X A L for the current month.  This gives you the regular hours when the station is on the air, and will enable you to tune in for programs that promise something of particular interest to you.  If you already have a copy of this schedule, you may wish to share it with a friend who is interested in hearing our programs.

With all good wishes,

Sincerely yours,

WORLD WIDE BROADCASTING FOUNDATION

*William J. Flanders*

Station   W 1 X A L

*Above and facing page:* The World Wide Broadcasting Foundation (WIXAL, later WRUL) was a leader in producing high-quality programming on shortwave (1935).

Despite hope and confidence after the 1939 change in policy, and some initial successes, shortwave broadcasting never proved commercially feasible. By the time the government took it over in November 1942—with the resulting transformation of shortwave from an adjunct of domestic broadcasting to an element of international politics—most of the private shortwave broadcasters were glad to give it up.

NBC was receiving the most revenue from its shortwave operation, and that was only $150,000 yearly, leaving NBC, like the others, deep in the red.

Only WRUL (formerly WIXAL) wanted to stay in the business. The Boston station was the brainchild of Walter Lemmon, who had been an aide to Woodrow Wilson at the Paris Peace Conference. His vision was of a radio university to promote international culture, a kind of National Public Radio of shortwave. In 1931 Lemmon had enough money to build the Boston experimental station W1XAL. In 1935, with the aid of several large companies and foundations but with still modest resources (and no more financial success than the other stations), he formed the World Wide Broadcasting Foundation. Among the company's financial resources were the $2 membership fees of members of the station's World Wide Listeners League. WRUL, known as Radio Boston, was born.

What distinguished WRUL was its program production capability and its educational rather than entertainment orientation. Instead of just transmitting domestic U.S. programming over shortwave frequencies, WRUL produced separate programming for foreign audiences (much of it in English, however).

DECEMBER PROGRAM

WORLD WIDE BROADCASTING FOUNDATION

(A NON-PROFIT ORGANIZATION)

OVER
WIXAL
SHORT
WAVE

BROADCASTING STUDIO
UNIVERSITY CLUB
BOSTON - - MASS.

The 1930s were the golden age of shortwave broadcasting. There were also lots of shortwave sideshows in that decade. The world was not as small as it is today, and shortwave found a niche in accelerating the reporting of events. For example, the Pilot company was there when the Graf Zeppelin arrived in 1929, providing live transmissions to WOR; and shortwave helped speed news of the verdict in the Lindbergh kidnapping trial.

Shortwave also facilitated communication with people in remote areas. Amateur radio became a basic ingredient of all expeditions. Pilot promoted the fact that

# Radio Helps Explorer in the Jungle

*Dr. and Mrs. Herbert S. Dickey. Mrs. Dickey was the first white woman to enter the land of the head hunters in South America.*

WHEN Dr. Herbert S. Dickey, explorer of world-wide renown, left New York this Spring on his eighth expedition into the wilds of South America, he took with him a complete Super-Wasp receiver, a donation of the Pilot Radio & Tube Corporation. It was his intention to use the set for the reception of radio time signals, by means of which he could check his chronometers and thus be able to determine accurately his position in uncharted territory. His purpose on this expedition was to map the source of the mysterious Orinoco River, in Venezuela, and to study the Indians inhabiting the territory.

As companions on his hazardous journey Dr. Dickey had Sidney F. Tyler, Jr., who acted as his assistant, and Charles F. Polsten, as radio operator and navigator. They were the only white men in the original party, which also included a number of Indians. Later they picked up an itinerant Spaniard named Felix Cardona, an ex-sailor who had been prospecting unsuccessfully for diamonds in the vicinity of the Orinoco. Dr. Dickey returned to New York on August 15th, and through his kindness we are able to describe some of his experiences with the radio set in the jungles.

Leaving New York on the steamer "Dominica" of the Furness-Trinidad Line, the party reached the Port of Spain, Trinidad, off the northern end of South America. Here it boarded the steamer "Delta", which took the explorers 300 miles up the Orinoco River to Ciudad Bolivar, from which the actual expedition started. While in this city Dr. Dickey wrote the following letter, which is self-explanatory:

> Dickey Orinoco Expedition.
> c/o American Vice Consul.
> Ciudad Bolivar, Venezuela.

Pilot Radio & Tube Corporation.
Brooklyn, N. Y.

Dear Sirs:

In thanking you for your gift of a Pilot Super-Wasp to my expedition, I wish to state that this set has given us the greatest satisfaction. We assembled it shortly after arriving at this place and have been enjoying programs from all over the United States since that time.

Your apparatus will not only be of incalcuable value to us in getting time for our observations, but will also prove a very welcome addition to our scant means of entertainment when we are in the wilds of the Upper Orinoco.

Reiterating my thanks, I am,
Sincerely yours,
Herbert Spencer Dickey.

Shortwave radio provided a new dimension to world exploration (*Radio Design*, Fall 1929).

its equipment was on both the 1928–30 Byrd Antarctic expedition and the 1929 Dickey Orinoco expedition to the Venezuelan interior. As early as 1923, using newly established KDKA shortwave station 8XS (and later the shortwave channels of other Westinghouse stations), Canadian Westinghouse Company instituted a series of broadcasts for inhabitants above the Arctic Circle. The company distributed receivers to the Royal Canadian Mounted Police, and soon other organizations—like the Hudson Bay Company and the Oblate Fathers—were equipping their outposts with shortwave. The Westinghouse programs consisted of messages from relatives, employees, and friends of those posted to these small habitations in the icy north. The airings were often their only communication with the outside world for months at a time. As Westinghouse vice president H. P. Davis stated, "We have sent messages that have saved lives, have rearranged winter plans, have caused heartache or happy reunion—all over that great area starting from Greenland in the east, thence over the coast of Labrador and all the way across Northern Canada. These Far North broadcasts are among the most important things that broadcasting has ever accomplished."[16] Ten years after its start, production of the program was assumed by various Canadian medium-wave stations who dubbed it the Northern Messenger Service and continued to broadcast it at least into the late 1940s.

Maintaining radio contact with the other end of the globe—the Byrd Antarctic expedition of 1934—was big news, and the subject of frequent comment. From *Short Wave Radio* magazine the following report is provided:

> The Byrd "mailbag," as it has come to be known, is broadcast regularly to Little America through the facilities of [GE] short-wave station W2XAF at Schenectady, N.Y.... Practical advice on various matters has become more the rule of late, crowding out the more routine comments on the weather and the penguins which predominated in early letters. Some time ago, when a member of the airplane crew was injured in a fall, W2XAF broadcast a prescribed treatment from a chiropractor on the Pacific Coast. Only recently, when it was made known that Admiral Byrd's flapjacks were sticking in the pan, seasoned advice on what to do about it was forthcoming from a number of housewives....
>
> Birthdays are the occasion for a flood of messages from relatives and friends and the broadcast takes on the semblance of a party....
>
> The most striking feature of the short-wave broadcasts to date has been the practically perfect reception of the messages reported by the expedition. The listeners, totally enclosed by the Antarctic night, say that the voice of the broadcaster comes through as clearly as if it were in the next room.[17]

Radio provided contact with excursions to other faraway places as well, like the MacGregor Arctic expedition, the Norcross Bartlett expedition, and the round-

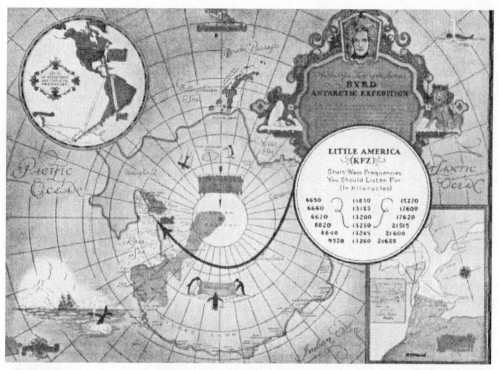

Members of the Radio Division of the Byrd Antarctic Expedition, left to right, are: John M. Dyer (Columbia), radio engineer for communication; Stanley Pierce, electrical engineer and relief operator; Guy Hutcheson, radio operator "S. S. Jacob Ruppert," and Clay Bailey, chief radio operator. Above, official map of the Second Byrd Antarctic Expedition. Insert shows frequencies used by the short-wave radio transmitter of the expedition; arrow points to location of little America.

**The Byrd expedition was an event of international importance (*Radio News*, July 1934).**

Endorsements of power radio users, such as this one from the Norcross Bartlett expedition to Arctic waters, were sought after by equipment manufacturers (*Short Wave Radio*, March 1934).

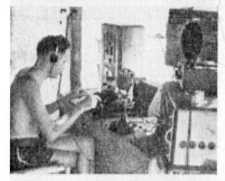

## VP3THE

### JUNGLES OF BRITISH GUIANA SOUTH AMERICA

Confirming ~~reception~~ on Nov 29 1937
            contact

Transmitter: RCA Model ACT-200. RCA 838's in final stage.

Receivers: RCA Model AR-60S Communication Receiver.
RCA Victor Broadcast Receiver.

Remarks:_____

### "Two Homesick Explorers"

● On November 14, 1937, VP3THE went "on the air" after weeks of treacherous travel over river rapids, sun-parched savannas and dense tropical jungles to inform the world of the activities of the Terry-Holden Expedition for the American Museum of Natural History direct from the base camp.

● VP3THE was set up approximately 500 miles from civilization at Long. 2° 19' North—Lat. 58° 22' West. The station was operated by O. W. ("Bill") Hungerford, radio operator, and Neil ("Mac") MacMillan, field assistant.

● Several NBC programs originated from the base camp which were picked up by R.C.A. Communications, Inc., at Riverhead, N. Y., and furnished to the NBC broadcast network.

● In spite of the humid, equatorial climate, not a single failure was experienced with this RCA equipment.

● On January 15, 1938, VP3THE went "off the air." We greatly appreciate your acknowledgment of our signals.

73,

A verification from the Terry-Holden expedition to British Guiana (QSL, 1937).

the-world jaunt of the windjammer Seth Parker, undertaken with much fanfare and publicity by Phillips H. Lord, who played New England philosopher Seth Parker on NBC Sunday night radio. Zenith had its shortwave equipment on the MacMillan Arctic expedition of 1923–24. On MacMillan's second expedition in 1925, Zenith's leader, Commander Eugene F. McDonald, Jr., not only supplied equipment

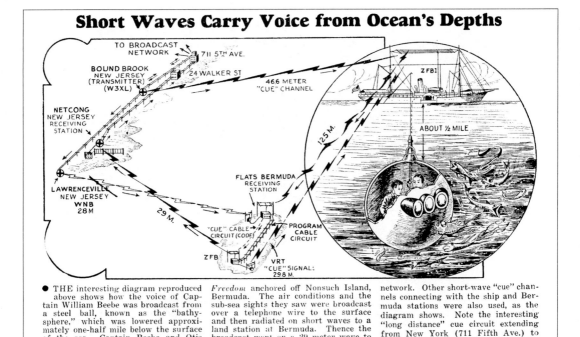

# Short Waves Carry Voice from Ocean's Depths

● THE interesting diagram reproduced above shows how the voice of Captain William Beebe was broadcast from a steel ball, known as the "bathysphere," which was lowered approximately one-half mile below the surface of the sea. Captain Beebe and Otis Barton, inventor of the "bathysphere," were lowered over the side of the S. S. *Freedom* anchored off Nonsuch Island, Bermuda. The air conditions and the sub-sea sights they saw were broadcast over a telephone wire to the surface and then radiated on short waves to a land station at Bermuda. Thence the broadcast went on a 29 meter wave to Netcong, N. J.; over a wire circuit to New York City, and out over the N.B.C. network. Other short-wave "cue" channels connecting with the ship and Bermuda stations were also used, as the diagram shows. Note the interesting "long distance" cue circuit extending from New York (711 Fifth Ave.) to Bermuda, thence by radio to the sender ship *Freedom*.

A diagram illustrating how shortwave can traverse long distances, in this case from Bermuda to the NBC network (*Short Wave Craft*, February 1933).

but went along as captain of one of the vessels. Shortwave's role in speeding police or physician response in emergencies was also stressed, and *Short Wave Craft* magazine even theorized that Amelia Earhart might have survived had she had different radio gear aboard her plane.

Shortwave radio not only covered the news—sometimes it was the news. The radio press reported on how the natives responded to seeing radio for the first time during the Terry-Holden exploration of the Amazon jungles of British Guiana, and on the role of radio in the 1931 "Trader Horn" moviemaking project in Kenya. Pilot staged a special international goodwill flight of its flying radio laboratory to South America, and promoted it widely.

The notion that something happening in one place could be experienced thousands of miles away was completely new. The magazines of the day often depicted graphically the ability of shortwave to bridge long distances, with diagrams showing how an event in one place was picked up and sent from place to place via shortwave, eventually reaching its intended, faraway destination.

It was in news and entertainment that shortwave broadcasting, with its ability to instantly put us in touch with other peoples and cultures, was expected to excel. Prepackaged international entertainment and live, worldwide TV news was still a very long way off. The gulf between people was wide, and it was natural that shortwave

## News Broadcasts

## Sunday, May 22

# On Short Waves

## Edited by Chas. A. Morrison

President, International DX'ers Alliance

Times Indicated on this page are for Eastern Daylight Saving Time. For EST and CDT subtract 1 hour; for CST, 2 hours; for MST, 3 hours; for PST, 4 hours

SEVERAL new short-wave stations to be officially inaugurated within the near future will add considerable variety to the already numerous programs from Europe. Claude Jones of Portsmouth, England, writes that 2RO8, one of the new Rome, Italy, transmitters, is conducting initial tests on 17.82, in conjunction with 2RO4 on 11.81 megs. He is also hearing a new Finnish station on approximately 9.5 megs . . . The highly publicized new 20,000-watt station nearing completion near Ankara, Turkey, to be officially inaugurated on July 22, will transmit on either 9.465 or 15,195 megs . . . According to reports, the new 10,000-watt short-wave transmitter under construction at Belgrade, Jugoslavia, will be completed before fall.

Raymond Messer of South Portland, Me., writes that he intercepted an announcement over 2RO3 (9.635) of Rome, Italy, to the effect that on May 9, a new short-wave station at Addis Ababa, Ethiopia, took the air on a frequency of 9.6 megs.

A new Latin broadcaster, TIGX, located at San Jose, in Costa Rica, operating on a frequency of 11.92 megs, was first heard on April 23, at 9 p.m. EDT.

*Arturo Toscanini will conduct the second and third concerts of the BBC Symphony Orchestra in the current London Music Festival at Queen's Hall, on Monday, May 23, at 3:15 p.m. and on Friday, May 27, at 3:15 p.m. EDT.*

SHORT-WAVE SHORTS: Albania may now be added to short-wave logs. Listen for Amateur Station ZA1CC (14.3) near 8 a.m. and 3 p.m. EDT . . . The short-wave station broadcasting irregularly near 10.03 megs, reported by many listeners as the mysterious anti-Stalin Soviet station, is, according to Eugene Rein-

hard, of Locust, N. J., the unauthorized anti-Nazi transmitter "Der Deutsche Freiheits Sender" . . . The first ultra-high-frequency non-commercial broadcast station to be licensed under the Federal Communications Commission's new ruling, owned by the Cleveland City Board of Education of Cleveland, O., has been assigned the call, WBOE . . . Guy Bigbee of Fort Benning, Ga., informs me that the call of the Vilarrica, Paraguay, station on 6.15 megs has been changed from ZP15 to ZP14 . . . Although supposedly operating on a new frequency of 8.735 megs, LZA, Sofia, Bulgaria, is still being heard on approximately 14.96 megs from 2 to 2:45 a.m. EDT by L. B. Brewer of Phoenix, Ariz. . . . W8XWJ (41), the ultra-high-frequency station in Detroit, Mich., is being heard with fair consistency in Germany . . . Jacques Jacquemard of Algiers writes that CSW of Lisbon, Portugal, has been testing near 8 a.m. EDT on a frequency of 11.82 megs and Radio Tananarive, Tananarive, Madagascar, is being heard on a frequency of 10.95 megs Sundays to 5:30 a.m. EDT, when the station signs off with the "Marseillaise" . . . VP2LO (6.384) of St. Kitts, British West Indies, is testing a new transmitter with aerial directional to the United States, on Saturdays from about 11:45 p.m. to Sundays at 12:45 a.m. EDT, according to John DeMyer of Lansing, Mich. . . . To his other aids for identifying Station TI4NRH (9.7), in Heredia, Costa Rica, Senor Amando Cespedes Marin has added a cuckoo call and a clock, whose chimes may be heard striking the hour . . . Andrew Young, the present operator of VR6AY (14.346) on Pitcairn Island, is keeping a nightly schedule with Amateur W2IXY in New York City, at 2 a.m. EDT.

*Sir Henry J. Wood will conduct fourteen South Wales choirs, including more than 1,000 voices, together with four solo artists and the Welsh Symphony Orchestra, in the broadcast of the famous Three Valleys Festival from the Pavilion, Mountain Ash, South Wales, on Saturday, May 28, at 4:10 p.m. EDT.*

Listeners to the "GS" stations of England hear W. M. Shewen, senior Empire announcer, who makes a specialty of broadcasting news bulletins

The national radio weekly, *Radio Guide*, devoted a section to the stations and programs that could be heard on shortwave (*Radio Guide*, May 28, 1938).

should try to bridge it. The bimonthly *Official Short Wave Listener* magazine gave prominence to shortwave programming, and featured news about the artists and the entertainment on particular shortwave stations. Some publications, like the national American AM radio weekly *Radio Guide*, had a special page describing the programs that would be available on international shortwave during the coming week.

The utilization of shortwave for nonradio purposes was also the subject of frequent comment. The term shortwave was generally taken to refer to anything above 1.5 mc., without upper limit, and so the frequencies above what today we think of as the top of the shortwave band, 30 mc., were considered part of the short waves. Transmissions in this part of the spectrum were fair game for shortwave hobbyists, leading to occasional coverage in the shortwave literature of such over 30 mc., non-broadcasting subjects as airplane landing beams, metal detection, insect extermination, ultra-shortwave diathermy and various other medical subjects, radio control of models, paging and facsimile, and a subject about which much was written in the 1930s: television.

# Part 2

# SHORTWAVE COMES OF AGE: THE 1930S

## Chapter 4

# Stations of the 1930s

In 1985 the Canadian DXer Tom Williamson reminisced about what it was like listening to shortwave in England some 50 years earlier.

> [I]t is very difficult to imagine what a thrill it was all those years ago to "hear America." Even on shortwave … it was not a regular daily event to tune in the U.S.A., and even the radio hams of that time used to refer to "getting across the pond" when they made transatlantic contacts…. The usual Europeans were heard, as in modern times, including Radio Moscow. Switzerland was heard on various channels with call signs like HBJ, HBQ, and HBO, and the slogan "Radio Nations" (it was the site of the League of Nations). France was one of my favorite sources of jazz music, but mainly on AM from Radio Paris. Each Saturday we could tune in to a period of musical history in the form of the "Hot Club de France," which featured a session of toe tapping, hot rhythms from the immortal Stephane Grappelli (still playing that fabulous violin in the United States today), Django Reinhardt, and others. They really set the air waves jumping.
>
> From the good old U.S.A. we had the era of big-band swing. My generation was brought up on this, and I well remember the orchestras of Artie Shaw, Glenn Miller, Benny Goodman, and others. "Swing and Sway with Sammy Kaye" was a favorite, heard over W3XAU, Philadelphia. Many happy "small hours" were spent listening to W4XB. "By the palm-fringed shores of blue Biscayne Bay in tropical America" was their slogan, and they had 5 kw. output on 6040 kHz. Operated by the Isle of Dreams Broadcasting Co., they relayed WIOD, Miami, still on the air on 610 kHz…. From the northern region, familiar voices were VONG, St. Johns, Newfoundland, then not yet part of Canada, and the amazing, low-power CHNX,

# PHILIPS RADIO-LABORATORIES

## EINDHOVEN HOLLAND

wish to convey to you their appreciation of your kind communication on the subject of their experimental transmission of

4 November 1934.

N.V. PHILIPS' RADIO

Bird's eye view of Philips' Laboratories, Eindhoven, Holland

Experimental shortwave broadcasting transmitter of Philips Radio.
Address to: Shortwave station PCJ
N.V. Philips Radio, Eindhoven, Holland.

Frequency: 15220 kc/s; Wavelength: appr. 19·71 m
9590 kc/s; „ „ 31·28 m
Power: Four 20—kW tubes type Philips
TA 12/20000 K in the final stage.

Position: Lat. 51°27'40" N      Long. 5°27'15" E
Times of operation: Irregular. Broadcasts on Sundays
on wavelength 19·71 m from 13.30
G.M.T. the program of the PHOHI
(Station PHI, Huizen, Holland).

**Announcements in NETHERLANDS - ENGLISH - FRENCH - GERMAN and SPANISH**

program over PCJ, the historic Philips station at Eindhoven. PCJ programs were intended mainly for the Dutch East and West Indies, but they were heard worldwide. "Shortwave signal magnificent," read a telegram from Bandung. The Startz theme song, "A Nice Cup of Tea," would become familiar to SWLs for decades to come.

The main Axis station was Deutscher Kurzwellensender. It boasted four transmitters, and, like the BBC, used two frequencies in parallel. It was known informally as "Zeesen," after the village near Berlin where it was located. Using various three-letter DJ and DZ calls such as DJR and DZA, it was the first station to have a highly developed directional antenna system (along with its own airfield, antiaircraft guns, and barbed-wire perimeter). With a staff numbering 1,000, Zeesen produced extensive news programs, as well as musical productions that

Still a strong presence on the shortwave bands today, PCJ in the Netherlands was one of the pioneer shortwave broadcasters, with Edward Startz as one of its premier international personalities (QSL, 1934).

drew an international following. One listener noted: "[W]e've danced here several times to music from DJD. They broadcast a German orchestra one evening playing 'Stormy Weather' and we just had to dance."[5] The station received 3,000 letters in 1933, 45,000 a mere three years later. This should be compared to a total of 3,500 letters received by CBS shortwave in 1937, of which 1,200 were from within the United States. The station engaged in elaborate promotions, distributing maps, picture placards, records, speeches, and language lessons. The estimated audience in the United States was one-half million, but it dropped by approximately two-thirds when Nazi excesses became known.

By 1938 Zeesen was broadcasting 24 hours a day in 12 languages.[6] The goal of the station was to "bind all German racial comrades firmly to their homeland and the new national community which has been brought into being [in Germany]," beginning with Germans in North America (the station's first foreign beam was to the United States and Canada). The German foreign ministry estimated that there were 3 million German citizens living abroad, plus a potential audience of 15 million German "racial comrades" overseas. Listener clubs were formed in places where German citizens resided. The station played a lot of German folk songs, and offered radio plays, German lessons, and strong educational programming about National Socialist politics.[7] Observed the *New York Times*, "Germany is ... not alone in directing broadcasts beyond its frontiers. But no other country has developed the technique so fully."[8]

MINISTÈRE DES POSTES
TÉLÉGRAPHES & TÉLÉPHONES

DIRECTION de la RADIODIFFUSION

**STATION RADIO-COLONIALE
DE L'ETAT FRANÇAIS**
98 bis, Boulevard Haussmann, 98 bis
PARIS (8ᵉ)

$296 \frac{3}{2}$

Paris, le _____ 19

Monsieur,

J'ai l'honneur de vous accuser réception de votre lettre du _19/8/36_. Je vous remercie des renseignements que vous avez bien voulu me communiquer sur les résultats que vous avez obtenus dans l'écoute de la Station Radio-Coloniale de l'État Français et en particulier : *sur les longueurs de 25 m 60.*

Nos émissions se font tous les jours sur les longueurs d'ondes ci-après : 19 m. 68, 25 m. 23, 25 m. 60.

Veuillez agréer, Monsieur, l'assurance de ma considération très distinguée.

*Le Directeur du Service de la Radiodiffusion.*

**Radio Coloniale was the early French shortwave station (QSL, 1936).**

Studio N.º 1

Studio N.º 2

Amplificadores e controle
Amplifiers and controle room

ESTAÇÃO

# CT1AA

(Rádio Colonial)

Emissor de ondas curtas
Short-wave transmitter

ABILIO NUNES DOS SANTOS JUNIOR

Aspecto parcial
Parcial view

STUDIO: Av. Antonio Augusto de Aguiar, 136, r/c d.   Telefone 4 0593      LISBOA
EMISSOR: Av. Antonio Augusto de Aguiar, 144            Telefone 4 0594      Portugal

Another Radio Coloniale, this one CT1AA, Lisbon, Portugal (QSL, 1935).

Ente Italiano Audizioni Radiofoniche (EIAR), station I2RO in Rome, transmitted with 25 kw. (increased to 100 in the late 1930s) on 9635 and 11810 kc., usually rebroadcasting the daily program of Italian domestic stations, but also presenting special programs for the Americas. The "American Hour" was broadcast on 6085 kc., Monday, Wednesday, and Friday, at 6:00–7:30 P.M. EST.[9] EIAR utilized an interesting form of propaganda: Italian language lessons based on Il Duce's own speeches. You sent your homework to Rome for correction and received Fascist propaganda by return mail.

Beginning in 1931, Radio Coloniale, Pontoise, France, transmitted with 15 kw. on 11710, 11900, and 15250 kc. The station maintained a high cultural level that was welcomed by the well educated, but overall it was neither very entertaining nor very well heard. In 1938 Pontoise was supplemented by a 25 kw. transmitter at Essarts-le-Roi, and programs from the two sites were thereafter known as "Paris Mondial." The *New York Times* stated: "Early morning" in 1938 "finds the French on 25 meters reaching out to the Society and Marquesas Islands in the Pacific. Later, with waves on 19 meters, beams from Paris are turned on the Asiatic possessions of Indo-China and the little-known French city colonies of Pondicherry and Karikai on the East Indian coast; toward noon Paris entertains for Madagascar and African colonies on the borders of the Sahara. Then at 6:15 waves are focused on Devil's Island, the French West Indies, Canada, and America."[10]

EAQ, Radiodifusion Ibero-Americana, Madrid, Spain, used 20 kw. on 9870 kc., and concentrated on maintaining contact with South America and the Spanish colonies. "Apparently Madrid is pumping tremendous power into its ethereal arteries and has erected a directional aerial that megaphones the broadcasts to the United States and Canada. On these Spring nights this voice on the 9.4 megacycle channel is so loud that it equals the strength of the most powerful local stations; it seems as if the speaker was at the open window of the American home."[11]

Also heard from Europe were Belgian station ORK, 10330 kc., in Ruysselde, which was used for broadcasting as well as point-to-point communication with the Belgian Congo; and 12 (later 50) kw. station HVJ, Vatican City. "HVJ is easily recognized by the announcement, 'Radio-Vaticano,' and by the ticking of a clock in the studio."[12] And, unlike modern times when only pirate radio stations operate on shortwave from Ireland, the Irish shortwave station at Athlone transmitted on 17840, 15120, and 9595 kc. Portugal had both a government outlet, CT1AA, 9600 kc. (also called Radio Colonial), and a private station, CT1GO, Radio Clube de Portugal, Parede, on 6200 and 12400 kc. The Hungarian stations HAS and HAT, "Radio Labor, Station of the Royal Hungarian Post," were widely heard and sent a QSL card with a little photograph pasted in the middle.

The Soviet Union was a major player in the shortwave game of the 1930s. This was consistent with its early use of high-powered medium-wave transmitters for broadcasting beyond its borders, and low frequency shortwave for domestic coverage of the country's huge territory. As early as 1930, Radio Centre Moscow was broadcasting on shortwave in 50 languages. Russian stations heard in mid-decade were RV15 in Khabarovsk, said to be an easy log on 4273.5 kc., and Moscow channels RV59, 6000 kc., RAN, 9600 kc., RNE, 12000 kc., RKI, 15145 kc., and RV96, 15183 kc. Reported one DXer: "I was turning the dials this afternoon around 1:45 and I heard a station on 25 meters, something new to me, playing violin music. The music stopped and a voice, 'This is Moscow calling....' He talked entirely in English, asking for reports of reception, giving the address as Radio Station RNE, Gorki St., No. 17, Moscow, U.S.S.R. It signed off before 2 P.M.... They are experimenting with the United States."[13] During the war, Radio Centre Moscow began and ended its English programs with the call, "Death to the German Invaders." Slogans like "Death to Fascism, Liberty to the People" were also used by Eastern European countries that were overrun by the Soviets.

Twenty kilowatt League of Nations station HBL was also well received. It was reported in May 1934 that "the station broke into New York's short-wave limelight with unusual clarity. For nearly an hour the waves crossed the Atlantic without audible ethereal blemish; in fact, the signals were so strong that a listener might be tempted at times to glance at the dial of the all-wave receiver to make sure the talk was not coming from a local studio."[14]

U.S.S.R.
Radio Centre Moscow

Dear Listener,

We are glad to verify that you heard our broadcast on 20/12
1937, at ___24___ G.M.T. on a wave length of ___41.25___
metres ___7400___ kcs. through Radio Station RAN.

We shall always be glad to hear from you and to have your reports
on reception. We shall also welcome criticisms of our programs and
suggestions for improvement in the future.

Radio Greetings
Radio Centre Moscow.

Moscow was omnipresent on shortwave for many years, but has been less reliable since the fall of the Soviet Union (QSL, 1937).

## Africa

There were some stations here, but in radio terms it was still the dark continent. Many stations in Africa (and elsewhere) were not dedicated broadcasters, but combination utility and broadcast senders, carrying both regular broadcast programming and government or commercial traffic, depending on the need. One such station was CNR, Radio Maroc, which transmitted on 8036 and 12825 kc. Another was VQ7LO, "Kenya Colony," on 6060 kc. The station was located at Kabete, five miles from and 1,000 feet above Nairobi. Programs consisted of music, twice-daily news bulletins, and relays of the British Empire Service.

An often heard African station was CR6AA, 7170 kc., in Lobito, Angola. In South Africa there was the African Broadcasting Company, with the same Johannesburg address—P.O. Box 4559—that would be used by the South African Broadcasting Corporation 50 years later. An interesting station was EA9AH, Tetuan, Spanish Morocco, a combination amateur-broadcast station and one of Franco's key propaganda outlets during the Spanish Civil War. Radio Tananarive, Madagascar, was also on shortwave. As it reported: "The transmissions begin with a piece of recorded music entitled 'Ramona,' and end with the French National Anthem. The station operates on 6000 kcs. with a power of 400 watts antenna. We transmit every day except Monday, programs consisting of musical selections rendered by artists, or recordings, as well as news flashes."[15]

## The Americas

There were many shortwave stations in Latin America, as there would be for

LA ESTACIÓN EXPERIMENTAL NACIONALISTA

# EA9-AH

Marruecos    DE LA RUEDA DEL OESTE    España (Spain)

Saluda a la ~~Estación~~ *Secretary* de *Baltimore* y tiene el gusto
de acusarle recibo del Q S O celebrado el día *18 de* *May* de 193*7*
a las *5.15 & 5.45* G M T significándole que su ⌐⌐⌐⌐ ha sido recibida
con Q R K *R* ⌐⌐ Q S A ⌐⌐, comprensibilidad ⌐⌐⌐ T ⌐⌐, modulación
⌐⌐⌐⌐ y que esta Estación ha utilizado un emisor 500 W Output con
antena "Johnson Q" y modulación Clase B y un receptor F B X NATIONAL
*20 wti . foue*

*Fernando Díaz Gómez*

aprovecha esta ocasión para ofrecerse como colega y amigo, deseando se repitan esos Q S O
tan agradables y le comunica su Q R A APARTADO, 124 TETUAN

MARRUECOS ESPAÑOL

OBSERVACIONES: *Very much obliged—OK Writing — 73's*

Station EA9AH was a combination amateur-broadcast station. It was Franco's key propaganda station in Morocco during the Spanish Civil War (QSL, 1937).

many years to come. By 1940 there were 32 stations on the air in Venezuela, 23 in Colombia, 10 in Peru, even 2 in Bolivia (the still familiar R. Illimani and R. Fides).[16] Then, as now, Latin America was the preserve of private rather than governmental broadcasting, the product of a laissez-faire regulatory climate and the influence of American diplomacy and culture and U.S. radio manufacturers.[17]

Stations were commonly identified by their slogans, but they were often referred to by their call letters as well. Among the more familiar stations in Venezuela were YV2RC, Broadcasting Caracas, 5800 kc., YV3BC, Radiodifusora Venezuela, Caracas, 6145 kc., and YV5RMO, Ecos del Caribe, Maracaibo, 6070 kc. As YV5RMO reported: "Every Monday evening we broadcast operas or other classical music and the rest of the week is dedicated to lovers of the more popular variety, especially local music. Our programs open and close with the playing of the 'Blue Danube March.' YV5RMO announces as 'Ecos del Caribe' (Echoes of the Caribbean), and one stroke on a gong usually precedes this announcement."[18]

LSX, Transradio Internacional, Buenos Aires, Argentina, transmitted on 10350 kc. and often relayed programs from the Byrd expedition. Other widely reported stations included HJ1ABG, Emisora Atlantico, 6042.5 kc., Barranquilla, Colombia, HJ7ABD, Radio Bucaramanga, 9630 kc., and HJ4ABL, Manizales. The *New York Times* advised that "[a]t the present time [1935], HJ4ABL announce their schedule

# Leading Short Wave Stations of the World and Schedules of Operation

| METER BAND | METERS | MEGA-CYCLES | STATION CALL | STATION LOCATION | SUN. | MON. | TUE. | WED. | THU. | FRI. | SAT. |
|---|---|---|---|---|---|---|---|---|---|---|---|
| | 51.60 | 5.80 | YV2RC | CARACAS, VENEZUELA | ★ | ★ | ★ | ★ | ★ | ★ | ★ |
| | 50.30 | 5.96 | HVJ | VATICAN CITY, ITALY | ★ | ★ | ★ | ★ | ★ | ★ | ★ |
| 49 M | 49.92 | 6.01 | COCO | HAVANA, CUBA | ★ | ★ | ★ | ★ | ★ | ★ | ★ |
| | 49.90 | 6.00 | XEBT | MEXICO CITY, MEXICO | ★ | ★ | ★ | ★ | ★ | ★ | ★ |
| | 49.83 | 6.02 | DJC | ZEESEN, GERMANY | ★ | ★ | ★ | ★ | ★ | ★ | ★ |
| | 49.70 | 6.03 | VE9CA | CALGARY, ALBERTA, CAN. | ★ | ★ | ★ | ★ | ★ | ★ | ★ |
| | 49.67 | 6.04 | W4XB | MIAMI, FLA. | ★ | ★ | ★ | ★ | ★ | ★ | ★ |
| | 49.60 | 6.04 | PRA8 | PERNAMBUCA, BRAZIL | ★ | ★ | ★ | ★ | ★ | ★ | ★ |
| | 49.59 | 6.05 | GSA | DAVENTRY, ENGLAND | ★ | ★ | ★ | ★ | ★ | ★ | ★ |
| | 49.50 | 6.06 | W3XAU | PHILADELPHIA, PA. | ★ | ★ | ★ | ★ | ★ | ★ | ★ |
| | 49.50 | 6.06 | W8XAL | CINCINNATI, OHIO | ★ | ★ | ★ | ★ | ★ | ★ | ★ |
| | 49.34 | 6.08 | W9XAA | CHICAGO, ILL. | ★ | ★ | ★ | ★ | ★ | ★ | ★ |
| | 49.30 | 6.07 | OER2 | VIENNA, AUSTRIA | ★ | ★ | ★ | ★ | ★ | ★ | ★ |
| | 49.18 | 6.10 | W9XF | CHICAGO, ILL. | ★ | ★ | ★ | ★ | ★ | ★ | ★ |
| | 49.18 | 6.10 | W3XAL | BOUNDBROOK, N. J. | | ★ | | ★ | | | ★ |
| | 49.10 | 6.10 | ZTJ | JOHANNESBURG, AFRICA | ★ | ★ | ★ | ★ | ★ | ★ | ★ |
| | 49.10 | 6.10 | CRCX | TORONTO, CANADA | ★ | ★ | ★ | ★ | ★ | ★ | ★ |
| | 49.02 | 6.12 | W2XE | NEW YORK, N. Y. | ★ | ★ | ★ | ★ | ★ | ★ | ★ |
| | 49.00 | 6.11 | VE9HX | HALIFAX, N. S. | ★ | ★ | ★ | ★ | ★ | ★ | ★ |
| | 49.00 | 6.11 | GSL | DAVENTRY, ENGLAND | ★ | ★ | ★ | ★ | ★ | ★ | ★ |
| | 48.86 | 6.14 | W8XK | PITTSBURGH, PA. | ★ | ★ | ★ | ★ | ★ | ★ | ★ |
| | 48.70 | 6.15 | CO9GC | SANTIAGO, CUBA | ★ | ★ | ★ | ★ | ★ | ★ | ★ |
| | 48.60 | 6.16 | VPB | COLOMBO, CEYLON | ★ | ★ | ★ | ★ | ★ | ★ | ★ |
| | 44.93 | 6.67 | HC2RL | GUAYAQUIL, ECUADOR | ★ | | | | | | |
| | 37.33 | 8.04 | CNR | RABAT, MOROCCO | ★ | | | | | | |
| 31 M | 31.80 | 9.43 | COCH | HAVANA, CUBA | ★ | ★ | ★ | ★ | ★ | ★ | ★ |
| | 31.55 | 9.51 | GSB | DAVENTRY, ENGLAND | ★ | ★ | ★ | ★ | ★ | ★ | ★ |
| | 31.55 | 9.51 | VK3ME | MELBOURNE, AUSTRALIA | | ★ | ★ | ★ | ★ | ★ | |
| | 31.48 | 9.53 | W2XAF | SCHENECTADY, N. Y. | ★ | ★ | ★ | ★ | ★ | ★ | ★ |
| | 31.40 | 9.53 | LKJ1 | JELOY, NORWAY | ★ | ★ | ★ | ★ | ★ | ★ | ★ |
| | 31.38 | 9.56 | DJA | ZEESEN, GERMANY | ★ | ★ | ★ | ★ | ★ | ★ | ★ |
| | 31.35 | 9.57 | W1XK | SPRINGFIELD, MASS. | ★ | ★ | ★ | ★ | ★ | ★ | ★ |
| | 31.29 | 9.58 | GSC | DAVENTRY, ENGLAND | ★ | ★ | ★ | ★ | ★ | ★ | ★ |
| | 31.28 | 9.59 | VK2ME | SYDNEY, AUSTRALIA | ★ | | | | | | |
| | 31.28 | 9.59 | W3XAU | PHILADELPHIA, PA. | ★ | ★ | ★ | ★ | ★ | ★ | ★ |
| | 31.27 | 9.59 | HBL | GENEVA, SWITZERLAND | | | | | | | ★ |
| | 31.25 | 9.60 | I2RO | ROME, ITALY | | ★ | | ★ | | ★ | |
| | 31.20 | 9.59 | HP5J | PANAMA CITY, PANAMA | ★ | ★ | ★ | ★ | ★ | ★ | ★ |
| | 30.43 | 9.86 | EAQ | MADRID, SPAIN | ★ | ★ | ★ | ★ | ★ | ★ | ★ |
| 25 M | 25.60 | 11.71 | HJ4ABA | MEDELLIN, COLORADO | ★ | ★ | ★ | ★ | ★ | ★ | ★ |
| | 25.60 | 11.72 | VE9JR | WINNIPEG, CANADA | ★ | ★ | ★ | ★ | ★ | ★ | ★ |
| | 25.55 | 11.72 | FYA | PONTOISE, FRANCE | ★ | ★ | ★ | ★ | ★ | ★ | ★ |
| | 25.53 | 11.75 | GSD | DAVENTRY, ENGLAND | ★ | ★ | ★ | ★ | ★ | ★ | ★ |
| | 25.50 | 11.73 | PHI | HUIZEN, HOLLAND | ★ | ★ | | | ★ | ★ | ★ |
| | 25.50 | 11.76 | DJD | ZEESEN, GERMANY | ★ | ★ | ★ | ★ | ★ | ★ | ★ |
| | 25.40 | 11.81 | I2RO | ROME, ITALY | ★ | ★ | ★ | ★ | ★ | ★ | ★ |
| | 25.36 | 11.83 | W2XE | NEW YORK, N. Y. | ★ | ★ | ★ | ★ | ★ | ★ | ★ |
| | 25.30 | 11.86 | GSE | DAVENTRY, ENGLAND | ★ | ★ | ★ | ★ | ★ | ★ | ★ |
| | 25.27 | 11.87 | W8XK | PITTSBURGH, PA. | ★ | ★ | ★ | ★ | ★ | ★ | ★ |
| | 25.20 | 11.90 | CTIGO | PAREDE, PORTUGAL | ★ | ★ | | ★ | | | ★ |
| | 23.39 | 12.82 | CNR | RABAT, MOROCCO | ★ | | | | | | |
| | 21.2-1 | 14.15-14.25 | | AMATEUR PHONE | | | | | | | |
| 19 M | 19.90 | 15.04 | RKI | MOSCOW, U. S. S. R. | ★ | ★ | ★ | ★ | ★ | ★ | ★ |
| | 19.84 | 15.12 | HVJ | VATICAN CITY, ITALY | | ★ | ★ | ★ | ★ | ★ | ★ |
| | 19.82 | 15.14 | GSF | DAVENTRY, ENGLAND | ★ | ★ | ★ | ★ | ★ | ★ | ★ |
| | 19.74 | 15.20 | DJB | ZEESEN, GERMANY | ★ | ★ | ★ | ★ | ★ | ★ | ★ |
| | 19.72 | 15.21 | W8XK | PITTSBURGH, PA. | ★ | ★ | ★ | ★ | ★ | ★ | ★ |
| | 19.70 | 15.22 | PCJ | HUIZEN, HOLLAND | ★ | ★ | | | ★ | ★ | ★ |
| | 19.68 | 15.24 | FYA | PONTOISE, FRANCE | ★ | ★ | ★ | ★ | ★ | ★ | ★ |
| | 19.65 | 15.27 | W2XE | NEW YORK, N. Y. | ★ | ★ | ★ | ★ | ★ | ★ | ★ |
| | 19.57 | 15.33 | W2XAD | SCHENECTADY, N. Y. | ★ | ★ | ★ | | ★ | ★ | ★ |
| | 19.50 | 15.37 | HAS3 | BUDAPEST, HUNGARY | ★ | | | | | | |
| | 16.87 | 17.78 | W3XAL | BOUNDBROOK, N. J. | ★ | ★ | ★ | ★ | ★ | ★ | ★ |
| | 16.86 | 17.79 | GSG | DAVENTRY, ENGLAND | ★ | ★ | ★ | ★ | ★ | ★ | ★ |
| | 16.80 | 17.78 | DJE | ZEESEN, GERMANY | ★ | ★ | ★ | ★ | ★ | ★ | ★ |
| | 13.90 | 21.54 | W8XK | PITTSBURGH, PA. | ★ | ★ | ★ | ★ | ★ | ★ | ★ |

Crosley Radio Corporation provided its customers with a list of what could be heard on the short-wave bands (c. 1935).

OUR MODERN
5 K. W.
R. C. A. VICTOR
TRANSMITTER
———
NUESTRO MODERNO
TRANSMISOR
R. C. A. VICTOR
DE 5 KILOVATIOS

CONTROL
ROOM
———
CUARTO DE
CONTROL

ONE OF THE STUDIOS
CAV. ADOLFO BRACALE
CONDUCTING
———
UNO DE LOS ESTUDIOS.
EL MAESTRO ADOLFO
BRACALE DIRIGIENDO

*Above and facing page:* **Glimpses of station YV1BC (later, on shortwave, YV2RC), Broadcasting Caracas, Caracas, Venezuela, circa 1933.**

REMOTE
CONTROL
—
CONTROL
EN LA
PLANTA

PART OF
THE ENGINE
ROOM
—
VISTA PARCIAL
DEL CUARTO DE
MAQUINAS

OTHER VIEW
OF THE
ENGINE
ROOM
—
OTRA VISTA
DEL CUARTO
DE MAQUINAS

HCJB, "Heralding Christ Jesus Blessing," has been a strong shortwave voice for many years. Its powerful signal is widely heard today (QSL, 1935).

as Saturday nights only, from 11 until about 11:30 P.M., EST, at which time they broadcast a program for English-speaking people, although announcements are made in Spanish, German and Dutch as well as English. HJ4ABL uses the slogan 'Ecos del Oriente' (Echoes of the West), and was heard using an automobile horn a few times as an identification signal."[19] In the same year a *RADEX* reader observed that HJ1ABB, La Voz de Barranquilla, "was picked up a few nights ago dedicating a program to the Chicago Short-wave Club. An 'International Orchestra' provided the music, beginning at 10 P.M., New York time."[20]

The 1930s also saw the birth of well-known religious shortwave station HCJB in Quito, Ecuador. The station was the joint effort of Clarence W. Jones, an American evangelist who dreamed of introducing missionary radio to South America, and Reuben Larson, an American preacher who had gone to Ecuador in 1924 to establish a small ministry. La Voz de los Andes, as it was (and still is) known, began broadcasting on Christmas Day, 1931, on 5986 kc. with 250 watts. The antenna was a horizontal wire stretched between two 85-foot telephone poles set 200 feet apart.[21] During the first few years the station was reported on such out-of-band frequencies as 3998, 4107, 5710, and 8103 kc. A medium-wave channel was added, and, in 1940 a 10 kw. shortwave transmitter was connected to the Clarence Jones–invented Cubical Quad, an antenna soon to become known worldwide as an efficient design for use on the short waves. One of the first programs to be broadcast over HCJB was "Morning in the Mountains," a program that is still broadcast from this station.

Central and South American stations abounded on the shortwave bands. They usually simulcasted their sister AM stations (QSL, 1938).

One of the most promising of the early companies, Pilot Radio and Tube Corporation, produced some of the best early shortwave receivers, including the Wasp, the Super Wasp (AC kit $35, battery version $30), and the Universal Super Wasp (AC kit $85). Alas, organizational problems overtook Pilot, which fared poorly in the superhet revolution.

Hallicrafters arrived later than the others, but also started with two presuperhets: the H-13 regenerative in 1933, and in 1934, a five-tube, $39 TRF receiver that introduced a name that would become a household word among shortwave hobbyists for the next 40 years, "Skyrider."

"Screen grid" was a term spoken with reverance. Screen grid tubes were introduced by RCA in 1927. They contained a screen around the anode, yielding high audio gain, high gain as an RF amplifier, improved stability as an oscillator, and improved amplification at low wavelengths. Some receiver manufacturers took advantage of these features, promoting the screen grid concept in their advertisements. Other receivers were sold "less tubes," because tubes were a high-profit item and the subject of great competition among manufacturers.

An editorial in *Radio News* likened the proliferation of receivers to the seasonal changes in women's hats.[34] Radio exhibitions, which brought together manufacturers, dealers, and consumers, were held regularly. Many "radiotricians," as the technically inclined were called, became custom-set builders, making radios for nontechnical people on a full-time or part-time basis. A new profession, radio serviceman, developed, as did dreams of striking it rich in the new industry.

Many of the companies got into receiver manufacturing as an offshoot of some other already established business. And it didn't take much to get involved.

> In a small tool and die shop on Jerome Avenue in the Bronx, Frank Angelo D'Andrea, the son of a junk dealer with a fervent desire to be rich, began producing crystal detectors. Soon forty young women were busy making his "FADA" detectors. The crystals cost 96 cents to make and sold for $2.25. By early 1922, sales had risen to $50,000 a month, and he was branching out into simple vacuum tube sets and radio kits. On Washington's Birthday 1921, Powel Crosley, owner of an automobile accessories company and a phonograph cabinet manufacturing plant in Cincinnati, built a small crystal set with his son, which allowed them to hear broadcasts as far as seven miles away. With little regard for proper licensing of [Edwin] Armstrong's invention, he soon was selling a low-priced set of his own design that employed a regenerative circuit and was housed in a handsome wooden cabinet. On Stenton Avenue in Philadelphia, Arthur Atwater Kent, sometime manufacturer of sewing machine motors, gunsights, and automobile ignitions, decided he would create a line of handsome radio parts cast in expensive Bakelite. Beginning with audio transformers, he soon moved on to complete radio sets, each

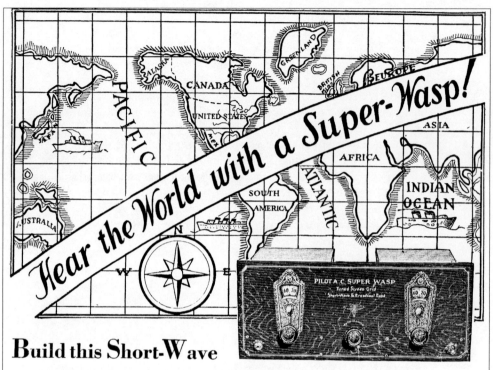

## Hear the World with a Super-Wasp!

## Build this Short-Wave

### Receiver *with the* **10,000** *Mile Range!*

*[Also covers the entire broadcast band from 14 to 500 meters, by means of interchangeable plug-in coils]*

**A. C. Operated Kit K-115**

**$34.50**

(Power Pack Extra)

This combination short-wave and broadcast receiver, designed by Grimes, Geloso and Kruse, utilizes the super-sensitive screen-grid tube and specially developed Pilotron 227. Thousands of fans attest the world-spanning ability of this four-tube short-wave wonder! Made for both A.C. and battery operation. (With the A.C. job use power pack K-111.) You, too, will get more "kick" per dollar from international short-wave reception with the Super-Wasp than from anything else in radio!

**BATTERY OPERATED KIT K-110**

**$29.50**

*If your nearby radio dealer is not yet supplied, write direct to*

# PILOT RADIO & TUBE CORP.

*World's Largest Radio Parts Plant*
*Established 1908*

Trade Mark

323 BERRY STREET
BROOKLYN, NEW YORK

Pilot Radio and Tube Corporation captured the romance of the shortwaves in its Wasp line of short-wave receivers (*Radio Design*, Winter 1929).

Founded in 1932, HC2JSB, Ecuador Radio, on 7850 kc., claimed to be the first commercial broadcaster in the country. Other out-of-band Ecuadorians included Station PRADO in Riobamba on 6620 kc., and HC2RL, Guayaquil, on 6670 kc. *RADEX* described the latter station thus: "Their regular schedule is Sundays from 5:45 to 7:45 P.M. and Tuesdays from 9:15 to 11:15 P.M., EST. These programs open and close with the playing of the Ecuadorian National Hymn, and the expression 'Quinta Piedad' is used often in the announcements [Marie Piedad Castillo de Levi was the station owner]. The January 14 [1934] program from this station will feature primarily Ecuadorian national music, and as Dr. Levi [station director Roberto Levi] has planned to have artists from the National Conservatory of Music and the Academia de Artistas Nationales, we believe the program will be a very interesting one."[22]

Peru didn't have anywhere near the large number of shortwave stations it has today, but nine were on the air by 1937, including the widely heard OAX4J, R. Internacional, on 9520 kc. Bolivia had 1 kw. CP5, R. Illimani, La Paz on 6080 kc. Brazilians were not as plentiful as Spanish stations, but one that was well heard was PSH, Radio Internacional do Brazil, Rio de Janeiro, on 10220 kc. Others included Short Wave Radiotelephone Station PRF5, Rio de Janeiro, on 9501 kc., and PRA8, Radio Clube de Pernambuco, on 6040 kc.

Many Central American stations, and a great many Cubans and Mexicans, simulcasted on shortwave, that is, they broadcast their regular AM programming on shortwave frequencies. Among them were HP5, R. Miramar, Panama, on 6030 kc.; HI1A, La Voz del Yaque, Santiago, Dominican Republic, on 6185 kc.; TIPG, La Voz de la Victor, San Jose, Costa Rica, on 6410 kc.; TIGPH, Radio Alma Tica, also in San Jose, on 5830 kc.; TGTQ, Radio Internacional, "La Voz de la Capital," Guatemala City, on 6285 kc.; the widely heard 200 watt TGW, Radiodifusora Nacional, 9450 kc., also in Guatemala City; and HI9T, Broadcasting Tropical, Puerto Plata, Dominican Republic.

Among the Cubans were COBZ, Radio Salas, 9030 kc.; COCX, La Voz del Radio Philco, 11435 kc.; COCW, The Voice of the Antillies, 6330 kc.; Transradio Columbia, 9833 kc.; and CO9GC, Laboratorio Radio-electrico, 6150 kc. COCD, La Voz del Aire, operated on 6130 kc. According to *RADEX*, "This station relays the programs of CMCD from the Palace Hotel and is heard most regularly between 2200 and 2400. Announcements are nearly always in Spanish, English being used only once in a while. Four chimes precede the announcements, as a rule, and Ted Lewis' familiar 'Good Night Song' closes the programs at midnight."[23]

Mexico boasted XEBR-XEBH, Radio Difusora de Sonora, on 11820 kc.; XEFT, La Voz de Veracruz, on 9510 kc.; XEBT, El Buen Tono, on 6010 kc.; XEWW on 9500 kc.; and countless others. It was from another early Mexican station that one of the best known long-distance listeners, August Balbi of California, received his

**Small in size but powerful in its influence on shortwave listeners, TI4NRH, Heredia, Costa Rica, was one of the earliest, and best known, of the Latin American broadcasters (QSL, c. 1936).**

very first QSL: XETE, Empreso de Telefonos Ericsson, broadcasting on 6130 and 9600 kc., and heard by Balbi on June 15, 1933. As one observer pointed out, "XETE tends to remind one of that other popular Mexican station, XEW, which has been missed for a long time. Some of the most beautiful programs ever heard on short waves were transmitted from XEW, and XETE seems to be continuing the good work."[24]

The most famous Central American broadcaster was TI4NRH, San Jose, Costa Rica. Starting out with a mere 7.5 watts in 1928 (which was increased to 500 watts during the 1930s), the station's owner, Sr. Amando Cespedes Marin, gained worldwide recognition for his promotion of friendship and understanding via shortwave. A renaissance man of his day, he carried on extensive correspondence with shortwave fans in all corners of the globe. He was a well-known personality among long-distance listeners, dedicating special programs to radio clubs and going the extra mile for shortwave listeners. TI4NRH issued some of the most impressive QSLs of all time: oversized, multicolored certificates more decorative than almost any other verifications ever issued, before or since.[25]

U.S. shortwave broadcasting is described in chapter 5. In Canada, as in the United States, shortwave broadcasting was in private hands, and numerous stations changed calls and metamorphosed over the years. James Richardson and Sons, of Winnipeg, Manitoba, purveyors of stocks, bonds, and grain since 1857, was a company that became the first shortwave broadcaster in Canada, starting out with 2 kw.

Halifax, Nova Scotia, still using only 500 watts on the same old frequency of 6130 kHz.[1]

Except in the Americas, broadcasting, including shortwave, was a government monopoly, or nearly so, usually supported by an annual fee on receiving sets.

## Europe

Europe was the home of many of the biggest international broadcasters.

The BBC transmitter base at Daventry had eight transmitters and 18 antennas, and would remain in service until the site's eventual closing on March 29, 1992. The results of the early (1927) tests of the BBC experimental station, G5SW, with 20 kw., were not very auspicious.

> Australia—Good and clear reception of one of three broadcasts only—namely, a midday organ recital and a message of greeting.
> United States—Picked up 5SW, but it was suffering from excessive fading and local static.
> Canada—Successful rebroadcast of speech by Prince of Wales and other items in evening program.
> India—Not even a carrier wave heard; Buenos Aires—Speech by Prince of Wales received; Lagos—Speech received badly; music only passable.
> There were no definite reports from New Zealand or South Africa, which seem to indicate that reception there was a failure.[2]

Soon two frequencies would be used on each of five beams, some of them still familiar BBC channels today; for example, 15260 (GSI), 11750 (GSD), and 9510 (GSB). (In the early days of shortwave, individual transmitters were often assigned their own call letters, a practice that has now been largely abandoned.) The international service, which began on December 19, 1932, was known originally as the Empire Service. Later it would be called the General Overseas Service, and then the World Service. According to the *New York Times*, "Big Ben comes in so regularly from London at 6 o'clock in the evening (Eastern Standard Time) that one family in Washington has dubbed it 'our dinner bell.'"[3]

Like most of the major European shortwave broadcasters, a major BBC goal was preserving contact with the colonies. Foreign language programming did not commence until 1938, long after the Axis stations had begun their foreign language services. Indeed, the success of German shortwave was a major factor in gaining British commitment to a shortwave service of its own.[4]

During the 1930s in Holland, Edward Startz, who would go on to become one of shortwave's best known personalities, was already the host of "The Happy Station"

# Amateur Broadcasting Station 10-BQ
## BRANTFORD, ONTARIO

CHIEF OPERATOR
HAROLD BROWN

TELEPHONE
CITY
CANADA

ASSISTANT OPERATORS
ALBERT ELLIS
WILBERT BROWN
EDGAR BROWN

### 250 METRES   —   1200 KILOCYCLES

**Regular D-X Programs**
First Saturday Morning
in the Month
2-3.30 a. m. E. S. T.

Nov. 5—1932
Dec. 3—1932.

Dec. 11—1932. { Special 3-3.30
a. m. E.S.T.
Atlantic
Radio Club

Jan, 7—1933
Jan. ?—1933—Special ?
Feb. 4—1933
Feb. ?—1933—Special ?
March 4—1933
March ?—1933—Special ?

**Our Power at time of** { Regu
**D-X Programme** { Spec

Power Output (Tube Rating 7½ Watts)
Using 2 Tubes as Oscillators - 15 Watts
and Home-Made Double Button Michrophone.
Antenna Current 15 Amps.
Input Volts 500.     Milliamps 75 on Oscillators.
Input Volts 500.     Milliamps 30 on Modulators.

WE APPRECIATE YOUR REPORT.
This will verify your reception.

*Thos Brown*

Manager

---

# "Radio Club Océanien" Papeete, Tahiti
### ( ETABLISSEMENTS FRANÇAIS DE L'OCÉANIE ).

à Radio W3-SWS. Heureux de confirmer notre émission QSO du 26/1/37

Carroll H. Weyrich

de 18.00 à 19.10 (heures locales) UR Sigs QSA   R   T   tc

# FO8AA

*Transmetteur*          *Remarques*          *Récepteur*

Quoique nos émissions sont destinées spécialement pour les Etablissements Français de
l'Océanie, nous sommes très heureux d'apprendre que vous avez eu le plaisir de nous enten-
dre. Notre station n'est qu'expérimentale. Puissance: 200 watts.     7.100 Kcs

73s     Le Président :

---

Two amateur stations that seconded as broadcasters in Canada (QSL, 1932) and Tahiti (QSL, 1937).

*Top:* A view of the equipment room at early Canadian shortwave station CJRX (QSL, 1937). *Bottom:* Station VE9GW in Bowmanville, Ontario, carried the programming of standard broadcast station CKGW (QSL, 1934).

as VE9JR (11720 kc.) and VE9CL (6150 kc.), later becoming CJRX and CJRO, and then (in 1943) CKRX and CKRO. There were many others: CFCX (on 6005 kc. even then), CJCX on 6010 kc., CFRX on 6070 kc., and VE9HX (later CHNX) on 6110 kc. VE9HX read "notes and letters to the trappers of the North each Saturday night from 11 o'clock to 1 A.M."[26] A popular station was 200 watt VE9GW, Bow-

## MTCY

*Hsinking Central Broadcasting Station*
*Hsinking, Manchoukuo*

Dear Mr. Eugene S. Allen:

We are in receipt of yours of April 13th, reporting reception of our SHORT-WAVE RADIO PROGRAM over MTCY on April 13th. We hereby verify your report and thank you sincerely for it.

It is our hope that you will continue to send us such reports, including receiving set and reception details as well as any criticisms and suggestions you may have regarding our programs.

Although transmission times and wavelengths are subject to change with atmospheric and other conditions, we are pleased to give you our present transmission details herewith:

TIME: 6:30 to 7:20 GMT.
STATION: MTCY 20 Kw,
WAVELENGTH: 25.47 meters
PROGRAM: NEWS, MUSIC, EYE-WITNESS ACCOUNTS, AND INFORMATIVE TALKS.

Thanking you for your kind help,
Yours very truly,

SHORT-WAVE SYSTEM
Hsinking Central Broadcasting Station
**Manchuria Telephone & Telegraph Co., Ltd.**

### Identification Signal

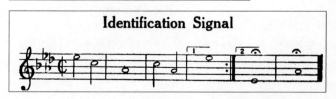

manville, Ontario which simulcasted CKGW's programming over 6095 kc. until its demise in 1933. Newfoundland had VONH, the Broadcasting Corporation of Newfoundland, on 5970 kc. It was eventually absorbed by the CBC, becoming first CBNX and then CKZN. Some of these stations are still on shortwave today, and their call letters are familiar to listeners the world over.

## Asia

The Asian continent was a happily mysterious place on the shortwave bands.

In Japan, Nippon Hoso Kyokei (NHK) controlled all broadcasting activity. Hour-long programs were beamed to all parts of the globe from the 20 and 50 kw. facilities of the International Wireless Telephone Company of Japan in Nazaki. According to the *New York Times*:

> There is a discussion of current topics from Tokyo for ten or fifteen minutes in Japanese and ten minutes in English. This is followed by thirty minutes of entertainment and information.... Station JVH, Nazaki, will use 20,000 watts, but is prepared to step this power up as much as necessary to reach the important countries of the world. It is expected that JVH will generally use a wave length of 20.5 meters, or frequency of 14,600 kilocycles, but if, on account of weather

Well heard in the early days of shortwave broadcasting was MTCY in Manchuria (QSL, c. 1939).

**600 KC**
**11910 KC**
*11,860 Kc./Hol.*

**500 M**
**25.19 M**

*"The call of the Orient"*

This station's broadcast on ___July 2, 1939.___
as received by you is hereby verified.

**XMHA**

445 Race Course Road,
Shanghai, China.

XMHA was one of Shanghai's private shortwave stations (QSL, 1939).

or other conditions, it seems desirable, the station may try twenty-eight meters, 10,600 kilocycles, or forty meters, 7,510 kilocycles. Japanese stations are being heard regularly in the afternoon, according to a report by Charles A. Morrison, president of the International DXer's Alliance, at Bloomington, Ill. "There is really nothing particularly remarkable in my reception of Japan in the afternoon," reports Mr. Morrison.[27]

There was some interesting activity from Manchuria, known as Manchukuo (or Manchoukuo) after the Japanese takeover in 1932. There had been intermittent broadcasting from Manchuria telephone and telegraph stations JQAK and JDY at Dairen on the Kwantung Peninsula. From July 1939, however, MTCY, the Central Broadcasting Station in Hsinking, began regular international shortwave broadcasts, including an English program to Western North America at 6:30–7:20 A.M. (GMT) on 11775 kc., 20 kw. The Japanese distributed free or low-cost receivers to the Manchurian population (who often used them to listen to the "enemy" Chinese station in Nanking).

Western onslaughts and the absence of restrictions made the Chinese broadcasting scene one of near pandemonium, with many private shortwave stations. The main Chinese shortwave station was XGOA, located in the prewar capital of Nanking. When the Sino-Japanese war started in 1937, the Chinese government moved to Chungking and reestablished the station there.

Shortwave broadcasting then became the responsibility of the Central Broadcasting Station, or XGOY. It transmitted in 20 languages, and was staffed mostly

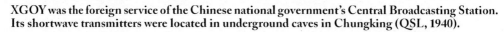

# The Voice of China

*THE CHINESE INTERNATIONAL BROADCASTING STATION*

## Chungking, China

### XGOX

### XGOY

| 19.75m. | 15.2m.c. | 25.21m. | 11.9m.c. |
| 16.85m. | 17.8m.c. | 31.10m. | 9.65m.c. |

This is to verify your report

dated FEB 14 1940

Thank you and tune in again

XGOY was the foreign service of the Chinese national government's Central Broadcasting Station. Its shortwave transmitters were located in underground caves in Chungking (QSL, 1940).

by students returning from the United States and other countries. The chief engineer, Professor Feng Chien, had been trained by General Electric in Schenectady. The station received many letters, varying "from simple reception reports to criticisms and long discussions, with digressions bordering on the fantastic. One said the writer had invented a secret weapon that he offered to China. Another had worked out a foolproof strategy that would 'annihilate' the Japanese in two months.... A Hollywood studio cabled a request for a broadcast describing life in Chungking's airraid shelters, which was urgently wanted for a picture with the war in China as a background."[28] Following Pearl Harbor, XGOY transmitted a widely heard "Mailbag Hour," which featured radio messages from American missionaries and other civilians interested in informing family and friends of their whereabouts. The station also featured much entertainment for U.S. troops.[29]

There were numerous other "X's" freelancing under various Chinese authorities in the 1930s including XPSA, Kueiyang (Kweiyang); XTC, Shanghai; XTJ, the China Information Committee station, Hangchow (Hankow); XMHA, "The Call of the Orient," Shanghai; XTPA, the Canton Broadcasting Station; and the "Station Radiophonique Française 'Art et Culture,'" Shanghai. Many of these stations were heard in the United States, but all were eventually closed down as the war with Japan intensified. During World War II, reported one listener many years later, "one of our favorite newscasters, and certainly the most dramatic, was an American named

# VK3ME
## MELBOURNE..VIC.
## AUSTRALIA

**POWER**
5 KILOWATTS
**WAVE LENGTH**
31.55 METRES

**A.W.A.**
**Owns and Operates**

Beam Wireless Services to Great Britain, The Continent of Europe and North and South America.

Beam Wireless Picturegram Service for the transmission of Pictures between Australia and Great Britain and Nth. America.

Wireless Telephone Services to Great Britain, The Continent of Europe, North and South America, Java and New Zealand.

Coastal Radio Stations in Australia, Papua, New Guinea and Fiji.

Wireless Services on ships of the Australian Mercantile Marine.

Radio - Electric Works for the manufacture of every type of transmitting equipment and Radiola broadcast receivers.

Research and experimental laboratories.

WORLD-WIDE BROADCASTING SERVICE

AREA IN SQ. MILES:
2,974,581

POPULATION:
6,550,000

DISTANCES FROM
VK3ME
(Nautical Miles)

| | | |
|---|---|---|
| London | - - - | 9,230 |
| New York | - - | 9,044 |
| Chicago | - - - | 8,500 |
| San Francisco | - | 6,828 |
| Rio De Janeiro | | 6,800 |
| Tokio | - - - - | 4,420 |
| Shanghai | - - | 4,300 |
| Calcutta | - - - | 4,900 |
| Capetown | - - | 5,560 |
| Wellington | - - | 1,400 |

AMALGAMATED WIRELESS (A/SIA) LTD.
AUSTRALIA'S NATIONAL WIRELESS ORGANISATION.

AUSTRALIA CALLING !
THE WORLD AROUND AUSTRALIA
FROM
## VLG
### MELBOURNE
OFFICIAL VERIFICATION OF RECEPTION

OF *VK6-2 - 9.54 mc/s - 8:00 - 8:40 pm - EWT - July 20th, 1943.*
BY *Mr. P. Kary, 103 Suppes Avenue, Johnstown, Pennsylvania. U.S.A.*
VERIFIED BY

Carroll Alcott, who used the sanctuary of the International Settlement in Shanghai to rake the Axis over station XMHA three times a day. On the same 25 meter band was the German financed propaganda station in Shanghai, soon joined by a Russian station."[30]

Indonesia, a Dutch colony at the time, had several stations. The Netherlands Indies Broadcasting Company, or NIROM as it was called, was located in Batavia (Jakarta). Distant precursor of today's Radio Republik Indonesia, it transmitted from various locations in the islands. Java Wireless Station PLP, Bandung

**Australia has been a long-time shortwave broadcaster (QSLs, 1935, 1943).**

THE GARDEN OF THE PACIFIC
These islands were discovered in 1643 by Tasman and were ceded to Great Britain in 1874. There are about 250 islands in the group. The population is about 172,000. Principal exports: Sugar, Copra, Bananas, Rubber, Cotton and Shell.
Amalgamated Wireless (A/sia) Ltd. operates the wireless services of Fiji. At VPD, there are 3 transmitters. All these stations were designed and built in Australia by A.W.A., which also owns and operates Australian Beam Stations, Coastal Radio, Ship Stations, and Short Wave Overseas Broadcasting Station 2ME Sydney, and 3ME Melbourne.

AMALGAMATED WIRELESS (AUSTRALASIA) LTD.  ::  SUVA, FIJI

Fiji was one of the more exotic, but regularly heard, sources of shortwave programming (QSL, 1936).

(Bandoeng), was also often heard relaying broadcast programming over its 1.5 kw. transmitter.

India started shortwave broadcasting in May 1934, although VUB, Bombay, on 9570 kc. (4.5 kw.), and VUC, Calcutta, on 6110, appear not to have been very well heard. Southeast Asia and the Malayan Peninsula boasted some exotic stations, including HSP in Bangkok on 17750, and FZS, Saigon, on 11990. The 6 mc. band in this area was interesting, and included several stations in what were then known as the "Straits Settlements": ZHJ, The Penang Wireless Society, on 6080 kc.; ZGE, Kuala Lumpur on 6130 kc.; and ZHI, Singapore on 6010. A well-heard station from the area was ZHP, the British Malaya Broadcasting Corporation, on 9690 kc.

## The Pacific

Australia was home to the first major shortwave stations in the Pacific, Amalgamated Wireless twins VK3ME, Melbourne, 2 kw. on 9510 kc., and 20 kw. VK2ME, 9590 kc., in Sydney. Both were widely heard by U.S. listeners (as are today's shortwave broadcasts from Australia). The *New York Times* reported in November 1934: "VK2ME, Sydney, Australia, on '9,590,' was tuned in Sunday morning at 4:36 o'clock. For nearly an hour reception was extremely clear. VK2ME occasionally

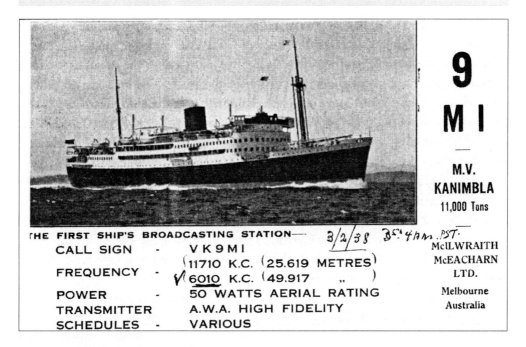

9

M I
___
M.V.
KANIMBLA
11,000 Tons

THE FIRST SHIP'S BROADCASTING STATION— 3/2/38 3⁵·⁴ʰᵐ PST·

| CALL SIGN | - | V K 9 M I | McILWRAITH |
| FREQUENCY | - | ⎰11710 K.C. (25.619 METRES⎱ ⎱ 6010 K.C. (49.917 „ ⎰ | McEACHARN LTD. |
| POWER | - | 50 WATTS AERIAL RATING | Melbourne |
| TRANSMITTER | | A.W.A. HIGH FIDELITY | Australia |
| SCHEDULES | - | VARIOUS | |

Station 9MI, aboard the merchant vessel *Kanimbla*, was an example of a novel vehicle for early radio (QSL, 1938).

sends Sunday programs dedicated to distant parts of the globe. On Nov. 25 a broadcast is to be dedicated to the District of Columbia. The regular Sunday schedule is from about midnight to 2 o'clock, 4:30 to 8:30 and 9:30 to 11:30 A.M."[31] These two stations were soon followed by another, VK3LR, Lyndhurst, on the still-used frequency of 9580 kc., and VK6ME in Perth. It was also in the 1930s that the Kookaburra interval signal first came into use. It would be well known to shortwave listeners for generations.

Another widely heard Pacific outlet was Amalgamated Wireless station VPD in Suva, Fiji. Operating with 10 kw., it took its programming from local mediumwave station ZJV. Although designed principally to cover the outlying islands, it was widely heard in the United States, and was a good verifier.

Less often heard but still reported and verified occasionally was VK9MI on board the merchant vessel *Kanimbla*. Promoted as the first shipboard broadcasting station, it was owned by McIlwraith McEacharn and operated at 12:00 noon GMT on 6010 and 11710 kc. with 200 watts. *All-Wave Radio* reported: "They have three studios facing the ballroom—beautifully fitted out and artistically furnished in green, cream, and chromium. A quartet of girl singers live permanently on board and under the direct control of Miss [Eileen M.] Foley, who claims the distinction of being the only woman in the world in full charge of a broadcasting station. The *Kanimbla* quartet render musical programs for the benefit of the passengers in addition to broadcasting from the ship."[32]

It was in the 1930s that shortwave was first used as a major propaganda weapon. Within a week after the start of the Spanish Civil War in July 1936, every major broadcasting station in Spain was directly controlled by either the rebels or the loyalists, with each side proclaiming its version of the truth. The broadcasting scene was as chaotic as the fighting, but a DXer's delight. "Since the outbreak of the Spanish rebellion," reported the *New York Times*, "new stations have appeared on various short waves, sending music and speech from both Nationalist and Rebel headquarters. Stations in the Canary Islands, Spanish Morocco, the Balearic Islands, and new stations in Spain itself may be tuned almost daily by shortwave listeners who know when and where to locate these transmitters.... [S]hort-wave broadcasting throughout the Spanish republic has grown by leaps and bounds since the war began."[33] An example was EAJ43, Tenerife, the Canary Islands, a government-owned station (later Radio Clube Tenerife) that fell into the hands of the rebels and broadcast worldwide in five languages on 10380 kc.

As the threat from the Axis powers escalated in the late 1930s, shortwave propaganda grew on a grand scale. It was at this time that some of the now familiar propaganda techniques—mailbag programs, favorable interviews with visiting tourists, and announcers speaking with the accent of the target population—were first developed. The Germans went so far as to urge North American listeners to contact them via cost-free telegrams, of which 10,241 were sent in February 1941 during the last week of the offer. South America was a favorite target of the Axis countries, particularly Germany and Italy.

It was also during the 1930s that jamming was first used. In the Spanish Civil War it consisted of sending an open carrier on the target station's frequency. Things soon got more sophisticated, however, with German *Störsenderen* emitting music, code, and shrieking whistles. By and large, however, stations respected one another's frequencies, preferring to avoid reprisals and the chaos that would inevitably follow.

## Chapter 5

# SHORTWAVE BROADCASTING IN THE UNITED STATES

THERE WAS NO UNITED STATES *government* shortwave broadcaster—no "Voice of America"—until 1942. Before that, U.S. shortwave broadcasting was in private hands, and occasional efforts to establish a government shortwave station were singularly unsuccessful.

## *The Early Years*

Following the discovery of shortwave, the entrepreneurial spirit led to a fairly large number of American shortwave broadcasting outlets, most of them simulcasting their standard-broadcast band parent stations. Some broadcasters were also in the radio manufacturing business, and were hopeful that broadcasting would help create markets for their new shortwave products. Some smaller stations went on shortwave just to satisfy an engineer's desire to dabble in a new medium, while others wanted to reach listeners directly, or provide programming for rebroadcast via local broadcast-band stations in other countries.

This last point is important. Although today we think of shortwave in terms of direct broadcasting, in the early days the usual goal was to use shortwave to get the signal to the target area for pickup and rebroadcast by local medium-wave stations. This is why the Federal Radio Commission called it experimental *relay* broadcasting: the transmission of broadcast material from one station to another, on high frequencies and over long distances, for rebroadcast to the public by the receiving station on its regular broadcast frequency. Subsequently, these shortwave stations were renamed international broadcast stations, and in 1936 the regulations were upgraded to require operation with at least 5 kw. of power and utilization of only one frequency at a time to a target area.[1] By the end of the 1930s, the comparative effect of U.S. vs. Axis shortwave broadcasting, especially to Latin America, was gauged in part by the number of local rebroadcasting arrangements that each side had available.[2] There were 117 stations in the NBC South American network; CBS had 76; and Crosley had 24. One-third of the Latin American stations were affiliated in some fashion with U.S. shortwave broadcasters.[3] Meanwhile, the Germans had 200–300 such relays.[4]

A complete examination of the early days of U.S. shortwave broadcasting would require a more detailed study of the alphabet soup of the experimental "X" call signs of the day. These calls consisted of the letter W, followed by the number of the radio district, then an X, and two or three letters, for example, W2XAF. (The experimental calls were exchanged for regular four-letter "W" and "K" calls in 1939.) In brief, however, and with some exceptions, America's first shortwave broadcasters were the offspring of the giants of the U.S. radio industry. In addition to W8XK (KDKA), Westinghouse operated W2XK (later WBOS) in Boston. The National Broadcasting Company had W3XAL (WBOU) in Bound Brook, New Jersey, General Electric operated W2XAF (WGEO) in Schenectady, New York, and W6XBE (KGEI) in San Francisco, California; and CBS put on the air W2XE (WCBX),

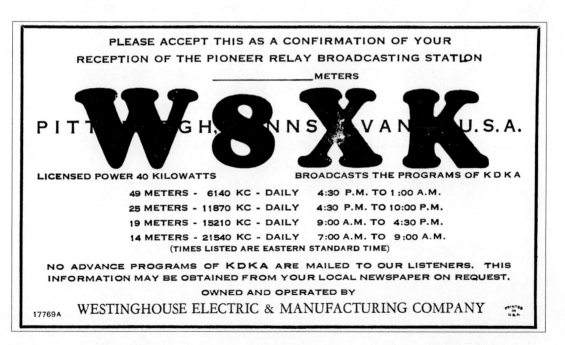

PLEASE ACCEPT THIS AS A CONFIRMATION OF YOUR
RECEPTION OF THE PIONEER RELAY BROADCASTING STATION
_____ METERS

# W8XK

PITTSBURGH, PENNSYLVANIA, U.S.A.

LICENSED POWER 40 KILOWATTS          BROADCASTS THE PROGRAMS OF KDKA

49 METERS - 6140 KC - DAILY     4:30 P.M. TO 1:00 A.M.
25 METERS - 11870 KC - DAILY    4:30 P.M. TO 10:00 P.M.
19 METERS - 15210 KC - DAILY    9:00 A.M. TO 4:30 P.M.
14 METERS - 21540 KC - DAILY    7:00 A.M. TO 9:00 A.M.
(TIMES LISTED ARE EASTERN STANDARD TIME)

NO ADVANCE PROGRAMS OF KDKA ARE MAILED TO OUR LISTENERS. THIS
INFORMATION MAY BE OBTAINED FROM YOUR LOCAL NEWSPAPER ON REQUEST.

OWNED AND OPERATED BY

17769A   WESTINGHOUSE ELECTRIC & MANUFACTURING COMPANY   PRINTED IN U.S.A.

KDKA programs were carried over Westinghouse shortwave station W8XK (QSL, 1935).

Wayne, New Jersey, and W3XAU (WCAU), Philadelphia. As noted earlier, Boston's World Wide Broadcasting Foundation, W1XAL (WRUL), was the most serious attempt to produce educational programming specifically for shortwave. It had an extensive program development department, and boasted a news connection with the *Christian Science Monitor*. Crosley was represented by W8XAL (WLWO) in Cincinnati, Ohio. (Powel Crosley was a ham operator himself, and was always interested in receiving reception reports from listeners.)

There were also some lesser known stations, among them W4XB (WIOD), the "Wonderful Isle of Dreams" station in Miami; Chicago's W9XAA (WCFL), operated by the Chicago Federation of Labor; and 10 kw. W9XF (WENR-WMAQ) in Downer's Grove, Illinois. All contributed to the growing interest in shortwave broadcasting in America and elsewhere.[5]

By 1929 American shortwave broadcasters had become quite busy. Three times in September of that year NBC relayed the activities of the Graf Zeppelin to Germany over G.E. shortwave stations W2XK, W2XAD, and W2XAF (WGY). General Electric had set up a 44-acre receiving site 10 miles from its Schenectady transmitters, and was picking up and rebroadcasting programs from England, Holland, and Australia, as well as from W6XN (KGO) on the West coast. It used a spaced antenna, a "group of widely separated and independent antennas all feeding into a device which levels the aggregate signal, passing it on to the transmitter in an even intensity or volume.... Thousands of letters indicate the great interest taken by foreign listeners in work carried on at Schenectady, and many hundreds have volunteered to act as observers when special propagation tests are contemplated."[6]

As these were the golden days of radio in the United States, so was American-style programming enjoyed by thousands of people everywhere. For example, although it was on the air only three hours daily in 1930, NBC station W3XAL received letters from all over the world: from shipboard radio operators, and from radio fans in cities and outlying areas.[7] During the war years, U.S. stations were relied upon for credible news. Said one South American listener: "[General Electric] [s]tation W2XAF is considered a semi-official news bureau here.... When we do not hear it, we ignore the news, particularly the foreign news."[8]

In 1939 some stations, including W4XB and W9XAA, fell by the wayside when the government, in order to nurture a system that could compete more successfully with Axis stations and ensure audibility of U.S. signals in faraway places, required that by July 1, 1940 (extended to July 1941), all American shortwave stations use directional aerials and a minimum of 50 kw. At the same time, the FCC permitted commercial advertising on shortwave for the first time (see discussion in chapter 2). With the approval of the State Department, it also promulgated a regulation requiring that "a licensee of an international broadcast station shall render only an international broadcast service which will reflect the culture of this coun-

# W8XAL

## The Short Wave Outlet for WLW Programs

*One of the most important short-wave stations in this country is W8XAL operated by the Crosley Radio Corporation at Cincinnati, Ohio. This station usually relays programs from WLW.*

Photo above shows the 10 K. W. short-wave transmitting station operating on the well-known call letters W8XAL. This station has been received in all parts of the world and has entertained listeners as far away at New Zealand and Australia. The photo at the left shows the power equipment of W8XAL.

As the country's only AM station using (for a time) 500 kw., WLW had an important history apart from its shortwave outlet, W8XAL (*Official Shortwave Listener*, April–May 1935).

try and which will promote international goodwill, understanding and cooperation." The broadcasting industry, the press, and the American Civil Liberties Union railed against this proposal, branding it a violation of free speech and basic democratic principles, and—more importantly to the industry—a perceived step along the road to censorship and government control of *domestic* broadcasting. This was one of the industry's constant fears.[9] However, the purpose of the "culture rule," as it was

*Opposite page and next two pages:* "Wonderful Isle of Dreams Station" W4XB carried the programs of AM station WIOD to the world via shortwave (QSLs, 1930, 1936).

## W4XB's Transmitter Is Located on Collins Island, a Small Island Situated in Biscayne Bay

Thank you for your report of 1/15/36 on reception of W4XB. We are glad to verify this report

By MCScott

We sincerely hope that you will be a regular listener to W4XB and that we may have the pleasure of further reports from you.

In the same building housing W4XB are also located the 1,000-watt transmitter of broadcast station WIOD, the 100-watt transmitter on 120 meters serving the Miami Police Department and the 15-watt transmitter on 8 meters which serves the Police Department of Miami Beach.

**6040 KC or 49.67 Meters**

W4XB operates on a power of 250 to 2,500 watts and is an experimental relay broadcast station operated in conjunction with broadcast station WIOD.

**Owned and Operated by Isle of Dreams Broadcasting Corpn.**
**Transmitter Collins Island, Miami Beach, Fla.    Studios News Tower, eta**
**Transmitter Collins Island, Miami Beach, Fla.      Studios News Tower, Miami, Fla.**

**Isle of Dreams Broadcasting Co.**

Wave Length-Frequency
247.8 Meters or 1210 KL
Power ~ 1,000 Watts
Western Electric Equipment

Miami Beach, Fla.
At The Rainbow's End
A Tropical Station
Dedicated to National Service

January 25, 1930

Mr. John T. Tweedie,
Box 145 E.,
R.F.D.#1,
Asbury Park, N. J.

Dear Sir:

    This letter is to verify your reception of station W.I.O.D., and to thank you for your courtesy in writing us.

    We operate on a frequency of 1300 kilocycles or a wave length of 230.6 meters.

    Inclosed are some interior views of the studio, which may interest you.

        Sincerely yours,

        ISLE OF DREAMS BROADCASTING CO.

        Jesse H. Jay,
        Manager

Radio Station WIOD is the community broadcasting station of Miami Beach, Florida, owned and directed by The Carl G. Fisher Company.

Entrance to W. I. O. D.

*Radio Station*
**W.I.O.D.**
(Wonderful Isle O'Dreams)
*at*
MIAMI BEACH
FLORIDA

called, was benign; its implementation was deferred, and it was eventually withdrawn altogether.

The 1930s also saw the inception of FM broadcasting in the shortwave bands. As today, FM signals were free from static, and of higher fidelity. In the early 1940s, before being allocated their present frequency range of 88–108 mc. (in 1944), FM stations operated in the 42–50 mc. band. Before that, in the mid to late 1930s, these stations were allowed to experiment on 11 meters, or 25–27 mc. (the "apex" band as

Mko Roto Corp'n, News Tower, Miami.

it was called). Many stations became active in this band. W9XTC, Minneapolis, simulcasted WTCN-1250 on 26050 kc; W6XKG transmitted from Los Angeles on 25950 kc. 24 hours a day; and WOR's 100 watt shortwave outlet, W2XJI, on 26300 kc., carried a program for the NNRC on Tuesday and Friday nights.

W9XJL, Superior, Wisconsin, 26100 kc., was the foremost SW-FM performer. *All-Wave Radio* reported: "The power is only 80 [later 250] watts, but ... reports

# W2XAF Can

*One of the world's most powerful short-wave transmitting stations is that located at South Schenectady, N. Y. The new equipment here shown can handle six different messages simultaneously; code, voice and pictures can be sent out at the same time.*

Above—Operator seen holding one of the large water-cooled tubes used in one of the power amplifiers at W2XAF, the new General Electric Company's powerful short-wave station at South Schenectady, N. Y.

Below—One of the short-wave experts at W2XAF's new, ultra-powerful short-wave transmitting station at South Schenectady, examining a one kilowatt short-wave unit, consisting of a crystal oscillator and vacuum tube multiplier.

Operating desk and control switchboard panels of the short-wave transmitter at W2XAF's new station. The high power vacuum tubes used as oscillators and amplifiers are located behind these switch panels.

Above we have a close-up view of one of the intermediate linear amplifiers at W2XAF. The powerful vacuum tubes used are water-cooled and the expert seen in the picture has his hand on one of the valves controlling the cooling water. This water line is connected to the tube by means of rubber hose.

General Electric station W2XAF was widely heard internationally. The above is the first page of a magazine article whose headline read in full, "W2XAF Can Send Code, Voice and Photos Simultaneously" (*Short Wave Craft*, February–March 1931).

The map below shows how "foreign" short-wave broadcasts to South America are counteracted by the two powerful S-W beams from the Schenectady, N. Y., stations; the new Belmont, Calif., S-W beam can also be "reversed" to cover South America, when that station goes on the air.

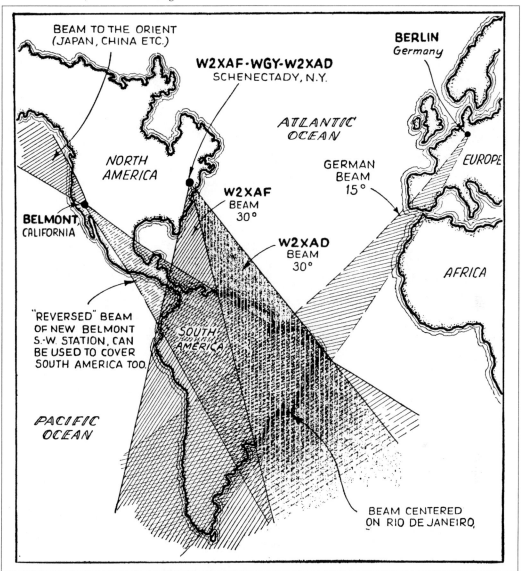

From *Short Wave and Television*, August 1938.

have been received from 11 countries. At this writing [1938], 20% of the received mail has come from England!"[10] There were so many 11 meter FMers that in December 1937 *All-Wave Radio* began a special column about the FM bands. Called Ultra-High, it was edited by a young man who would become well known to many contemporary SWLs, the late Oliver "Perry" Ferrell, founder, with his wife Jeanne, of Gilfer Shortwave, a major shortwave radio supplier in New Jersey.

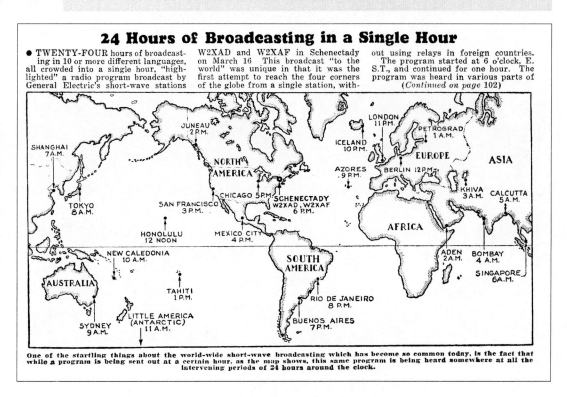

## 24 Hours of Broadcasting in a Single Hour

● TWENTY-FOUR hours of broadcasting in 10 or more different languages, all crowded into a single hour, "highlighted" a radio program broadcast by General Electric's short-wave stations W2XAD and W2XAF in Schenectady on March 16 This broadcast "to the world" was unique in that it was the first attempt to reach the four corners of the globe from a single station, without using relays in foreign countries. The program started at 6 o'clock, E.S.T., and continued for one hour. The program was heard in various parts of (*Continued on page 102*)

One of the startling things about the world-wide short-wave broadcasting which has become so common today, is the fact that while a program is being sent out at a certain hour, as the map shows, this same program is being heard somewhere at all the intervening periods of 24 hours around the clock.

From *Short Wave Craft*, June 1934.

## The Voice of America

The Voice of America was born officially on February 5, 1942.[11] It traces its history to the establishment of the office of the Coordinator of Information (COI) by President Roosevelt in July 1941 and the appointment of Wall Street attorney William "Wild Bill" Donovan to the post.

The proliferation of offices engaged in various governmental information activities at the time, and the absence of any central intelligence coordinating function within the government, made such an office highly desirable. However, Donovan's interest was less the collection and analysis of intelligence than the aggressive use of mass media techniques for psychological warfare, that is, the development of morale-subverting, anti–German fifth-column activities of the type that were widely perceived as having contributed to the German takeover of France. Donovan believed in the use of foreign propaganda as an attack weapon in territories that were about to be invaded, an activity complementary to the military action itself.

Within COI was the Foreign Information Service (FIS), whose responsibilities included monitoring Axis radio transmissions and countering those broadcasts abroad. The head of FIS was well-known playwright Robert Sherwood. At first, FIS

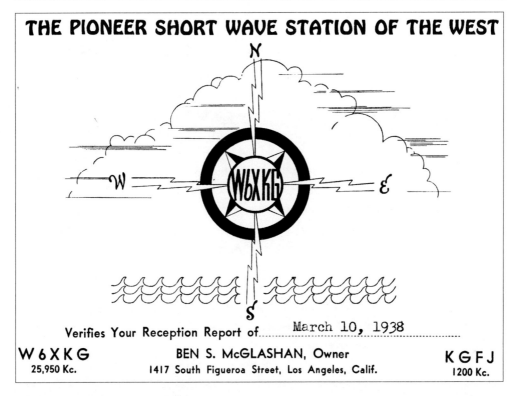

Operating just below 30 mc., and thus considered shortwave, were the "apex band" stations, including W6XKG in Los Angeles (QSL, 1938).

played a mentoring role for U.S. shortwave broadcasting by preparing weekly news and background information releases based on monitoring done by CBS, NBC, and the FCC. These writings, assembled in what amounted to an international city room at the COI's Madison Avenue headquarters, reflected U.S. policy, and were sent mainly to U.S. shortwave stations, all of which were still in private hands and producing programming of varying quality. There was no assurance that the releases would be used, however, and indeed many were not.

The government then began leasing 15-minute blocks of air time over the private shortwave broadcasters and producing its own programs, calling them, fairly casually, the Voice of America. They introduced them with the Yankee Doodle theme that is still familiar to listeners of the Voice of America. Thus, at the outset, the Voice of America was neither a station nor a government agency, but a series of short, government-produced programs.

The broadcasters, fearing any steps that might be a precedent for governmental interference in *domestic* broadcasting, employed their own coordinator of international broadcasting. His job was to act as a liaison with FIS, clean up the broadcasters' shortwave house in areas that needed it (such as the coordination of broadcasting times), and generally keep Uncle Sam at bay. The coordinator was

Stanley P. Richardson, an old Associated Press correspondent and former secretary to the U.S. ambassador in Russia and Belgium, Joseph E. Davies.

The FIS information dissemination function was not enough for Donovan, however, since he was more interested in projects like clandestine radio broadcasting. The eventual result was the replacement of COI by two separate agencies, the Office of War Information (OWI) and the Office of Strategic Services (OSS). The OWI inherited the functions being performed by FIS (thereafter known as the OWI overseas branch), which, in the radio field, was basically the management of foreign broadcasting. OWI tried to maintain high standards of truthfulness and consistency, while always emphasizing principles of U.S. democracy. The OSS, which Donovan headed, took on the task of intelligence gathering, sabotage, support for resistance movements, and the planning and operation of such special activities, including clandestine broadcasting, as were approved by the joint chiefs of staff. OWI efforts were essentially overt, OSS activities covert. The OSS was the predecessor to the Central Intelligence Agency, which was created in 1947, and Donovan went down in history as the father of the American intelligence community.

An important aspect of the transition from private to governmental shortwave broadcasting was the role given to Latin America before Pearl Harbor. The United States had long been the leading force in point-to-point communications in Latin America. A parallel U.S. media dominance in the region's mass communications would provide some control mechanisms to displace the interventionism that had been foresworn in President Roosevelt's good neighbor policy. During the war years, the competition from Axis propaganda activity in South America had become considerable in such fields as clubs and societies, movies, press agencies, and radio broadcasts. Radio, including community listening, was well established in the Latin countries, and shortwave was in use for both local and regional broadcasting.

The totalitarian countries were putting great emphasis on shortwave broadcasting to South America, where many people lived in isolation[12] and where there were few alternative sources of news and information (and where those that did exist were often affiliated with political interests). Millions of Germans and Italians lived in South America. Zeesen had extensive Spanish, Portuguese, and German language services devoted to the area, and Germany and Italy regularly bought time on local medium-wave stations, many of which were desperate for funds and eager to broadcast anything they could get their hands on from paying clients. Germany, in particular, wanted to build solidarity with the many German communities in Latin America. Fascist Spain was also active on the South American broadcasting scene, emphasizing a Spanish renaissance and Spanish–Latin American solidarity. So intense became the foreign radio war that Argentina and Chile passed (but held in abeyance) decrees forbidding the rebroadcast of foreign transmissions from their soil, or the acceptance of foreign program sponsorship.

While England was Germany's main enemy in Europe, the target in Axis broadcasts to South America was the United States. This was particularly so after the fall of France, when criticism of the United States jumped from 20 to 43 percent of Germany's program content.[13] The message was often an economic one: Latin American national economies would develop faster if South America would sell its raw materials to the Axis countries, which would sell back needed finished products. The Axis countries also promised to cooperate in the development of South America's national industries. The United States would not pay adequately for South American goods, these stations said, and Yankee imperialism would impose an unwelcomed American hegemony.

The United States was far behind in the international broadcasting race, but at least it was heading in the right direction. Through their shortwave outlets WRCA and WNBI, NBC began beaming special programs to Latin America, as did CBS (WCBX and WCRC), G.E. (WGEA, WGEO, and KGEI), Westinghouse (WBOS), and Crosley (WLWO). Latin America became the principal target audience for nonsimulcasted American shortwave programming.[14] By 1941 about 35 hours per day of specially produced Spanish and Portuguese language output was being beamed to the area by U.S. shortwave stations.[15] Additional relay arrangements were entered into with local medium wavers.

Most of the Spanish and Portuguese language programming was of the news and current affairs variety that appeared to be preferred by listeners. It was in this area that the U.S. reputation for truthfulness and objectivity paid off. By 1941 U.S. stations were transmitting 161 English newscasts each week, along with 136 in Spanish and 59 in Portuguese.

Entertainment tended to consist of rebroadcasts of standard English language U.S. network programming. For a time in 1937 and 1938 a Spanish language "Pan American Hour" was prepared by the Pan American Union and broadcast over U.S. shortwave stations. Major shortwave productions were staged on South American national holidays. There was considerable response to Department of Commerce distribution of U.S. shortwave schedules to American embassies for further dissemination within the respective countries, and the department was soon sending them to anyone who asked. An NBC offer to send a free picture postcard of the 1940 Godoy-Louis championship fight to anyone in the shortwave audience who wanted one brought 23,000 requests.[16]

One of Donovan's early bureaucratic conflicts as coordinator of information had been with the office of the Coordinator of Inter-American Affairs (CIAA), headed by Nelson Rockefeller. The objectives of CIAA were to promote goodwill with our neighbors to the south and counter Axis propaganda there.[17] Although Donovan fought hard to keep the information dissemination function for Latin America within COI, he was unsuccessful. When OWI was formed, responsibility

THE UNITED NETWORK

SAN FRANCISCO, CALIFORNIA, U. S. A.

Hankins PA

The United Network was part of the effort of the Office of the Coordinator of Inter-American Affairs to manage U.S. shortwave broadcasting to Latin America (QSL, c. 1943).

for Latin American activities, including shortwave broadcasting to the area, shifted to CIAA.

By 1942 there was little opposition to government assumption of national shortwave broadcasting responsibilities, and NBC, Crosley, Westinghouse, and General Electric were ready to turn things over. The need for better coordination, and for a single national voice in wartime, was evident. Moreover, governmental sensibilities to the concerns of the private broadcasters over the years had fostered close working relationships between the stations and the government. Perhaps most importantly, none of the stations was making any money on shortwave. Only CBS and WRUL opposed the takeover, CBS because it had been behind the others in shortwave and was just completing a system that it felt would be competitive, and WRUL because it was committed to international educational broadcasting for nonpropaganda purposes and did not want to lose its unique identity, even for the duration of the war.[18]

On November 1, 1942, American shortwave broadcasting was transformed from an adjunct of domestic broadcasting to an element of governmental information efforts.[19] On that date, the U.S. government assumed control of the 14 private U.S. shortwave transmitters by entering into leases with their parent organizations for the duration of the war. The stations were CBS stations WCBX, WCDA, and WCRC (Brentwood, New York); Crosley's WLWO (Cincinnati, Ohio); General Electric's WGEO and WGEA (Schenectady, New York), and KGEI (San Francisco); NBC stations WRCA and WNBI (Bound Brook, New Jersey); Westinghouse transmitter WBOS (Boston); three World Wide Broadcasting Foundation transmitters (WRUL, Boston); and Associated Broadcasters station KWID (San Francisco; the Associated Broadcasters BCB outlet was KSFO).

The parent companies continued to operate the stations without profit, with Uncle Sam paying the costs and OWI and CIAA preparing and transmitting the programs (some of which were produced in collaboration with CBS and NBC). OWI used the transmitters two-thirds of the time, CIAA one-third. All the takeovers were friendly save that of WRUL, which had to be seized by the government. The United States paid the actual costs of operation plus depreciation (an improvement for the owners, who had been operating at a loss). CBS and NBC were permitted to operate distinct services to Latin America for a time, but this eventually ended.

Although the owners retained the option of postwar resumption of private broadcasting, only WRUL would exercise that right. There was some hope that commercial shortwave broadcasting would resume after the war and play a role in the development of new markets, but by then the broadcasters had lost interest in international shortwave and were happy to have the government in charge. NBC and CBS continued to provide government programming under contract until 1948, then left shortwave broadcasting entirely.

To address the various inadequacies of the stations—mainly age, low power and outdated equipment—a major equipment upgrade, including 18 new transmitters in the United States, was undertaken in the years 1943–45. The equipment would be government owned, but still operated by the companies. The new facilities (separate call letters for each transmitter) were CBS stations WOOC and WOOW (Wayne, New Jersey, 50 kw.), and KCBA, KCBF, and KCBR (Delano, California, 50 and 200 kw.); Crosley stations WLWK (Mason, Ohio, 50 kw., a spare transmitter obtained from station KFAB, Lincoln, Nebraska), and WLWL, WLWR, and WLWS (Bethany, Ohio, 200 kw.); General Electric stations WGEX (Schenectady, New York, 25 kw.) and KGEX (Belmont, California, 100 kw.); NBC stations WNRA, WNRI, and WNRX (Bound Brook, New Jersey, 50 kw.), and KNBA, KNBI, and KNBX (Dixon, California, 50 and 200 kw., a mirror of the Delano installation); and Associated Broadcasters station KWIX (San Francisco, 50 kw.). The government also made antenna improvements at WRUL, WBOS, and the CBS Brentwood facility. New overseas transmitters were installed in Honolulu (KRHO, 100 kw.) and Algiers (50 kw.). Existing arrangements for relays via the BBC Woofferton transmitter were continued, and a few other initiatives, such as U.S. takeover of certain German and other Axis broadcasting facilities, came and went as the wartime geography of Europe changed.

At the end of the war the functions of both the OWI and the CIAA were transferred to the Interim International Information Service (IIIS) in the Department of State. OWI and CIAA were wartime agencies, ripe for elimination, and the

ALGIERS, ALGERIA, NORTH AFRICA

# THE VOICE OF AMERICA

## IN NORTH AFRICA

We are pleased to confirm your report of reception

of our station on ....*31·22*.... m., ....*9610*.... kc.,

....*Nov. 16*.... 19*46*., at ....*1700*....hours, G.M.T.

Long forgotten, the Voice of America in North Africa became a major broadcasting site for coverage of the Balkans, Germany, France, Italy, and the eastern Mediterranean (QSL, 1946).

transfers were accompanied by personnel and broadcast hour cutbacks of 60 percent. On December 31, 1945, IIIS was itself replaced by the Office of International Information and Cultural Affairs (OIC), and the Voice of America became OIC's International Broadcasting Division.

During its early history, Voice of America (VOA) was treated as a stepchild of both the executive and legislative branches. Congress had fundamental problems with the government taking on a major media role, even at the international level, and the Department of State had little knowledge of, or interest in, broadcasting. Some felt that the department could not be relied on to project a properly American image overseas. The VOA appropriations process was contentious, and the entire operation was highly unstable. By December 1947 Voice of America had only 226 employees, less than one-third the wartime number. The agency survived largely through the tireless personal efforts of the assistant secretary of state for public affairs, William Benton.

As world tensions increased, however, Congress rethought the need for an international radio service. It was becoming increasingly important to tell the U.S. story, and to counter propaganda from other sources. As a result, Congress passed and on January 27, 1948, the president signed into law, the Information and Educational Exchange Act of 1948, for the first time making the U.S. official voice, the Voice of America, a permanent instrumentality of government.

## Chapter 6

# RECEPTION

IN 1928 AN UNKNOWN MEDIUM-WAVE poet described DXing as follows:

> Comes now the season of my great content
> As I dash home ev'nings on pleasure bent,
> For the air's chockful of distant waves
> That I long to master and make my slaves.
> Winging away far out through the ether,
> Scanning away those waves meter by meter—
> Hopping all over—then fin'lly the Coast.
> Ah! That is what pleases a DX hound most![1]

The thrill was even greater if it was shortwave and you were young. DXer Jack Jones remembers when the DX bug bit him. It was around the same time, and he was 12 years old.

> In 1927 [my father] got another Atwater Kent (single dial) and late one afternoon—very probably October or November 1928—we heard [medium wave] KDKA relay 5SW, Chelmsford, England, 5:30 to 6:00 P.M. CST. I distinctly recall the midnight chimes of Big Ben and the announcer saying, "5SW, the experimental station of the Marconi Company, closing down. Good night everybody, good night." This really got me hooked, and I started reading about radio and those remarkable short waves. I started a campaign to get dad interested in a shortwave adapter I saw advertised, but he kept stalling until one day he said that Mr. Jess Huffman (two houses down, and a radio bug) wanted to show me his shortwave receiver! I didn't even know there was one within 100 miles of Tupelo, Mississippi! This was probably late 1929. Needless to say I hurried down to see Mr. Jess. There I found a Pilot Super Wasp four-tube shortwave set! I had seen them in magazines and approached his with the respect and awe due royalty. He plugged in the yellow ring coil and got 8XK on its 60

meter wave, 2XAF on 31 meters, and HKC [Colombia] on 49 meters (orange ring coil). I was absolutely enthralled. To top it off, he called me early one morning and said he had Australia. All the homes on our street had hedges, and I either ran through them or jumped over them getting down to his house. Sure enough, 3ME, Melbourne, was heard. I visited Mr. Jess often and he'd sit at the Super Wasp and fiddle around. Finally he'd say, "Jack, I can't get anything. Get over here and see what you can do." Mr. Jess would stomp out of the room in a bad humor and I'd be in seventh heaven.[2]

In many ways today's DXer would feel right at home in the 1930s. By the start of the decade the principles of shortwave propagation were well understood, including sky wave versus ground wave, skip, the seasonality of reception, the relationship of sunspots to radio propagation, and even diversity reception (simultaneous reception of a station over two receivers, each connected to its own antenna). There was also an understanding of the reflective properties of the ionosphere, known then as the Kennelly-Heaviside layer after Britain's Sir Oliver Heaviside and Harvard professor Arthur Kennelly, who had independently proposed the existence of an ionized layer in the atmosphere.

Likewise there was much knowledge of antennas. Most popular were wire antennas, like the inverted-L, the T, and the inverted-V, all connected to the receiver by a single wire lead-in. Also in use were "Hertzian" antennas—what we today call dipoles—connected by a twisted pair. DXers also understood the properties of vertical antennas and the concepts of directionality, antenna length, and grounds.

Frequency allocations for international shortwave broadcasting were first established at the Washington International Radio Conference of 1927, and expanded at the International Radio Conference in Madrid in 1932 and the International Telecommunications Conference held in Cairo in 1938. After the latter, the bands were defined as 6–6.2 mc. (49 m.), 7.2–7.3 mc. (41 m.), 9.5–9.7 mc. (31 m.), 11.7–11.9 mc. (25 m.), 15.1–15.35 mc. (19 m.), 17.75–17.85 mc. (16 m.), 21.45–21.75 mc. (13 m.), and 25.6–26.6 mc. (11 m.). The 60 and 90 meter bands came into use (especially by stations in Venezuela and Colombia) soon after, and there was much out-of-band broadcasting.

People were already longing for the good old days. Not unlike today, they complained about band overcrowding, stations that did not verify, and countries that did not accept international reply coupons, the international medium for prepaying postage. Already by 1935 the International DXers Alliance had a mint stamp service in operation, selling unused stamps of foreign countries to those who wished to accompany their letters with return postage in a form that was convenient for the recipient.

One thing that was different was the level of power needed to push a signal around the globe. In 1931 Maynard Marquardt, chief engineer of U.S. shortwave

A setup for the well-equipped DXer of 1935 (*Official Short Wave Listener*, April–May 1935).

station W9XAA, the International Voice of Labor, reported that "[i]nside of 45 days after W9XAA was put on the air [on 6080 kc.], every state in the United States, four Canadian provinces, Mexico, Brazil, and New Zealand had been heard from. Many of the letters were so complimentary that they were regarded as being more friendly than accurate. But, as evidence in the form of consistent reports by mail continued to come in, it became plain that W9XAA on only 500 watts is 'covering the world.'"[3]

Shortwave was a topic of discussion in the regular media, and the *New York Times* often included highlights of shortwave programs and stations in its Sunday edition. In both hobby circles and the popular press, the hours of shortwave broadcasts were almost always stated in Eastern standard time rather than Greenwich time. This was due in part to the number of countries that did not conform to the internationally recognized time zones. In part it was also a holdover from domestic broadcast-band DXing, where the use of EST was common, and made more sense.

The casual home tape recording of today was a long way off, but the most serious listener had equipment available for the recording of programs on celluloid or aluminum records. The process used in 1930 was described this way:

> Go to your local phonograph dealer and get a diamond point used for the purpose of recording, and also get some blank recording records, which come in different sizes to suit the amount of reproduction desired. Substitute the recording point for the present reproducer, which is attached to the movable arm connecting to the horn or sound chamber. Then place your radio speaker directly in front of the phonograph horn and when the radio program comes in, start the turntable with a recording record on it, at the proper speed, and set the recording point on the record in the same way that the records are ordinarily played. The volume of the radio should be quite loud but not distorted.[4]

Although the recording art advanced some by mid-decade, disk cutting was still the only available method. It was expensive, but some DXers made extensive use of recorded reception reports. One enthusiast wrote as follows:

> Usually, I send at least one record to the station heard as a form of report requesting verification.... In most cases, the response is almost immediate. Often, the station plays the record on one of its local programs and, occasionally, there is a newspaper write-up about the event. I have quite a few clippings from different corners of the globe....
> [T]he expense is usually terrific. The biggest item is the wastage of records.... I hate to think of the pile of wasted disks I have around the house.[5]

An author's description of Latin American DXing in 1935 will ring true with

overcome, however, the new technology transformed the shortwave receiver from an experimental instrument to a common household device.

The superhet receiver eliminated the instability of the variable frequency RF amplifiers by converting all received frequencies to a single frequency, called the intermediate frequency (IF). It did this by combining the incoming RF signal with a signal produced within the receiver itself, creating a third signal at the desired intermediate frequency. The receiver's amplification and selectivity circuits could then be built around this common frequency. Another important result of superheterodyne technology was the replacement of the usual two or three dials on the typical receiver (one dial for each RF stage) with single dial tuning.

Three basic types of superhet receivers with shortwave capability soon emerged: all wave home radios with shortwave bands, communications receivers, and high fidelity shortwave sets.[7]

Most prevalent were the regular home models, all wave radios covering both medium wave and shortwave. These were basic six to 11 tube superhets, usually including shortwave up to about 15–22 mc. (The range of even some "BCB only" sets went up to about 1750 kc., and thus included the police bands.) Most had automatic volume control (AVC) to even out the wild fluctuations on the audio side of the signal. These radios were manufactured by the companies that we instinctively associate with early home radios: the big three—Philco (Philadelphia Storage Battery),[8] RCA, and Zenith—along with Admiral, American Bosch, Emerson, Howard, Silvertone (Sears Roebuck), Stewart-Warner, Stromberg-Carlson and many others. By 1933–34, 66 percent of home radio receivers had a shortwave capability. By 1936 almost 100 percent of the console models and 65 percent of the table models were able to receive shortwave.[9] During most of the 1930s, Zenith promoted its line as "Zenith Long Distance Radio."[10] As a practical matter, the future of international shortwave radio as a source of consumer news and entertainment was tied to the performance of these popular grade all wave receivers.

The all wave sets were of either the console or table model ("mantle") variety. By 1933, 75 percent of the receivers sold were table models. They were typically housed in wooden cabinets, first of the "cathedral" shape, and then of the "tombstone" or more modern horizontal box design. They ranged in price from about $35 to $100. The consoles were waist-high pieces of furniture in the $70–200 range or higher, depending on cabinetry, number of tubes, and other features. (It should be noted that published information on original sales prices of radios is not always reliable. Prices indicated were obtained from various sources and have not been independently verified.)

Among both consoles and table models, the receiver usually had four or five controls. Generally there was a combination on-off switch and volume control, a band selector switch, a tone control, and a tuning knob. Sometimes there were two tuning controls, or a sensitivity control (like a modern-day attenuator). Dial arrangements varied, but the most popular was the so-called airplane dial, a round face on which three to five bands would be arranged in concentric circles. The band selector switch would work in one of several different ways: it would illuminate the particular band chosen, or a pointer would be engaged, or the scale itself would change position. Dial faces were usually calibrated in megacycles, and sometimes the principal short-wave broadcast bands were highlighted, along with the locations of some of the major stations of the world, for example, London, Paris, Berlin, or Moscow.

The tuning knob often had two positions, a high ratio position of roughly 6–10 to 1, and a low ratio, bandspread-type "pull out" position with a ratio of 30–80 to 1. Some of the more expensive models had an "electric eye" or similar tuning device, which displayed the signal as it was being brought into resonance. These went under various proprietary names like "Magic Eye," "Shadowgraph," or "Tune-A-Lite." Another mid–1930s tuning innovation was automatic tuning, wherein particular stations could be selected by push buttons or a telephone dial type of device, making it easy to later return to the same spot on the dial. Some receivers even had motor-assisted tuning. Built-in speakers were in the 6–15 inch range, the larger sizes usually reserved for the consoles.

The largest and perhaps the most popular line of all wave consumer radios were the Zenith "big black dial" consoles and table models made from 1935 to 1942. The big black dial was a circular, 8–12 inch diameter dial that held a center-pivoted airplane dial pointer. The shortwave band markings were spread out in five concentric rings around the circumference of the dial. This dial was introduced with the 25-tube Stratosphere model that sold throughout the remainder of the 1930s for $750, about the cost of a new midrange sedan in those days. Zenith soon adopted this design as the dial layout for all of their radios. By the late 1930s they introduced the Robot (Shutter) Dial, a simplified variant that was actually three dials: one fixed, the other two (each made of two half-moons) snapping in place as the band switch was rotated.

Another design innovation on a few of the top-of-the-line consumer radios was the abandonment of general shortwave frequency coverage in favor of three or four narrow frequency ranges, each devoted exclusively to one of the major international broadcasting bands. Thus a band (for example, 31 meters, 9.5–10 mc.) that measured less than half an inch on the normal general coverage shortwave dial could be stretched out to six inches or more on its own bandspread dial. This made finding a particular broadcaster much easier.

Although more common on communications receivers, some of the all wave sets had BFOs—beat frequency oscillators—which were promoted to broadcast listeners as station finders. You tuned with the BFO on, locating stations by way of the beat note, and then turned the BFO off and listened in AM (if you could still

An early reminder of the role that Zenith long-distance radios played in communications with the MacMillan Arctic expedition of 1923 (*Radio Age*, May 1924).

hear the signal). Receivers of the day were not stable enough for modern-day "exalted carrier" reception, that is, listening in AM mode with the BFO on.

How well did the all wave receivers perform? Here are some comments.

1. The Bosch Model 575, six-tube table model (1935): "On the short-wave bands, Italy and Rio came in, in fine fashion, but London on three bands and Berlin on two bands didn't show up well until later in the week. VK2ME was hauled in with moderate strength on a Sunday morning. The 49-meter band brought up almost the entire flock of Central and South American stations, and also Portugal."[11]

2. The Pilot Model 293, six-tube table model (1936): "A total of 39 stations in the broadcast band were hauled in during an early afternoon, and 63 at mid-evening. Starting at 7 P.M. one evening and tuning right through, no stations were heard on 16 meters, 3 on 19 meters, 8 on 25 meters, 12 on 31 meters, and 27 on 49 meters. Random tuning at different periods brought in 3 stations on 16 meters and there would have been more had we listened on this band at a more appropriate time.... London and Berlin were picked up well and consistently on all their bands from 16 meters up; Berlin closed the electron-eye on 25 and 31 meters and came through like a local broadcaster, with London and Radio Coloniale [France] almost as good on 25 meters."[12]

3. The RCA Victor Model T10-1 "Magic Brain," 10-tube table model (1936): "The 16-meter band brought in the inevitable GSG and DJE, as well as PHI and W3XL. On 25 meters the receiver picked up with no difficulty the station at Pontoise, PCJ, DJD, DJB, DJQ, GSF, GSI, HVJ, and W8XK. Without attempting to pick up calls, we ran through about 5.75 mc to 6.5 mc and hauled out 40 stations. In only two cases was interstation interference noticeable that particular evening, and in no other case did we have any difficulty in actually separating stations."[13]

From a modern perspective, the inexpensive prewar receivers that tuned short-wave appear to have had both poor sensitivity and poor selectivity. The dial mechanism and the small size of the shortwave dial ranges in most of the models made tuning shortwave stations difficult. On the other hand, it is surprising how well the very best prewar consumer radios could perform on shortwave. In modern evaluations the top-of-the-line radios (ten tubes or more) tended to be easy to tune, remarkably drift free, quite sensitive even on short antennas, and reasonably selective. Further, the tuning of some of their gear-driven dial mechanisms compares quite favorably with all but a few postwar, predigital communications receivers.

In all probability, people of average means in the 1930s bought radios that, while capable of tuning shortwave, would perform relatively poorly there. If their interest in receiving international programming was only casual, poor performance on short-wave was not much of an issue. However, for the wealthy or the person seriously

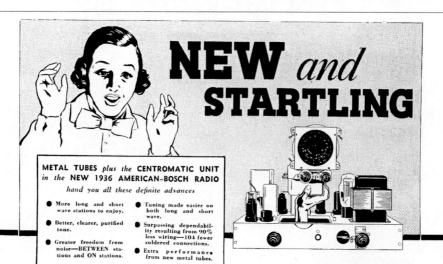

**NEW** *and* **STARTLING**

**METAL TUBES** *plus the* **CENTROMATIC UNIT** *in the* **NEW 1936 AMERICAN-BOSCH RADIO** *hand you all these definite advances*

- More long and short wave stations to enjoy.
- Better, clearer, purified tone.
- Greater freedom from noise—BETWEEN stations and ON stations.
- Tuning made easier on both long and short wave.
- Surpassing dependability resulting from 90% less wiring—104 fewer soldered connections.
- Extra performance from new metal tubes.

So MANY good radios! But the CentrOmatic Unit in the new American-Bosch helps you choose the best!

You not only can hear the difference which CentrOmatic Engineering introduces. You can actually *see* the difference! The chassis—as you can see—has a separate unit on which are centralized all the sensitive radio elments; armored and insulated from internal set noises.

That's why CentrOmatic Radio is so free from noise. That's why you can get more long and short wave stations. That's why even short wave tuning is so accurate and easy. That's why tone is so pure and rounded out. *That's why CentrOmatic Engineering means more to your enjoyment than metal tubes alone.* In American-Bosch CentrOmatic Radio you get both.

**UNITED AMERICAN BOSCH CORPORATION**

Springfield      Massachusetts

**Model 595M** — High Fidelity 10 tube, 11 tube performance, American, police and foreign, plus U. S. weather band, superheterodyne Console radio, with exclusive combination of new metal tubes and American-Bosch CentrOmatic construction. Range 540 to 18,500 Kilocycles and long wave U. S. weather band 150 to 350 Kilocycles. **$169⁵⁰**

**Model 565W**—6 tube, 9 tube performance, American, police and foreign superheterodyne Consolet with new metal tubes. Range: standard broadcast 540 to 1540 Kilocycles; police and short wave 1540 to 4200 Kilocycles; short wave 5900 to 18,200 Kilocycles. **$49⁹⁵**

American-Bosch Radio is licensed under patents and applications of R. C. A. and Hazeltine Corp.

**AMERICAN-BOSCH** *CentrOmatic* **RADIO**

One of the early names in radio receivers was American-Bosch (*All-Wave Radio*, February 1936).

interested in receiving shortwave broadcasts, consumer radios were available that performed very well, even by modern standards.

In a different category from the consumer radios were the communications receivers. The full story of the communications receiver is beyond the scope of this book.[14] Suffice it to say that they were intended to offer a level of sensitivity, selectivity, and signal handling that would get the most out of whatever signal was reaching the antenna, without regard to operational simplicity or decor. The term communications receiver was not entirely self-defining, for there were communications receivers that were "little more than broadcast receivers repackaged in metal communications-type cabinets,"[15] modest radios like the Hallicrafters Sky Champion and Super Defiant, and high-performance sets like some of the Hallicrafters Sky Riders and many of the Hammarlund and National models.

Raymond Moore, in his work on the history of these receivers,[16] says that the RME-9 by Radio Manufacturing Engineers of Peoria, Illinois, was the first bona fide communications receiver, although several earlier sets would have qualified under a slightly relaxed standard. The RME-9 was introduced in December 1933 and offered many of the features that would define communications receivers over the years: calibrated dials, bandspread, bandswitching, signal strength meter, separate RF stages, BFO, AVC, and selectable bandwidth filters. Wooden cabinets were replaced by metal, S-meters were substituted for tuning eyes, and single dial tuning was dropped in favor of the familiar two-control, main tuning–bandspread combination. Some communications receivers came with their own factory prepared dial calibration charts to convert 0–100 linear scales to actual frequencies. Kits were "out," and factory made was "in."

The biggest name in communications receivers was Hallicrafters. Lacking the necessary access to RCA licenses in the early days, company founder William J. Halligan collaborated with the Silver-Marshall Manufacturing Company of Chicago, a holding company for then defunct Silver-Marshall. The company had few assets other than its RCA licenses. Halligan produced receivers under the Silver-Marshall umbrella for a short time. In 1934 he contracted out the Hallicrafters manufacturing function. For a few months in 1936 he formed a partnership with Case Electric in Marion, Illinois, another company possessing the requisite RCA licenses, and he manufactured his receivers there. Later that year he bought the Echophone Company, turning its Chicago plant into the Hallicrafters headquarters, in which the company would remain until after World War II.

Hallicrafters was known for value and for the breadth of its line.[17] Although early Hallicrafters advertising emphasized craftsmanship, the company philosophy was to make maximum use of ready-made parts in order to minimize cost and get new models out quickly. It offered more models than any other manufacturer, and in just about every price range. They were large, well built units, the typical set mea-

Hallicrafters brought the concept of the specialized communications receiver home to the serious, albeit nontechnical listener (*All-Wave Radio*, July 1937).

suring roughly 20 inches across and 12 inches tall and deep. Most important, they were good performers.

The first of the Hallicrafters communications receivers, and one of the most popular, was the 1935 Super Skyrider. There would be many Super Skyrider incarnations over the years, but the first one was a 40 pound, seven-tube rig that came in six different versions: the S-4, S-5, and S-6, plus a crystal-equipped, "X" version of each (see below). Different models covered slightly different ranges, from the broadcast band through 30 mc., and were priced around $60–80. There was a large tuning dial with continuous bandspread, a preselector, BFO, transmit-receive switch, tone control, built-in loudspeaker, and no plug-in coils. According to a *RADEX* review, "Tuning is very easy and the logging of stations becomes highly accurate.... Because the Super Skyrider responds to a very narrow, knife-like width of the frequency band to which it happens to be tuned, the total amount of background noise is low in proportion to the amount of usable signal that can be amplified."[18]

Except for the 1935 Super Skyrider and the 1936 Super Seven (a joint project with Montgomery Ward, which sold the set as the Airline Professional Model 37), the Hallicrafters receivers of the 1930s and early 1940s are best categorized by their appearance. Generally speaking, those produced through 1938 featured a distinctive, calibrated "micro-vernier" dial made of an alloy of silver, copper, nickel, and zinc known as German-Silver. Beginning with the Skyrider 23 (SX-23), introduced in March 1939, Hallicrafters replaced this dial with a circular main tuning dial face located behind a raised housing. This basic design, with variations, was used through the war years and on many Hallicrafters units thereafter.

Just the names of the Hallicrafters receivers were enough to get the DX juices flowing. Super Skyrider, Ultra-Skyrider, Sky Challenger, Super Defiant, Sky Champion, and Sky Ranger; each receiver offered its own particular array of features. Prices ranged from $29 to about $159, with a few costing more. Some covered only up to 18 mc., but most went well beyond today's 30 mc. upper limit, into the 40–60 mc. range. The lower-priced units usually had a built-in speaker, with the better models requiring a separate speaker unit.

Many of the 1930s Hallicrafters receivers came in two versions, the standard S version, and, for $10–15 more, an SX version. The latter version was equipped with a crystal filter, and offered improved selectivity. Thus, for example, one might buy the 1937 Sky Challenger as either the S-15 for $69.50 or the SX-15 for $81.95. From 1939 on, the availability of the crystal filter as an option was dropped; the receiver either came with it or it didn't.

A few additional Hallicrafters models are worthy of note. The Sky Buddy series was the company's budget line. Introduced in September 1936 as the 5T, the receiver had five tubes, 36–1 bandspread action and built-in speaker, and tuned up to 18 mc. The Sky Buddy S-19 version, also with five tubes, came along two years later, and the six-tube S-19-R, which tuned up to 44 mc., went into production in 1939. Like other Hallicrafters receivers, the Sky Buddy was housed in a metal cabinet. The price of the Sky Buddies was $29.50. The S-19-R was the first low-priced receiver with electrical bandspread, and it was very popular. The company is said to have sold about 10,000 S-19s and 20,000 S-19-Rs.

The Super Skyrider SX-16 came to market in June 1937 and sold for $111 ($99 for the S version). The matching 12 inch speaker was $12. The receiver weighed 60 pounds and had much to offer, including 11 tubes, better than one microvolt sensitivity, variable selectivity, separate bandspread control, and an S-meter. Hallicrafters's "inertial tuning mechanism" made dialing very smooth. A new version of this receiver, the S-17, was introduced the same year. It sold for $125.50 and offered 13 tubes, two stages of preselection and an automatic noise limiter for the high-frequency range. Its successor, the SX-17, was widely used in FCC monitoring stations until it was replaced by the SX-28.

The Skyrider 23 (SX-23), introduced in 1939, was a little out of the ordinary for Hallicrafters. With its stylized gray, heavy steel case and high-tech vent grills, it was the first departure from the usual German-Silver dial design. It had 11 tubes and featured a new, eight-position bandswitch, reduced drift, and an unusual Venetian blind-type dial. It was only a fair performer, however, and was overshadowed by the SX-24 Skyrider Defiant that was introduced a few months later with more features and a $69.50 price tag (the SX-23 was $115.50).

Another major player in the communications receiver market was the National Company. National started out in 1914 as a manufacturer of an eclectic line of power plant specialty items, toys, airplane parts, and household wares.[19] Eager to profit from the radio boom, and always interested in new products, it began making variable capacitors in 1922, and then started producing the Browning-Drake broadcast receiver kit. The company decided to concentrate on radio components and, under the leadership of chief engineer and general manager (and prolific writer) James Millen, it soon grew into one of the major names in the high-frequency communications business.

The first National shortwave superhet designed principally for the amateur market was the FB-7, a less expensive, seven-tube, 1933 version of the high-performance, nine-tube AGS (Aeronautical Ground Station) shortwave receiver that National had built for the Civil Aeronautics Authority the year before (and which listed for $165–265, depending on when you bought it). A *RADEX* review stated that "The National FB-7 model is designed primarily for the experienced amateur operator and advanced DX listener. It has exceptional sensitivity, selectivity and stability throughout the crowded short waves…. A crystal is available which may be added to the receiver at any time and when it is used the selectivity is said to be measured in cycles rather than kilocycles. Interference due to heterodyning of adjacent signals is almost entirely eliminated."[20] A variety of FB models filled the company's line during the early 1930s, all in the under $50 range.

The AGS itself was a rugged set, definitely in the ultimate receiver category at the time. It was a major improvement over most receivers of its day, with two tuned IF stages, a crystal filter, good AVC, National's Velvet Vernier dial, and a tuning range of up to 20 mc. Band changing was by means of front panel plug-in coils.

The AGS served as the testing ground for features that would be refined and incorporated into what would eventually become National's two main contributions to shortwave listening: the HRO line and the NC line. In addition to being an outstanding DX receiver, the HRO—with its large, linear-reading dial, plug-in coils (a fixture of the HRO long after other manufacturers had gone to band switching), gear arrangements, and ganged capacitors—was a mechanical marvel, reflecting James Millen's background as a mechanical engineer. It went through countless hollow state (tube) versions from 1934, when it was first introduced in a nine-tube, $167 edition, until the solid state HRO-500 was announced in 1964.[21]

The NC series was inaugurated in 1936 by way of the 12-tube, $105 NC-100. Through the years there were many NCs of both more and less grand design, including—in the 1930s—many other models in the 100 series, such as the NC-101, which featured over eight feet of dial space on each of its four bands. Also available were the less expensive, 10-tube NC-80X, introduced in 1937 for $88, and the seven-tube $49 NC-44, brought to market in 1938. National also produced a number of receivers for the frequency range above 30 mc.

The third major player in the communications receiver market was Hammarlund Manufacturing. Founded in 1910 in a loft on Fulton Street in Manhattan, at first (like National) Hammarlund manufactured an odd collection of items, including metal watch cases, fire alarms, an antirattling device for windows, liquor decanters, and clips for Christmas tree ornaments. It started producing variable capacitors in 1916 and other parts soon thereafter, and entered the receiver business in 1925.[22] In the 1930s Hammarlund invented the wide-range crystal filter, which permitted variable selectivity within the receiver's IF amplifier. This was a major breakthrough in shortwave technology.

The two principal Hammarlund shortwave superhet lines were the Comet and the HQ series. The eight-tube Comet, introduced in 1931 for $130, and the improved 1932 Comet Pro ($88), were the company's first shortwave superhets. They covered the shortwave range up to 21 mc. There were many variations of the Comet Pro, and within a short time the receiver was in wide use. The first of the Comet Super Pro line—soon shortened to just Super Pro (SP)—appeared in 1936. It was the SP-10, and sold for around $195. It had 16 tubes and featured two RF stages, crystal filter, BFO pitch control, variable bandwidth, high-quality audio, and an external power supply.

Many variations of the SP series would be offered over the years, including—in the 1930s—the 16-tube SP-100 series ($239 in 1937) and the 18-tube SP-200 series (list was $279 in 1939). The HQ series likewise began in the 1930s, with the HQ-120, introduced in 1938. It cost $230 in 1940, had 10 tubes, covered the range up to 30 mc. (as would most future Hammarlunds), and featured calibrated bandspread on the amateur bands (a first), adjustable antenna trimmer, multiple bandwidths, and a highly effective noise limiter. Hammarlund receivers contained few compromises. They were built with high-quality components, most of which were manufactured by Hammarlund itself.

There were many other quality communications receivers available. Although McMurdo Silver ultimately made his mark in the hi-fi shortwave market (see below), he got his start with a line of fairly modest communications receivers, including the seven-tube Ham Super (1933), the 5C Single Signal Super (1934, $75), and the 5D Radio Silver (1935, $110). In 1939 E. H. Scott, who was also interested mainly in hi-fi shortwave receivers, produced a 26-tube communications receiver, the Scott Special, which contained many of the features of the Scott hi-fi sets. It boasted two completely separate front ends, one for the broadcast band and long wave, the other for shortwave up to 64 mc. The set had 22 controls, and by flicking the Wavechange switch you could move back and forth between the broadcast band and shortwave. An early Scott observer reminisced as follows: "It is extremely interesting, when one of the local stations is rebroadcasting war news from Europe, to switch over and receive the same program directly from the European station, then by throwing the control switch, make an instant comparison between the reception direct from Europe, and the same program being rebroadcast from the local station."[23] The Scott Special had a very low production run, however, owing mainly to its price: $650.

RCA produced the top-of-the-line AR-60 communications receiver for $495 in 1935 (when U.S. annual per capita income was $474). Later in the 1930s, RCA offered a series of communications receivers in the $69–189 range, including in 1938 the 10-tube AR-77 ($139), and the following year the AR-88, a 100-pound, 14-tube receiver with very high sensitivity, gain, and selectivity. Other popular communications receiver manufacturers included Howard, Meissner, Midwest, and Patterson.

A third category of shortwave radio, between the all wave set and the communications receiver, though closer to the latter, was the so-called high-fidelity receiver. Containing many more features than the standard all wavers but lacking some of the technical features of communications receivers, these radios were geared to the listener who was less concerned with DXing than with getting the best fidelity possible out of the more common shortwave signals.

One of the leading manufacturers of this genre was E. H. Scott Radio Laboratories. The bridge between the early Scott sets and the Scott hi-fi radios was the factory-made Scott Allwave series. It included the Allwave 12, introduced in 1930, and the Allwave Deluxe which came to market two years later. The Allwave Deluxe improved upon the 12 by eliminating the plug-in coils and utilizing single dial tuning. In 1934 these were followed by the first truly hi-fi set, the Allwave 15, which featured an improved visual tuning system, improved antenna tuning, and a BFO for station finding; and in 1935 by the 23-tube Scott Full Range High Fidelity Receiver, which featured a larger amplifier and power supply.

The Allwave series was the start of the Scott line of classic receivers—sturdy, well-built affairs—"The Stradivarius of Radio," as they were advertised. Workmanship was excellent, and the sets were guaranteed for five years. In the Allwave series and all subsequent models (except some made during World War II), the chassis, tube shields, coil shields, and transformers were chromed. Scott receivers were purchased either direct from the factory or in Scott salons located in New York, Detroit, and Los Angeles.

A lengthy ad in *Radio Craft* (June 1932) touted the 'round-the-world reception that could be expected from Scott's receivers. The ad began:

> Seven years ago, newspaper and magazine editors gave columns and columns of space to the amazing performance of a theretofore unknown receiver. They heralded the advent of transoceanic reception, on the broadcast band (200-500 meters) as the greatest radio achievement of the age. They named the receiver "World Record Super," because it brought in 117 programs from 19 stations, ALL OVER 6000 miles away, and WITHIN THE SHORT SPACE OF 13 WEEKS.
>
> This receiver was the work of E. H. Scott, who believed that a radio set designed in accord with certain advanced ideas of his own, and engineered to micrometric precision, would do things no other receiver was ever able to do. These sets were built in the laboratory. Not even a screw was touched by an unscientific hand, and the radio industry was given a new target.

This introduction was followed by a grand headline and "four pages of FACTS":

> They say you CAN'T, but I say you CAN get Enjoyable Programs from dozens of Foreign Stations Every day of Every month of the Year
>
> MANY prominent radio engineers STILL contend that dependable daily reception of extremely distant foreign stations is impossible.
>
> "It can't be done!" they shout. They insist that the distance is too great—that atmospheric conditions are too variable—that signal strength is insufficiently constant—that if foreign reception is to be obtained at all, an ideal location must be had—and, last, that there is no receiver generally available today that is sensitive enough to bring in foreign stations regularly.

Many of those making these statements are receiver manufacturers; men who have been forced to conclude that mass production methods cannot produce receivers capable of regular foreign reception. Seeming disbelief in the practicability of foreign reception is therefore the result of someone's failure. The only reason for *sincere* disbelief is ignorance of the facts.

You are entitled to the truth. It is your privilege to know the FACTS, because the most interesting—the most enjoyable world of radio is to be found between 15 and 200 meters. Hence, I have written this answer to disbelievers and to the unadvised, and I am spending my own money to publish these four pages of FACTS.

You will find in them a full explanation of what foreign reception is; how regularly it comes in; what the programs are and how they sound. In addition—you'll find undeniable PROOF that the Scott All-Wave 15-550 meter Superheterodyne is certain to give you enjoyable round the world reception every day of every month of the year. Yes, EVERY day, even during the summer months! I say, "You CAN do it!"

### The AUSTRALIAN TEST
*first proved regular reception possible*

For a considerable period, short wave broadcasts from England, France and Italy have been picked up by the broadcasting chains in this country, on highly developed laboratory-type short wave receivers and re-broadcasted on the 200-550 meter band to listeners in America. The fact that these broadcasts were always planned, weeks in advance, convinced us that their reception was contemplated with absolute certainty. Why, then, couldn't *all* foreign broadcasts be depended upon? To ascertain whether or not they could be, we selected the station farthest from Chicago that broadcasted regularly, and set out to see how many of its programs we could pick up with the Scott All-Wave.

### All Programs Recorded

VK3ME at Melbourne, Australia, is 9560 air miles from Chicago. This station broadcasts two times a week on a wave length of 31.55 meters. The reception test was begun June 6th, 1931. Ten months have elapsed, and *every* broadcast (excepting three) was received with sufficient loud speaker volume to be clearly heard and logged. The three programs were missed only because an illegal code transmission interfered.

Each broadcast from VK3ME has not only been clearly heard, and its reception verified by the station, but they have all been recorded just as they came from the amplifier of the Scott All-Wave on aluminum discs. These recordings are available to anyone who wishes to hear them.

### Program Returned to Australia by Phone

The engineer of VK3ME was curious to know with what quality his program was received in Chicago. He realized, of course, that clarity was sufficient to permit logging of details, but beyond that he was skeptical. So on January 23rd, 1932 Mr. Scott telephoned VK3ME from Chicago, and while VK3ME's program was being received, the telephone mouthpiece was pointed toward the speaker and the program sent back to Melbourne—another 9560 miles, and with perfect clarity as verified by the engineer's written acknowledgment.

This 10 month test on reception from a point nearly 10,000 miles away, proves, beyond any doubt, that enjoyable foreign reception can be depended upon, IF the receiving equipment is competent. It PROVES the DISTANCE is *no* obstacle! And it PROVES that variable conditions of the atmosphere are not insurmountable obstacles! To further substantiate our contentions we began a test of VK2ME at Sydney.... Both of these tests PROVE that there IS a receiver having more than enough sensitivity to detect and reproduce the broadcast from foreign stations regularly and with adequate volume!

*Other Owners Do Even Better*

This remarkable performance was not a stunt. It was not a freak happen-stance occurring to one Scott All-Wave ideally located and installed. To the contrary, it appears as mediocre performance when compared to the 9,535 logs of foreign reception sent to us during January, February and March from Scott All-Wave owners located in all parts of the country!

The ad reproduced two of the logs as examples of what listeners had pulled in on their Scott All-Waves. It also described what other listeners could expect to there:

### What Countries Will You Hear?

Any Wednesday, Saturday or Sunday morning you can tune in the Australian stations and listen to a three hour program, in English, of course. Then if you wish something with a decidedly foreign flavor, you can dial Saigon, Indo-China, and listen to the weirdest, Eastern music you have ever heard.

Right after breakfast, most any morning, you can tune in the Radio Colonial at Paris, France—or Chelmsford, England, from which station comes an English version of the World's latest news.

From 11:30 A.M. until 5 P.M. you have your choice of musical programs, talks, plays, etc. from Italy, France, Germany or England. In the late afternoon, the offerings from Portugal will be found very entertaining.

In the evening you may have your choice of a dozen or more different stations including Colombia and Ecuador in South America. Then, too, there is Spain, and Cuba.

Is this all?—Indeed not!—These are just a few of the many foreign stations that will be found on the dial of the Scott All-Wave. A complete list showing the exact time to tune dozens of foreign stations, is furnished with the receiver.

## What Will You Hear?

From a large number of these foreign stations you'll hear news in English, and you'll delight in the variety of aspect the different countries give to an item of international interest.

You'll hear music from everywhere. Weird chants from Indo-China, and in contrast, a tango from the Argentine. From Rome you'll hear the real Grand Opera—you'll hear the voice of the Pope, the Vatican Choir and solo voices mellowed in Italian sunshine. From Germany you'll hear political speeches, music and news. From France, Spain and Portugal you'll hear a wonderful musical program that will thrill you hour after hour. From England you'll hear plays—drama— comedy and musicales; delightful presentations, refreshingly different from those to which you are accustomed. You'll never tire of foreign reception, because it never loses its novelty.

## Will the Reception Be Clear?

Foreign stations are tuned easily and smoothly with a Scott All-Wave. As the dial is turned to the correct spot, the station comes on, in most cases, with the same naturalness, clarity, and roundness of tone that characterizes *domestic* reception.

Usually, you can have more volume than you wish, which means simply that the sensitivity may be lowered beneath the noise level, thereby permitting the program to come through with truly enjoyable bell-like clarity. There's no doubt about it. Dependable foreign reception is here; yours to thrill to; yours to enjoy as you have never enjoyed radio before.

The ad ended with a coupon to send for further information, and the promise of a money-back guarantee.

Scott took a quantum leap in 1937 with the introduction of the 30-tube Scott Philharmonic, which incorporated improved RF circuitry, variable bandwidth, variable sensitivity, volume expander, and a record scratch suppresser (similar to an automatic tone control). The receiver covered the range from 150 kc. to 80 mc., and produced 40 watts of output to a 15 inch speaker (later models also contained two 5 inch high-frequency speakers). Scott also produced two lesser variations of the Philharmonic, the Scott 16 and the Scott 18, each of which adopted certain features of the parent set.

In 1938 Scott introduced the Phantom, a receiver similar to the Scott 18 but more useful for DX purposes. This was followed by the Phantom Deluxe, and in 1939 the 14-tube Scott Masterpiece (introduced after Scott purchased McMurdo Silver, parent company of the Masterpiece line; see below). A Scott expert stated: "[T]he Masterpiece was an ideal instrument for those who desired a much finer receiver than the average mass-production radio. The Phantom Deluxe was designed for the music lover and radio listener who desired unequaled record reproduction, increased

| Call. | Location. | Identification. |
|---|---|---|
| GSH...... | Daventry, England.... | (See GSB).  [Stations appear in order of frequency] |
| PMC...... | Bandoeng, Java....... | (See PLF). |
| LSY....... | Buenos Aires, Argentina | Begins transmissions by sounding E, E, G sharp, and A, on xylophone. |
| PLF....... | Bandoeng, Java....... | Begins transmissions with three tone auto horn.   Notes are F, D, C. |
| GSG...... | Daventry, England.... | (See GSB). |
| DFB....... | Nauen, Germany...... | Sounds three tone whistle at beginning of transmissions.   Notes are D, C, G. |
| DJB....... | Zeesen, Germany...... | (See DJC). |
| GSF....... | Daventry, England.... | (See GSB). |
| GSE....... | Daventry, England.... | (See GSB). |
| I2RO...... | Rome, Italy.......... | Woman announcer announces "Radio Roma Napoli." |
| DJD....... | Zeesen, Germany...... | (See DJC). |
| GSD....... | Daventry, England.... | (See GSB). |
| PHI....... | Huizen, Holland...... | Announces "This is Huizen." |
| FYA....... | Pontoise, France...... | Plays the "Marseillaise" at beginning and end of transmissions. |
| ORK...... | Brussels, Belgium..... | Plays Belgium national hymn at close of programs. |
| EAQ...... | Madrid, Spain........ | Announces "Ay-ah-coo, transradio Madrid." |
| CT1AA.... | Lisbon, Portugal...... | Sounds the cookoo calls between selections. |
| VK2ME.... | Sydney, Australia...... | Laugh of Kookaburra bird at beginning and end of transmissions. |
| HBL....... | Geneva, Switzerland... | (See HBP). |
| DJA....... | Zeesen, Germany...... | (See DJC). |
| GSC....... | Daventry, England.... | (See GSB). |
| VK3ME.... | Melbourne, Australia... | Opens programs with clock chimes. |
| GSB....... | Daventry, England.... | Big Ben Chimes on quarter hours. Announces "London calling on—(stations and wavelengths)." Begins and ends transmissions by playing "God Save The King." This song has the same tune as our "America." |
| IAC....... | Piza, Italy.......... | Calls "Pronto, pronto—(name of ship)." |
| PSK(PRA3) | Rio de Janeiro, Brazil.. | Plays chimes like the NBC chimes when signing off. |
| CNR...... | Rabat, Morocco...... | Announces "Radio Rabat dans Maroc." Uses metronome between selections. |
| HBP....... | Geneva, Switzerland... | Announces "Hillo, hillo, radio nations." |
| TIEP...... | San Jose, Costa Rica... | Announces "La Voz del Tropico." |
| HC2RL.... | Guayaquil, Ecuador.... | Plays the Ecuadorian National Anthem at beginning and end of transmissions. |
| PRADO.... | Riobomba, Ecuador.... | Announces "Estacion el Prado, Riobomba, Ecuador." |
| HJ1ABB... | Barranquilla, Colombia. | Announces "Achay-hota-uno-ah-bay-bay." |
| HJ5ABD... | Cali, Colombia........ | Announces "Achay-hota-thinko-ah-bay-bay." |
| HI1A...... | Santo Domingo...... | Plays "Anchors Aweigh" at start and finish of programs. |
| YV3RC.... | Caracas, Venezuela..... | Announces "Ee-vay-trays-erray-say." |
| W2XE..... | Wayne, New Jersey.... | Announces in English, German, French, Spanish and Italian. |
| YV2RC.... | Caracas, Venezuela..... | Announces "Ee-vay-dos-erray-say."   Sounds four strokes on chimes every fifteen minutes. |
| VE9HX.... | Halifax, Nova Scotia... | Sounds four strokes on a gong at beginning of transmissions. |
| OXY...... | Skamleback, Denmark.. | Midnight chimes at 6 P. M. E. S. T. |
| VE9CS..... | Vancouver, B. C...... | Sounds two bells between selections. |
| GSA...... | Daventry, England.... | (See GSB). |
| DJC....... | Zeesen, Germany...... | Announces in German, and English. Eight notes of old German song played over and over at beginning of transmissions. |
| XEBT..... | Mexico City, Mexico... | Sounds auto horn after each selection. |
| RV59...... | Moscow, U. S. S. R.... | "International" is played at beginning and end of transmissions. |
| HVJ...... | Vatican City, Italy.... | Announces "Pronto, pronto, radio Vaticano."   Clock ticking. |
| TGX...... | Guatemala City, S. A.. | Two tone high frequency signals. |
| YV5RMO... | Maracaibo, Venezuela.. | Strikes gong before announcing. |
| HCJB..... | Quito, Ecuador....... | Sounds 2-tone chime after announcements. |

Stations often play "tuning signals" prior to sign-on so that listeners can recognize their signals and adjust their sets (*Official Short Wave Listener*, April–May 1935).

today's DXers. "The numerous Spanish-speaking stations of South and Central America are, without doubt, the source of the average fan's most difficult identification problems! Few of these stations ever give English announcements; many of them shift wavelength at will, and new ones are appearing almost daily, to add to the listeners' confusion."[6]

The biggest factor in the growth of shortwave in the 1930s was the development of the supersonic heterodyne, or "superhet," radio, a design that remains basic even to today's high-tech receivers. Although superhet technology was well understood by the mid–1920s, its growth was retarded for almost ten years by RCA's withholding of its superhet patents from receiver manufacturers. This left early superhet development to the experimenters and custom-set builders. Once the patent problem was fidelity, and comparatively noise-free distance reception. The Philharmonic was for the discriminating taste of those who were satisfied only with the best instrument Scott could build regardless of cost."[24] Scott got well-known musicians like concert vocalist Ezio Pinza, symphony conductor Eugene Ormandy, violinists Yehudi Menuhin and Jascha Heifetz, and pianist José Iturbi to attest to the performance of his products.

Scott's principal (and worthy) competitor was McMurdo Silver, founder of the Silver-Marshall and McMurdo Silver lines. Starting out in the parts and kit business in 1924, within four years Silver was one of the nation's largest dealers. His receivers paralleled Scott's in many ways, and sometimes surpassed them. Silver was a prolific writer, and some Scott receivers bore an uncanny resemblance to sets described in Silver articles. Unlike Scott, who cherished the image of a radio craftsman, Silver's dream was to become a large manufacturer. By 1929 his plant had a capacity of over 1,000 receivers a day.

Silver-Marshall went bankrupt in 1929, whereupon McMurdo Silver, Inc., with a custom-set orientation, was formed. Intensified competition with Scott soon followed. Scott considered Silver an upstart, in part because some of his receivers were manufactured for Silver by Howard Radio Company of Chicago.

The heart of the McMurdo Silver line was the Masterpiece series. A new Masterpiece was introduced each year, starting with the Masterpiece I in 1932 and ending with the Masterpiece VI in 1937. The Masterpiece I was similar to the Scott Allwave Deluxe, and the Masterpiece IV was like the Scott Full Range High Fidelity Receiver. The receivers varied in tubes and features, but were similar to the Scotts, up to and including the chrome. Among the features available in the Masterpiece V were modified Jensen electrodynamic speakers, volume expander, and "mechanical band spread dialing through planetary ball bearings and split gears that are able to resolve … 18 mc. to a couple of hundred hertz with almost imperceptible backlash." In a 1981 comparison of the Masterpiece V (1936) with a Scott Phantom (1938), National HRO-50 (1950), Drake SSR-1 (1975), and Barlow-Wadley XCR-30 (1970), the Masterpiece received the highest overall rating.[25]

Silver was no amateur in the promotional department either. A 1938 Silver advertisement contained a letter from none other than Lee De Forest himself, attesting to the merits of the Masterpiece VI. Silver also advertised that Admiral Byrd had a Masterpiece II with him in the Antarctic. (Admiral Byrd seems to have taken with him one of every radio ever made. Companies made the most of such promotional opportunities. A 1938 advertisement of the Ward Leonard Electric Company noted that a Ward Leonard Plaque Resistor was used as the terminating resistor on a MacGregor Arctic expedition rhombic antenna.)

Unfortunately, bankruptcy hit McMurdo Silver again in 1938, whereupon Scott bought the assets of the company. Silver died in 1948 at age 45.

Gateway to the World!

THERE NEVER WAS BEFORE THERE MAY NEVER BE AGAIN A RADIO SUCH AS *This!*

## LET McMURDO SILVER *Build* A RADIO— ESPECIALLY FOR YOU!

Just as a radio for operation in Tokio should be quite different from a radio intended for operation in St. Louis, your radio should undoubtedly be quite different from that of a friend three blocks away. The MASTERPIECE is the world's only truly custom-built radio — built especially for each owner — not just built for the finest average reception conditions.

It's NEW! The McMurdo Silver MASTERPIECE V is as startlingly different as the first inter-planatary rocket flight will be! When you first see it — even before you roll the controls — you'll know why it is called "The Radio of 1940." It has fourteen points of construction never found before in any equipment for the reception of radio signals! Scientists, case-hardened to radio phenomena, have been frank in their curiosity to tear one apart to see what makes it "tick." Never before have we been so proud to present a new model of "The World's Only Truly Custom-Built Radio!"

### $34.00 DOWN – $17.08 MONTHLY

For the first time it is possible for anyone to own the finest there is. Our own easy payment plan puts the "millionaire's radio" into any home.

Send this coupon TODAY for complete technical details.

McMURDO SILVER **MASTERPIECE**

CHICAGO STUDIO—3354 NORTH PAULINA STREET
NEW YORK DEMONSTRATIONS—63 CORTLAND STREET

"THE WORLD'S ONLY TRULY CUSTOM-BUILT RADIO"

### MAIL THIS COUPON

McMurdo Silver Corp.
3354 N. Paulina St.,
Chicago, U. S. A.

Please send me full details on the new MASTERPIECE V.

NAME_____

ADDRESS_____

McMurdo Silver was Scott's main competitor (*Radio News*, September 1936).

There were two other main contenders in the hi-fi market. William H. Hollister's Lincoln Radio Corporation produced eight models during the 1930s. The Lincoln SW-33 (1933) competed favorably with the Scott Allwave Deluxe and the McMurdo Silver Masterpiece I, and the Lincoln Symphonic roughly paralleled the Scott Full Range High Fidelity and the McMurdo Silver Masterpiece IV. The other notable company, Midwest Radio Corporation, sold its hi-fi receivers by mail at substantially lower prices than Scott, Silver, and Lincoln, and, while not quite in their class, offered good value for the money.[26]

Finally, mention should be made of the 26-tube Hallicrafters Skyrider Diversity receiver that was introduced in June 1938. Diversity reception involves reducing the effects of fading by combining the audio output of two separate receivers, each connected to a different antenna. The DD-1 weighed 225 pounds, tuned the broadcast band through 61 mc., and featured a 12 inch speaker as standard equipment (with a Jensen Giant Bass Reflex speaker console as an option). The cost was $422 in 1938, jumping to $627 in 1939. The Jensen speaker package added another $135.

The DD-1 consisted of two identical receivers through the second detector, followed by a common audio stage and combined AVC. Hallicrafters promoted the receiver as reducing fading to negligible proportions while increasing signal strength and signal-to-noise ratio. The set was poorly engineered, however, with one recent commentator equating its performance to a $50 receiver.[27] Only a few hundred were manufactured, and advertising for it ceased in mid–1940.

## Chapter 7

# THE POPULAR SHORTWAVE PRESS

THE SHORTWAVE ENTHUSIAST Tom Williamson has observed that "the biggest single difficulty in the hobby was getting accurate information about stations in respect to address and wavelengths used at different times of the day."[1] From this need there developed an active shortwave press.

## *Magazines: The Gernsback Trilogy*

The biggest name in early radio publications was Hugo Gernsback. Born in Luxembourg, Gernsback came to the United States and made his mark as the founder of the Electro Importing Company. In 1908 "EI" was New York's principal source of electrical parts and equipment, and, in effect, the nation's first amateur radio supply house. The EI catalog was the bible for radio experimenters.

Often described as the father of science fiction, Gernsback was an "author, inventor, scientific prophet, magazine publisher, and broadcast pioneer;"[2] to some an eccentric, to others a man far ahead of his time. His penchant for mixing fantasy with art led to magazine covers depicting electronic gadgetry and futuristic machines of all kinds. Gernsback believed that science fiction, a term that he is said to have coined, could actually help bring about many of the wonders of the future. He "tossed out predictions as if scattering birdseed, occasionally pausing to elaborate with glossy illustrations."[3]

Gernsback's interests went far beyond radio. His other publications included *Amazing Stories* ("the magazine of scientification"), *Electrical Experimenter*, and *Science Wonder Stories*, plus *Television News*, which he published in the 1920s. Gernsback was also the originator of *Modern Electrics*, one of the earliest magazines devoted to electrical experimentation and radio, published from April 1908 to December 1913.

Gernsback created two of the most important shortwave publications of the day, *Radio News* and *Short Wave Craft*, plus their "little brother," *Official Short Wave Listener*. He also published *Radio Craft*, a widely read magazine that carried occasional shortwave news but concentrated on more technical topics.

One of the interesting things about the Gernsback publications and some others of the time was their pagination. Rather than each issue being paginated separately, Gernsback publications paginated continuously by volume. For example, volume 6 of *Radio News* began with issue no. 1, published in July 1924, and ended with issue no. 12, published in June 1925. The July 1924 issue was paginated 1–144 and the August issue 145–280, through the June 1925 issue that contained pages 2193–2328. Volume 7, no. 1, published in July 1925, resumed with page one.

Of all the early radio magazines, *Radio News* was probably the most widely read, with an advertised circulation of 400,000 by 1925. Although it concentrated at first on circuits and technical topics, what eventually set *Radio News* apart was the breadth of its coverage. There was something for everyone: amateur radio, equipment, patent news, antennas, broadcasting, radio servicing, DXing, clubs, and program listening. It also had contests, humor, one-act plays, extensive advertising for all kinds of parts, receivers and other equipment, and monthly Gernsback editorials on every conceivable radio subject. It even addressed such arcane questions as whether Esperanto or Ilo was the better international language (it ran a series of Esperanto lessons in 1925).

A distinctive feature of *Radio News* through 1925 was the magazine's covers. Here were the Norman Rockwells of the radio world, collectors' items in themselves. They were original, and often humorous: kids being diagnosed by a "Radio Doctor" machine, burglars enjoying the radio while gathering their booty, a headphone-donned radio fan suffering "interference" from his wife and child, and a "radio fiend" dreaming of lying in a receiver-bed surrounded by antennas and other gear.

*Radio News* began coverage of the standard broadcast band in the early 1920s when it started carrying a monthly list of U.S. stations. The magazine's first organized coverage of shortwave was a three-page column, "On the Short Waves," which ran from July 1928 through June 1929. It contained information on receivers and circuits, along with readers' letters, reception notes, and some sketchy information about shortwave stations. It was preceded in April 1928 by a list of shortwave broadcasters, and the following announcement:

> Radio stations in many parts of the world are now broadcasting on
> short wavelengths (i.e. below 200 meters), but because most of their
> transmissions are still only of an experimental nature, Radio News
> has found it difficult to obtain, even from the stations themselves,

The old generation and the new (*Radio News*, January 1921).

accurate information about their operating frequencies, hours of broadcasting, etc. Readers owning short-wave receivers are therefore requested to report to Radio News any strange short-wave broadcast (not code) stations that they hear; giving the wavelengths as closely as they can guess the figures from the dial settings, by comparing the latter with the settings for such consistent transmitters as [the short-wave relays of] KDKA, WGY, and WLW.[4]

In December 1928 *Radio News* began carrying lists of the shortwave stations of the world on roughly a bimonthly basis. In later years many other magazines would also carry such lists as the interest in shortwave developed. However, as the International Short Wave Club would warn in its September 1934 bulletin, such lists were not always reliable. Said the club: "The average short wave station list contains hundreds of stations that have closed down, changed wavelengths or schedules, or have never really operated. The only reliable and helpful information comes direct from listeners, and even this must be published quickly in order to be of help." The club observed that the information in its bulletin was corrected up to within three days of mailing. "Other magazines usually make up copy from two to four months in advance of publishing." It was a problem.

In May 1929 *Radio News* was sold, and the omnipresence of Hugo Gernsback disappeared. The magazine retained the same general feel, but shortwave fans did not benefit from the new management: "On the Short Waves" was dropped, and with it the regular albeit limited coverage of shortwave in *Radio News*.

The station lists continued, but it wasn't until April 1933 that *Radio News* presented a new shortwave column, "DXer's Corner." Laurence M. Cockaday, *Radio News* editor and well-known inventor-developer in radio's early days, introduced the column this way:

> What was only a year ago considered a fad, the reception of long-distance short-wave transmissions from the far corners of the earth, is now taking hold among a much larger group of listeners than heretofore thought possible. Thousands of new recruits have joined the ranks of the short-wave listeners during the last few months in America and they are persons in all walks of life.... [They] have been "bitten by the bug" and have purchased the finest type of equipment they could find for this purpose.... With a good short-wave set today it is possible to sit down and pull in stations 3,000 to 12,000 miles distant and receive them enjoyably and comfortably. If one knows how to tune, there is certainly more thrill and adventure on the shortwaves in a half hour than on the broadcast waves in many hours' listening.[5]

Broadcast band DXers might disagree with that last statement, but it illustrates the attraction that shortwave was thought to have.

*Radio News* provided its "Official DX Listening Post" reporters with this certificate. Such official designations were designed to promote the submission of station information that would be of interest to other readers (1937).

Cockaday's column was impressive. It featured a monthly "World Short Wave Time-Table," showing the stations that operated each hour of the day. It also had loggings, best bets, and station news supplied by readers and "Official Radio News Short Wave Listening Post Observers" (people who had registered their listening posts with the magazine). Later it included DXers' photos, pictures of QSLs, feature articles, distance maps, and club news, along with extensive shortwave station lists that contained addresses, ID texts, and interval signals.

In August 1934 *Radio News* supplemented its shortwave coverage with "Captain Hall's Short-Wave Page," an interesting monthly world tour of shortwave broadcast (and sometimes amateur) DX activity by Captain Horace L. Hall. Hall was already a well-known shortwave listening personality. He had a regular Saturday column, "Below the Broadcast Band," in the *New York Sun*, and he had written for another excellent (though short-lived) shortwave magazine, *Short Wave Radio*. For a few months in 1934 and 1935 he also edited a column, "Capt. Hall's Short-Wave Page," for *The Globe Circler*, the bulletin of the International DXers Alliance. He lived in Manhattan and got started in shortwave as an offshoot of his post–mer-

**Captain Hall was well known among shortwave authors (*Short Wave Radio*, April 1934).**

chant marine retirement vocation: building museum-quality ship models. He worked best in the late night hours, and during breaks he would smoke and listen to the radio, discovering shortwave after the BCB stations signed off. Captain Hall was married to Dorothy Hall, W2IXY, whom he introduced to shortwave and who, according to *Radio Craft*, was "known in radio amateur circles all over the world as America's No. 1 female radio ham."

In October 1933 *Radio News* actually changed its name to reflect the increased attention to shortwave. It became *Radio News and the Short-Waves* through December 1934, and *Radio News and Short-Wave Radio* from January 1935 through June 1938, at which time references to shortwave in the title were dropped. The addition of the word was a sign of the medium's anticipated importance.

> [T]he short waves have actually become, during the last two years, the greater part of radio. The technical reason for this is that although the average layman has become used exclusively to the broadcast band ... the shortwave bands below 1500 kilocycles include usable wavelengths thousands of times as great in number....
> In the possibilities of these short waves for distance reception, as

well as for local usage for short-distance transmission on the ultra-short waves, are thus something that interests everyone from the broadcasters to the listeners, including government officials, engineers and technicians, scientists, experimenters, servicemen, and the people who actually do the puttering around with their own receivers.

Therefore, in order to bring to the attention of the multitude of new recruits to the radio game through the short waves, we have added these words to our cover and are also incorporating all the shortwave articles in the magazine in a shortwave section that will be found this month in the front of the book.[6]

In April 1938 the magazine took on a slicker, modernized look. Cockaday joined the navy and his column was replaced with "Short Wave Flashes" by Charles A. Morrison, president of the International DXers Alliance. The column was dropped in 1939, however, a victim of the magazine's growing emphasis on amateur radio.

It would be five years before *Radio News* would get back in the shortwave business, but when it did it went first class. In June 1944, as a result of "many requests received from ... readers," the "International Short-Wave" column began under the editorship of Kenneth R. Boord. It soon grew into a major source of shortwave information.

By the 1950s Ken Boord would become the shortwave DXing hobby's leading spokesman, and a look at his *Radio News* columns over the years shows one reason why. They usually began with a profile of a station or a particular country's short-wave broadcasting activities, and a comprehensive look at its origins and operations. The columns also featured news about clubs and general hobby events. Most important, they contained extensive loggings and station information supplied by some of the great DXers of the day, both in the United States and overseas. August Balbi, Arthur Cushen, Paul Dilg, Grady Ferguson, Gil Harris, Paul Kary, Charles Sutton, and many others were active contributors to Ken Boord's columns. It was the most extensive magazine coverage of shortwave loggings ever.

*Radio News* became *Radio and Television News* in August 1948, and then *Electronics World* in May 1959. There was a hiatus in Ken Boord's column from May to September 1945, but otherwise it lasted for another ten years, through April 1955, when the shortwave news was transferred to the magazine's sister publication, *Popular Electronics*, "because short-wave listening, as a hobby, has been somewhat replaced by ever-increasing 'graduation' to Novice amateur activity."[7] Thereafter, Ken Boord authored a few feature articles for *Radio and Television News*, but his efforts were mostly redirected to other hobby outlets, including a round robin DX "Flash Sheet" in which this author was privileged to participate.[8] Ken was one of the fathers of the hobby, and he got his start in *Radio News*.

The second in the Gernsback trilogy was *Short Wave Craft*. When this maga-

Ken Boord, shown in his radio room, started editing the shortwave column in *Radio News* in 1944 (*Radio and Television News*, June 1953).

According to this cover, when you were hooked on shortwave, it even invaded your dreams (*Short Wave Craft*, January 1935).

zine first appeared in 1930, shortwave was usually taken to include all channels above 1500 kc. These frequencies were thought to hold much promise for broadcasting, and they were still surrounded with mystery. It was felt that they were important for nonbroadcasting purposes as well, hence *Short Wave Craft*'s occasional attention to such VHF topics as paging, TV, the relationship of microwaves to the treatment of disease, and the development of plants and animals.

Hugo Gernsback caught the mood of the times in his introduction to the first issue of *Short Wave Craft*:

> Today's widespread enthusiasm for the great and unlimited possibilities of short waves recalls, in many ways, the days of 1921–1922 when the first real boom in radio had arrived.
>
> Just now, short-wave activities are certainly the hotbed of new radio developments. There are no longer revolutionary possibilities in the highly-standardized medium-wave broadcasting, or in the commercial receiving set of today, which has tended more and more to reduce radio to automatic reception of local stations.
>
> But radio history, in the present cycle, is repeating itself. There are over 100,000 short-wave enthusiasts, in the United States and Canada alone, who are daily listening to short-wave voice and music broadcasts from ... 10,000 miles away and more.... Then, there are in this country alone some 20,000 radio amateurs who are in regular telegraphic communication with each other in all parts of the globe.
>
> But short waves are very much more than just a hobby—they are important from a commercial standpoint. Television in the home, toward which our largest commercial laboratories are feverishly working, is possible by no other means than through the use of short waves. The trans-oceanic telephone, to Europe and to liners at sea, depends upon short waves; which are also relied upon to bring all sorts of international events to us for rebroadcasting over our American networks on the higher waves. Airplane radio cannot do without short waves today; for they are essential to make flights safe for passengers and property. Explorers in our days find it absolutely necessary to carry with them short-wave equipment. The success of Admiral Byrd cannot very well be imagined without short waves for his communication during his entire stay in the Antarctic.[9]

The scope of coverage of *Short Wave Craft* was considerable. Many pages were devoted to equipment reviews. Each month the magazine ran part of a list, "Short-Wave Stations of the World," which purported to contain all known shortwave stations, listed by frequency. This list grew over the years. "When To Listen In," a short column of SWBC station information written by Robert Hertzberg—another famous name in early radio development and one of the brains behind the Pilot Radio and Tube Corporation—was also featured in the early years. (The column was later taken over by Hugo Gernsback's son, M. Harvey Gernsback.) In November 1936 *Short Wave Craft* inaugurated "Let's Listen In" with Joe Miller. It was a high-quality, well-illustrated column featuring narrative news of serious DX value, mostly SWBC but with some utility and ham news included as well.

In January 1937 the magazine took an important step by changing its name to *Short Wave and Television*. "Short waves and television are so closely linked," said Hugo Gernsback, "that they have become inseparable, and at the present state of development of the art, it seems unthinkable that in the future we could have television without short waves, and vice versa."[10] Thirty megacycles had not yet been established as the top of the shortwave band; anything over two megacycles (including TV transmissions in the 40–60 mc. range) was considered shortwave.

Guest editorials on the future of shortwave and TV followed the change of name. David Sarnoff, Lee De Forest, early television inventor James L. Baird, Dr. Frank Conrad of KDKA fame, and many others, appeared as guest writers. In June 1937 *Short Wave and Television* upgraded the format and content of the monthly "World Short-Wave Station List," turning it into arguably the most authoritative list of its kind. It was arranged by frequency, and showed station name and call, operating times, and some addresses. Occasional supplemental lists provided valuable information on identifying stations.

In October 1938 the magazine changed its name again, this time to *Radio and Television*. A new emphasis on amateur radio was announced, the notion of experimentation and set building having gradually lessened among listening enthusiasts. Joe Miller's column was dropped at the end of 1939. It returned briefly in June 1941 with an inquiry as to reader interest, but nothing materialized.

*Radio and Television* merged into *Radio Craft* with the November–December 1941 issue of the latter. War was on the horizon. The reader market was shrinking, resources for publishing were getting scarce, advertising was down, and amateur radio and TV development were at a standstill. Rather than run two magazines at a loss, Gernsback decided to try to produce one at a profit. It was promised that *Radio and Television* would eventually resume publication as a separate magazine, but it was not to be. *Radio Craft* itself became *Radio-Electronics* in 1948.

The third of the Gernsback trilogy was the much shorter lived *Official Short Wave Listener*, a general circulation, newsstand magazine devoted exclusively to shortwave broadcast listening. The cover message, "4,600 Short-Wave Stations Listed," was a slight overstatement, 4,600 being the number of stations multiplied by the number of frequencies used by each. OSWL was nontechnical, concentrating on station lists, tuning information (antennas, station identification, and interval signals), and station and program information.

*Opposite: Official Short Wave Listener was short lived, but, as this advertisement suggests, it was full of useful information (Short Wave Craft, April 1935).*

# An Announcement by
# HUGO GERNSBACK

THE OFFICIAL SHORT WAVE LOG AND CALL MAGAZINE, of which three issues have been published, will hereafter come out every other month under the name of

## OFFICIAL SHORT WAVE LISTENER MAGAZINE

I have created an entirely new magazine for the short wave listener, such as has not existed before. This new magazine is totally different in get-up and contents from the former magazine, and nothing like it has ever been published before.

To begin with, the new magazine comes with a *four-color cover*, and it is beautifully printed throughout. It contains a great variety of material, all of which is *essential* today to the short wave listener.

IT IS NOT A TECHNICAL MAGAZINE. It is designed for the short wave listener only. The first, the *February-March issue*, which is now on all newsstands, contains the material you find listed below.

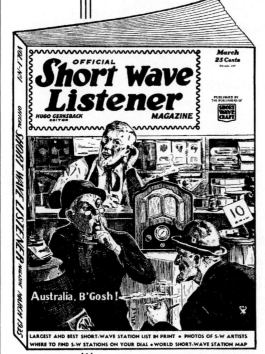

Australia, B'Gosh!

LARGEST AND BEST SHORT-WAVE STATION LIST IN PRINT • PHOTOS OF S-W ARTISTS
WHERE TO FIND S-W STATIONS ON YOUR DIAL • WORLD SHORT-WAVE STATION MAP

## ASK YOUR NEWS DEALER FOR A COPY OF THIS NEW SHORT-WAVE MAGAZINE

## 25c *the Copy*
### *Well Illustrated*

## Contents of the March Issue:

Over **800 short-wave** stations in various parts of the world await the touch of a finger on the tuning dial of your "short" or "all wave" receiver.

Photos and descriptions of short wave broadcasting stations in various parts of the world, with photos of short wave studio artists.

Where to find the important short-wave "DX" stations on the dial of your receiver.

Verification cards—what they are and how to get them.

Up-to-the-minute grand list of short-wave stations of the world with call letters and frequencies, including "Police," "Television" and short-wave stations.

Special list of the best or **star** short-wave stations, with their frequencies and call letters.

Valuable hints to the "short-wave listener"—how to locate the "weak" distance stations, etc.

Different time zones in various parts of the world, together with a map showing the location of short-wave stations of the world.

How To Use Earphones on Standard Receivers.

Short-Wave Fiction Story—"Short Waves by Heart"—by Hugo Gernsback.

W1XAL's S-W Educational Programs.

Fading and Ship Distance Explained.

How to identify short-wave stations by their "musical note" signatures.

Question and Answer department for the Short-Wave Listener.

Notes on "foreign" as well as "domestic" short-wave programs, meaning of foreign language phrases spoken in stations, etc.

How to erect special types of short-wave antennas, etc., SILVER CUP TROPHY for best photo of readers' listening "Posts."

### ● I ASK YOU A FAVOR ●

You have been an enthusiastic reader of SHORT WAVE CRAFT and your letters to me have always shown that I give you your money's worth. Now, I ask you as a special favor to me, that on or after January 25th you get from your nearest newsstand a copy of The Official Short Wave Listener Magazine. Take it home and look over it carefully.

If, after you have bought your first copy and have studied its contents and have read the new magazine, you are not fully satisfied with it in any way or form, I authorize you herewith to return the copy of the magazine to me and I will promptly refund you your quarter, as long as you state in your letter the reason why you do not like the magazine or if you do not think it is worth the money I ask for it. You to be the sole judge. This is my special promise to you.

*Hugo Gernsback*

From this, you will see that the magazine has been designed as a companion magazine to SHORT WAVE CRAFT.

If you are now a reader of SHORT WAVE CRAFT magazine, you will not wish to be without THE OFFICIAL SHORT WAVE LISTENER MAGAZINE. The new magazine will help you tremendously in your short wave reception at all times, and will give you priceless and invaluable **information, such as you cannot get anywhere else.** Nothing like it appears in print anywhere today. THE OFFICIAL SHORT WAVE LISTENER MAGAZINE, in other words, is a necessity.

**P. S.—If you cannot get the magazine at your newsstand due to sell-out, send 25c in cash, stamps, or money order, and we will send the magazine to you direct, prepaid.**

It was the emphasis on program content that made *OSWL* unique. The magazine featured many articles and photos about shortwave programs and shortwave radio personalities. Here are some examples of *OSWL* articles:

1. "London Calling";
2. CT1GO, Station of the Portugal Radio Club;
3. The Short-Wave Voice from Germany;
4. W8XAL—The Short-Wave Outlet for WLW Programs;
5. How NBC Broadcasts on Short Waves;
6. Short-Wave Beauties from Holland;
7. When Moscow Turns On the Short Waves;
8. New Stations in Latin America;
9. 3LR's Short-Wave Voice from "Down Under";
10. Bright Spots in U.S.S.R. Programs;
11. Musical Artists from Australia;
12. Hungarian Short-Wave Artists; and
13. Novel Programs from India.

It was the first time anyone had thought of catering to people who were interested in listening to shortwave *programs*, as opposed to DXing. Unfortunately, *OSWL*'s short life—it was nominally combined with *Short Wave Craft* in June 1936 after only seven issues—did not prove that an exclusively SWL magazine could make it. But *Official Short Wave Listener* was good while it lasted.

## Other Magazines

A great little DX magazine—perhaps the greatest ever published—was *RADEX* (*Radio Index*). For most of its life, which extended from 1924 through February 1942, *RADEX* was published ten times a year (monthly, except for a single June–July–August issue). Each magazine contained 100 pages.

DXer and *RADEX* staffer Carleton Lord described *RADEX*'s beginnings thus:

> It was intended for [broadcast band] listeners who did not have access to a newspaper with daily listings of programs. The listener would check the evening programs in RADEX, select those he would like to hear, and then note the nearest stations that would be carrying them. During the late 20's, many listeners would report the distant stations they had heard, and this led to a growing section for "Letters to the Editor."
>
> Editor/Publisher Fred C. Butler boasted that monthly letters ran from a few hundred to over 1,000 and, of those requiring a reply, every one received a note in the magazine or a personal response.[11]

N.S.E.

**THE MAY 1937**

**RADIO INDEX**

The All-wave DX Log of the World

25c

South American Stations
The New Television
Revised Frequency Checks
Most Complete Shortwave List

No. 109

*RADEX* was widely read by long-distance listeners (*RADEX*, May 1937).

Thus *RADEX*'s main appeal in the 1920s was its organization of station information. Each issue carried a listing of BCB stations arranged in frequency order, with three blank boxes next to each frequency. These boxes were used for entering one's receiver dial settings (in those days a set typically had two or three separate tuning controls, each with 0–100 markings). Interpolation between known frequencies permitted a rough identification of the channel you were tuned to. The magazine also contained separate station listings by call letters and state. From these listings came the magazine's official name, *Radio Index*, abbreviated *RADEX*.

Besides the indices, *RADEX* carried articles about stations, receivers, antennas, radio servicing, and many other topics. There were questions from readers, editorials, crossword puzzles, contests, and an hour-by-hour calendar of network programs. The magazine also featured articles by guest contributors, and the titles of the columns were colorful: "Riding the Ether Waves," "With the Midnight Marauders," "In the Wee Hours with the *RADEX*ers," and "Stories of the Log Builders."

*RADEX* carried commentary on many topics, including obnoxious advertising, reminiscences of the early days of radio, and various metaphysical aspects of QSLing. The entire magazine was written in a chatty, informative, DXer's style. It was more like a club than a magazine, and in fact a *RADEX* club was established in 1938. If you could have had only one DX magazine, it would have been *RADEX*.

Through the preshortwave 1920s *RADEX*'s orientation was, of course, toward the broadcast band. Late in 1930 it began carrying some shortwave information, and in June 1932 it presented its first list of shortwave stations of the world, soon to be a regular feature. *RADEX* belonged to DXers, especially broadcast-band DXers, but it was on its way to becoming the DXer's bible among shortwavers too. Letters from DXers in foreign countries began appearing, along with more articles about shortwave: "Breaking Into the Short Waves," "What's On the Short-Waves," and "Coming Treats On the Short Waves." Some columns spanned both broadcast band and shortwave, like "Leaves from a DXer's Scrapbook" by "Count de Veries" (Carleton Lord).

Since *RADEX*'s inception, Fred Clayton Butler had been its editor and publisher, and the only person on the masthead. In March 1933, reflecting the heightened interest in shortwave, Page Taylor, one of the great names in early DXing, was named *RADEX* shortwave editor. B. Francis Dashiell, a regular *RADEX* author, took the post of technical editor. In October 1935 Carleton Lord became DX editor (concentrating on the broadcast band), with Taylor and Dashiell retaining their positions.

Butler died on October 12, 1936. Page Taylor became editor, and Butler's wife, Elizabeth, became publisher. However, *RADEX* never missed a beat. It expanded its coverage to include amateur radio SWLing, SWL card swapping, early FM, and even stamp collecting. In September 1938 Ray LaRoque joined Lord and Dashiell as associate editor for shortwave. Soon he was splitting the shortwave editing responsibilities with respected West Coast DXer Anthony C. Tarr. *RADEX* had everything, and was better than ever.

An interesting *RADEX* anomaly was the magazine's cover, or frontispiece as it was called. As the emphasis on DXing grew, *RADEX* carried less and less program information, but every cover still featured the picture of a female program personality of the day: Clara Bow, Mary Nolan, Frances Langford, Annette Hanshaw, Alice Joy of the Prince Albert Quarter Hour ("she has a mellow voice of low register"), and dozens of others.

Likewise, throughout the magazine proper were many photographs of radio entertainers placed in the middle of articles that had nothing to do with them. There was Guy Lombardo in the middle of an article about radio salesmen, the "Cuckoo Hour" gang located in a discussion of volume controls, Lowell Thomas in the midst of some DX tips, and Ed Wynn surrounded by aerials and grounds.

The photos lasted through 1938, and the female covers were dropped in September 1939, long after *RADEX* had become a DX-oriented publication. Even as it took on a more businesslike appearance, however, hints of trouble started to appear. In January 1940 the magazine went bimonthly; six copies per year rather than ten. The cost of paper was rising, as was the cost of unsold newstand copies. However, despite some editorial staff changes and a reduction in the quality of the paper, the magazine looked as good as ever.

The cover of the September–October 1941 issue bore a special red imprint: "Very Important Announcement page 50." The news was positive. *RADEX* was upgrading its paper and going to eight annual issues, but it would be available by subscription only ($2 per year).

Subsequent issues seemed to be at full strength and there was little suggestion of further problems. However, publication was suddenly suspended after the February 1942 issue, even though it contained no hint of problems. It carried the regular subscription form, and a reminder to wartime readers to "K.O. the JO's" (JO being the radio call letter prefix for Japan). But it proved to be *RADEX*'s last appearance.

Although it had become a victim of wartime instability, *RADEX* had set a new standard in DX publishing during its almost 20-year history. In September 1943 some *RADEX* former staff members announced their intention to start publishing *RADEX* again as an annual yearbook of information for DXers, but it is believed that nothing ever came of the idea.

*All-Wave Radio* was another excellent magazine. It was published from September 1935 to mid-1938, when it was absorbed by *Radio News*. The main shortwave column was entitled "Globe Girdling," and was edited by J. B. L. Hinds, a

**J. B. L. Hinds was a widely regarded author on popular shortwave topics in the 1930s (*All-Wave Radio*, January 1936).**

resident of Yonkers, New York, and an accountant with the New York Central Railroad. Like Captain Hall of *Radio News*, Hinds had also written for *Short Wave Radio* magazine. He started DXing in 1930 with a Pilot Super Wasp, and by the time he began working for *All-Wave Radio* he had graduated to a Hammarlund Pro. He knew the shortwave scene well. His columns were full of loggings and DX news, and illustrated with numerous QSLs from his own collection. Supplementing his column were *All-Wave Radio*'s extensive monthly station lists of the day, showing frequencies and hours of operation for both shortwave broadcast and shortwave utility stations, plus separate, periodic lists of station addresses. *All-Wave Radio* knew what DXing was all about.

Short Wave Radio was an interesting, if short-lived publication, lasting only from November 1933 to October 1934 (the last issue, like *RADEX*, containing no hint of its imminent demise). Edited by Robert Hertzberg, it had its share of technical and semitechnical topics—receiver reviews, the development of TV, component evaluations, and general radio theory—but it also carried extensive information for the shortwave listener. It offered a comprehensive monthly shortwave station list, station addresses, and reader letters, plus feature articles on particular stations and things like the Byrd expedition, getting started in amateur radio, antennas, improving reception, and so on. It was in *Short Wave Radio* that Captain Hall got his start (until he moved over to *Radio News* in August 1934), and in July 1934 J. B. L. Hinds began an extensive column of loggings and station information in *Short Wave Radio* before going to *All-Wave Radio*.

## Station Lists and Other Literature

One of the challenges for both broadcast-band and shortwave enthusiasts was finding reliable information on frequencies, power, hours of operation, and addresses. Probably the first governmental publication covering shortwave broadcasting stations was *World Short-Wave Radiophone Transmitters*, published in August 1934 by the Department of Commerce (a second edition was published the next year).[12] This 96-page book listed all commercial and broadcasting stations above 1500 kc., showing frequency, call letters, location, power, and some schedule information.

However, most of the work in this field was done by private publishers, mainly through the radio log and call book. When radio fans talk of a call book today, they invariably mean the amateur radio call book, a listing of all amateur radio operators. But in the early days of radio there were many publications called logs or call books that featured lists of medium-wave and shortwave *broadcast* stations. Often they contained a section for noting stations heard, along with the listener's dial settings.

Radio logs and call books came in several forms. There were periodicals containing station listings that were updated and republished on a recurring basis. Particularly well known was *White's Radio Log*. Starting out in 1924 as the *Rhode Island Radio Call Book*, it was published by C. DeWitt White, a Providence (later New York) firm that specialized in street guides and city directories. The publication contained lists of all U.S. broadcasters, their ownership, frequency, wavelength, and power.

*White's* soon became *White's Mileage, Log and Radio Call Book*. Published quarterly, it contained the above information, plus a matrix for measuring distances between various U.S. cities, as well as a loggings section for recording dial readings. It then became known as *White's Air Line Mileage Book and Triple List of Radio Broadcasting Stations*, triple list because the stations were listed three ways: by call letters, state, and town.

*White's* eventually became just *White's Radio Log*, adding information on U.S. shortwave and TV stations, then national broadcast-band network programs, and, eventually, international shortwave stations. It originally cost 10 cents a copy, going to 15 cents in 1941, and 20 cents in 1947. It was published in various forms into the 1950s, eventually being incorporated into the bimonthly *Radio-TV Experimenter* and, from 1971 to 1981, the semi-annual *Communications World*. It reappeared in stand-alone form in 1985, but thus far no subsequent issues have been published.[13]

Similar to *White's* was *Stevenson's Directory of Radio Broadcasting Stations*, later *Stevenson's Bulletin of Radio Broadcasting Stations* and—eventually—*Stevenson's Radio Bulletin*. Published from the mid–1920s to the mid–1940s, it carried much the same information as *White's*. At first it was published monthly, then quarterly, then

*Above and facing page:* Many businesses, both radio related and otherwise, wanted to keep their customers informed about what was on the air. These are a few of the many logs and call books that helped listeners find and identify stations.

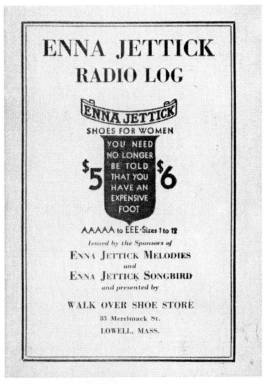

*Below:* Edward Startz, the famous and accomplished announcer, identifies Station PHI for local and world listeners. To make certain his call letters are clearly understood, this silver-tongued linguist repeats announcements in seven different languages — Dutch, Malay, English, French, German and Portuguese.

Programs from Station PHI are broadcast to the world from this transmitting plant, located in Huizen, Holland. Studios are maintained in Hilversum. This station is on the air Monday, Thursday and Friday from 7:30 to 9:30 A.M. and on Saturdays and Sundays from 7:30 to 11:00 A.M. (E.S.T.).

# DJB  BERLIN GERMANY
### 15.20 Megacycles   -   -   19.73 Meters

## "GERMAN ROUND THE WORLD SENDER"

is the name given to this station by its operators the German Broadcasting Company. Opened with a cheery "Hello, America, we hope you have good reception tonight," programs from this station bring to U. S. radio listeners gems of classical music and song. Broadcasting is done from early morning until late at night, two transmitters being used on each program to insure best possible reception. Announcements are made in three languages — first German, then English, then Spanish. Call letters used are DJA, DJB, DJC, DJD. Studios are in Berlin, the transmitting plant being located in Zeesen, Germany.

•

# EAQ   MADRID SPAIN
### 9.86 Megacycles   -   -   30.40 Meters

The daily broadcasts from this station are colorful and entertaining, and your enjoyment of them will be further increased by the fact that announcements are made in English as well as Spanish.
The programs, broadcast from approximately 5 to 7 P.M. (E.S.T.), offer music, literature and news. The Saturday broadcasts, noon to 2 P.M., are intended primarily for Europe, Canary Islands and other Spanish possessions. On stated evenings each week, one hour of the broadcast is devoted to the International Broadcast Club of London, an organization established for creating good will and a closer relationship among the radio listeners of the world.

# PHI  HUIZEN HOLLAND
### 11.73 Megacycles   -   -   25.57 Meters

The land of dikes and windmills and famous old cities is an interesting one to visit via radio. PHI is not only an outstanding station in Holland, but the world over. Through this station, Holland keeps in touch with her colonial possessions in Dutch East and West Indies. During the summer months, PHI leaves its regular wave band of 11.73 megacycles and broadcasts over 17.77 megacycles.

**Station J1AA, Kemikawa-Cho, Kiba-Chen, Japan**
sends listeners a program verification card on the front of which is a picture of the station. Broadcasts from Japan are received daily in the U. S. from approximately 5:00 to 7:00 A.M. (E.S.T.).

*Above and facing page:* Stewart-Warner invited interest in its shortwave receivers by publishing information about popular shortwave stations (*Stewart-Warner Simplified World Wide Radio Log*, 1934).

*Below:* The front of the card which YV3BC sends to listeners, upon request, to verify receipt of programs. When writing this station, address YV3BC, Radiodefusora Venezuela, Caracas.

*Above:* This orchestra is typical of those which play the tantalizing tangos and rhumbas broadcast from South American Stations and heard so regularly in the United States.

## YV3BC Caracas VENEZUELA

**6.15 Megacycles    -   -    48.78 Meters**

This station, located in the capital of the Republic of Venezuela — the most northerly country in South America — is heard consistently by Round-the-World radio listeners in the United States. Its entertaining programs offer a variety of typically South American tangos, rhumbas, songs, etc.

YV3BC broadcasts daily from 10:30 A.M. to 1:00 P.M., and from 4:30 to 9:30 P.M. (E.S.T.). Like several of the other South American stations, announcements are not made in English, but this station can be readily identified by a distinctive chimes signal.

"Ha-Ya-Une-Ah-Bay-Bay," says the station announcer in his best South American English, and you know you are listening to HJ1ABB, Barranquilla, Colombia. And, if you want your reception verified, this station upon request will mail you one of the above verification cards.

## VK2ME SYDNEY AUSTRALIA

**9.59 Megacycles    -   -    31.28 Meters**

"The Voice of Australia" is a welcome visitor each Sunday in many U. S. homes, with its diversified program of music, including an interesting and instructive talk on some section of Australia. The time of day is also broadcast, together with the chimes from the clock located on the Sydney Post Office.

Each program is opened and closed with the famous laughing call of the Kookabura bird. VK2ME broadcasts Sundays only, from 1:00 to 3:00, 5:00 to 9:00 A.M., and from 11:30 A.M. to 1:30 P.M.(E.S.T.).

●

## HBL Geneva SWITZERLAND

**9.59 Megacycles    -   -    31.27 Meters**

This station, together with HBP, is maintained by the League of Nations for a dual purpose. First: to broadcast discussions of the various problems placed before this tribunal and, second, to create good will and a better understanding among the nations of the world.

The program is Saturday — 5:30 to 6:15 P.M. (E.S.T.) — consists of three fifteen minute talks — given first in English, then French, then Spanish. Listeners who wish to communicate with this station will receive prompt, courteous acknowledgment of their letters. Answers to any questions will be cheerfully given. Address: Information Section, League of Nations, Geneva, Switzerland.

annually. Also available were *Duston's Radio Log and Call Book,* the *Blue Radio Station Finder and Log, Keller's Radio Call Book and Log,* and the quarterly *Official Short Wave Log and Call* magazine of 1933–34 (which was eventually merged into *Official Short Wave Listener*).

A lot of radio logs and call books were issued as one-time or occasional publications. Some were distributed as promotional items by radio manufacturers. Among these were the *Stromberg-Carlson Log of U.S. Broadcasting Stations* (1927), the *RCA Radiotron Broadcast Station Directory* (1930), the *Silvertone Radio Time Table and Log* (issued by Sears), the *Stewart-Warner Simplified Worldwide Radio Log* (1934), the *Victor Dial List,* the *National Co. Shortwave Station List* (1931), and the *Atwater-Kent Worldwide Radio Station Directory* (1934). These usually took the form of pocket- or magazine-size pamphlets. In addition to station information, they usually contained some advertising.

Radio-*related* companies also issued radio logs and call books, such as the *Tung-Sol* [tubes] *World Radio Log,* the *Burgess* [batteries] *Index of Radio Broadcasting Stations* (1926), the *Cunningham* [tubes] *List of Broadcasting Stations,* the *Green Mill* [radio shop] *Official Radio Log* (1929), and the *Spiegel/Air Castle* [radio products] *Long and Short Wave Radio Log Book* (1935).

Because logs and call books were of interest not just to radio hobbyists but to the general public as well, there were many that bore the names of companies that had nothing whatsoever to do with the radio industry. Examples are the *U.S. Light and Heat Corp. Radio Log Book,* the *J. M. Kralovec and Son Radio Log* [insurance agents] (1926), the *Enna Jettick Radio Log* [ladies shoes], and the *Songbird Radio Log and Call Book* [W. T. Grant] (1928), to name but a few. Sometimes stores got together, as did 20 or so who issued a *Radio Records* booklet, each page containing some logging blanks for the listener's dial settings, along with advertisements from a candy company, a lumber store, a decorator, a bank, an optician, and a florist. There was even a radio log inserted in the middle of a *Ripley's Believe It or Not* pamphlet. Everyone wanted to get into the act.

Many of these booklets were used as free promotional items, with companies preparing generic call books and customizing the covers for individual distributors. A copy of the 1924 *Radio Broadcasting Station Directory and Trouble Finder* by Bertram W. Downs of Saint Paul, Minnesota was one such. A sample stated: "Your imprint here without charge on orders for 100 or more." The same is true with the 1941 *RMS Radio Log*: "These excellent radio logs are supplied at 2 cents each. Use your rubber stamp or we'll imprint any quantity for $1.50."

Newspapers also were issuers of periodic (sometimes weekly) radio logs and call books. There was the *Chicago Daily News Radio Log* (1934), the *Boston Evening Transcript Directory of the Principal Broadcasting Stations* (1926), the *Boston Globe Radio Station Call Book* (1930), the *Newark Sunday Call Radio Guide* (1926), the

*Hartford Times Radio Directory* (a large fold-out card issued weekly during 1929), and many, many others. In 1927, before giving birth to the Newark News Radio Club (see chapter 8), the *Newark Evening News* published its own *Radio Guide and Log Book*. Although these publications seldom contained any program information, they were the distant precursors of today's Sunday newspaper TV section.

Some magazines had call book or log in their title, sometimes as a result of mergers with other publications. These included publications like *Radio Call Book Magazine and Technical Review* (absorbed by *Radio News* in December 1932), *Citizens Radio Call Book Magazine and Scientific Digest,* and *Radio Listeners' Guide and Call Book*. They were all full-fledged magazines. Although they carried station lists, their main orientation was usually technical: circuits, schematics, construction, and radio theory.

Another source of early shortwave listening information was the occasional "how to listen" monograph. One of the best was the 1935 Gernsback publication, *How to Get Best Short Wave Reception*. Seventy-two pages long, it contained a description of the various kinds of stations and when and where to hear them, practical hints for better reception, and information on interval signals, propagation, time conversion, receivers, antennas, and QSLs.

Other similar if less comprehensive booklets were also published, including the brief monographs on shortwave radio that companies sometimes issued in conjunction with the promotion of their products (usually receivers). Spiegel accompanied its Air Castle receivers with a copy of the Spiegel *Radio Log Book and Service Manual*. The *Short-Wave Radio Primer* was published by General Electric in 1934, and contained information on propagation, different kinds of stations, countries on the air, and how to tune, plus a station list and, for good measure, some pictures and descriptions of the GE shortwave receivers of the day. RCA published a booklet that accompanied its Globe Trotter Radio. It was an introduction to shortwave, with station lists and tuning tips.

Hammarlund issued an annual *Hammarlund Short Wave Manual* from the mid–1930s into the early 1940s. It was a pamphlet featuring articles on Hammarlund receivers, circuits using Hammarlund parts, and reception advice. Like items included *Worldwide Shortwave Reception* (1932) and *Peak Efficiency Design on the Short Waves* (1933), both published by the National Company and authored by its chief engineer and general manager, James Millen.

## Chapter 8

# ORGANIZING

THERE WAS A LOT OF LISTENER organizing by both clubs and magazines in the 1930s.

Just as there had been many amateur radio clubs in the days of the experimenter, so now were there many listener clubs. The Great Lakes Radio Club, the New England Radio Club, the Transcontinental Radio DX Club, Canadian DX Relay, the North American Radio Club, and the United States Radio DX Club are all gone now. *Radio News*, which had given the early amateur experimenter clubs generous coverage in its "Club Gossip" column of the 1920s, now did the same for listener clubs. So did *RADEX*. *Radio News* invited clubs to affiliate with its "DX Corner" shortwave column by becoming associate members and advising the magazine on shortwave activities and how to promote the hobby. The clubs were offered space for club news, and reader inquiries to clubs could be made via the "DX Corner" column.

Most of the clubs were small, with anywhere from 15 to 125 members, and they emphasized broadcast-band DX. Often they issued tip sheets, sometimes on a weekly basis. A major activity of many clubs was arranging, through what were called courtesy program committees, special broadcasts dedicated to club members. These broadcasts were often at late hours, increasing the likelihood that they would be heard over long distances. Club members were urged to send reports to these stations, even if they had verified them before, or at least write and thank them for putting on the broadcast. Probably the longest of these DX specials was a five-hour broadcast for the NNRC from 500 watt WFMD, Frederick, Maryland. It produced 358 reports, including 26 from Australia and New Zealand.

Although these programs were primarily a broadcast-band activity, special programs dedicated to particular clubs were sometimes arranged on shortwave as well, especially by the International DXers Alliance, the NNRC, and *RADEX*. Among

**LA VOZ DE LA VICTOR**
Apdo. 33—Colon, Rep. de Panama

April 8, 1940

Dear Friend and DX Listener:

We take this means to thank you for your response to our DX program's in the past and to assure you that we appreciate and cordially invite any comment that you may care to send us.

On Sunday April 28th, 1940 from 3:00 to 5:00 A. M. we shall again present another DX program, dedicated to all of you, who have responded to our past program's.

We shall broadcast on both the Long and Short Wave, Long Wave HOK-640 Kc. 468.75 meters, Short Wave HP5K-6005 Kc. 49.96 meters. Tell all your friends to listen in and send us their comment.

Thanking you in advance.

Alvin Lee
the "DXER"

Stations that broadcast "DX Specials" sometimes wrote to their listeners to inform them of upcoming programs (1940).

the broadcasters carrying such programs in the 1930s were U.S. stations W2XAD, W3XAL, and W8XAL, CFCX in Montreal, ZHI in Singapore, 2RO in Rome, stations in Russia and Poland, the Reichsrundfunk in Germany, and many Latin American stations.

The hundreds of special programs that were arranged each season produced numerous scheduling conflicts, and this led to shady practices among clubs. Some clubs would ask stations to dedicate to them a portion of a program arranged by another club. It became standard practice not to publish information on special programs arranged by other clubs, and interclub sniping abounded. As a result, the clubs eventually established an Inter-Club Cooperation Plan. It was chaired by Emily Griswald of West Hartford, Connecticut. Under the plan, which was adopted in 1935, stations and frequencies were allocated to particular clubs so that each station would receive only one request for a courtesy program, and programs would not compete with each other on the same frequency or at the same time. But the plan was often not adhered to. A few DXers disagreed with the courtesy program concept altogether. They felt that loading up the broadcast band with unnecessary specials (often on Sunday mornings) just blocked the chance to hear real DX. Over the years, courtesy programs became more difficult to arrange because stations were less interested in long-distance reception of their signals, and DXers who had already logged and verified them often did not participate. However, special DX tests have continued to be part of the medium-wave DX scene right up to the present time.

The only survivor of the early clubs is the National Radio Club (NRC). It was established in 1933 as an exclusively broadcast-band club, and remains so today. However, it covered shortwave as well from 1935 through 1944, and ham radio listening from 1937 to 1940. In fact, in those days there were as many members interested in shortwave as medium wave. The NRC's origins were typically modest. "I [Robert H. Weaver, first NRC president] discussed the formation of the National Radio Club with Art Brackbill and we decided to go ahead with it. We began to put out a weekly DX Bulletin containing DX news and tips. At first we made carbon copies, but we soon bought a small mimeograph machine and it was then that we began putting out a regular bulletin."[1] The NRC sold club stationery (55 cents per 100 sheets in 1934), stickers (20 cents per 100), photostamps bearing a picture of the member (25 cents for 50 in 1939) and other supplies. Most of the smaller clubs merged into larger ones, and these eventually ventured into shortwave. Most shortwave activity was oriented toward the Eastern and Central United States.

Radio club bulletins were an important source of station information. Of the clubs that carried shortwave information in the 1930s, the big three were the Newark News Radio Club (NNRC), with its early publication, *The Dialist*, precursor of the *NNRC Bulletin* of later years; the International DXers Alliance, publisher of *The Globe Circler*; and the Universal Radio DX Club, which published *The Universalite*.

The Newark News Radio Club was formed in 1927. Fifty-five people turned out for the organizational meeting of the Newark News *DX* Club, as it was known at first. Six years later the club, by then operating under the name Newark News Radio Club, had 1,800 members, making it the largest club at the time. The first president was Lee S. J. Cranse, a salesman from Summit, New Jersey. However, Irving Potts held the office from 1930 until his death in 1962 and provided the leadership that sustained the club throughout most of its lifetime. In 1927 dues were $2 for the first year, $1 thereafter.

In its early years the NNRC was principally a medium-wave club, and the vehicle for publishing DX information was the *Newark Evening News* itself. The newspaper carried various club features that were written by members. In 1934 the club commenced publication of *The Dialist*, a magazine of about 40 pages that bore a distant resemblance to *RADEX*. It took its name from Charlotte Geer, the author of a 1927 *Newark Evening News* column called "Broadcasts Winnowed." She sometimes reported on DX stations, and became known to thousands of Jerseyites as the Dialist. The magazine was commercially printed with a glossy cover, and featured club news, station information, articles about DXing, gossipy items about radio personalities, and a monthly list of U.S. BCB stations (again like *RADEX*). Unfortunately, its demise came after only six issues when it found itself in competition for advertising with its sponsoring parent, the *Newark Evening News*. Without the advertising revenue, *The Dialist* was not sustainable.

THE DIALIST

IRVING R. POTTS

JUNE                                          1934

*The Dialist* was the first professionally printed publication of the Newark News Radio Club. This is vol. 1, no. 1, containing the picture of long-time NNRC president and guiding light Irving R. Potts (*The Dialist*, June 1934).

September 1935 brought the less glitzy (mimeographed) and noncommercial *NNRC Bulletin*, which was published continuously until the club closed its doors in April 1982 (outlasting the newspaper by ten years). Although the soul of the NNRC was always in medium wave, a shortwave section, "High Frequencies," was begun in December 1935. Edited by Earl P. Roberts of Indianapolis, it soon became a major part of the bulletin. At first done in a narrative style, it eventually adopted a "by frequency" format, incorporating in one place news about broadcast stations, utilities, and amateurs, all of whom utilized the shortwave bands. Amateur coverage was dropped during the war, when the amateurs were silent, and resumed in November 1945. Statistics of members' stations and countries heard were added in 1946. The bulletin was issued weekly during the DX season (October through April), and monthly for the rest of the year. During the mid–1930s the NNRC also had a weekly DX program over WOR's shortwave channel, W2XJI, 25.3 mc. (later known as W2XOR, 45.5 mc.).

Although the bulletin was an essential means of exchanging information, the NNRC was as much a social club as a radio publication, at least in its early years. Many of its members traced their involvement back to the original 1927 meeting. The bulletin contained much good-natured ribbing among members, particularly those Maryland, New Jersey, and Pennsylvania fans who had been there at the club's birth—indeed, at the birth of radio itself. In addition to their common interest in radio monitoring, these early sustaining members knew each other personally, and valued their personal and social contacts as much as their listening activities. Among other things, the bulletin chronicled births, deaths, engagements, marriages, and illnesses of members and their families.

The International DXers Alliance was formed in 1932 by well-known Bloomington, Illinois, DXer Charles A. Morrison. Known over the years as the IDA, it emphasized foreign DX, mainly medium wave at first. Dues were $1 a year. The monthly bulletin, *The Globe Circler*, started out as a four-page mimeographed affair,

JUNE
Volume One

# The Dialist

1934
Number One

## CONTENTS

### EDITOR
IRVING R. POTTS

### ASSOCIATE EDITORS
ALFRED W. OPPEL        HERMAN A. WITTENBERG

Published monthly by The Newark News Radio Club, 215 Market Street, Newark, N. J.
Subscription price $1.00 per year.

1

Table of contents from the first issue of *The Dialist* (June 1934).

NOVEMBER 1934

# The GLOBE CIRCLER

Amateur Radiophone Station CX1AA,Montevideo,Uruguay
Owned by Sr.Wenceslao Sere, I.D.A.Official Representative for the Republic of Uruguay.

## IN THIS ISSUE

### *the* IDA CONTEST

Foreign Broadcast Calendar

Revised Short Wave  Station List

Captain  Hall's  S.W.   Page

BCB  Dx'ing  in  Hawaii

Charles A. Morrison
PRESIDENT

### International Dx'ers Alliance

The monthly publication of the International DXers Alliance was called *The Globe Circler* (shown is the issue for November 1934).

distributed to about 50 persons. Interest in shortwave began developing, and in August 1934 the club went "all wave." By 1935 the bulletin had grown to a 16-page pamphlet more closely resembling today's club bulletins, including loggings, station news, new member information, and club chapter news.

Publication of the bulletin was made possible in part by paid advertising from two companies, DX Radio Sales Company of Beverly Hills, California, distributors of the Patterson all-wave radio, and Postal Radio of New York City, a receiver manufacturer. The bulletin was sent to over 1,200 persons in 50 countries. For a time, Captain Hall was the IDA vice president in charge of shortwave activities. The club offered IDA stationery (70 cents per 100 sheets), and *RADEX* set aside a page in each issue for coverage of IDA activities.

There were IDA state managers and foreign representatives, and many local IDA chapters that organized small meetings at members' homes. There were also several IDA regional district bulletins, plus a *British Globe Circler* that was published in England for the benefit of the club's 100 European members. The IDA also offered a special publication for those interested in DXing amateur stations: *Ama-Touring* (which eventually became a section of the bulletin proper). The IDA deserves much credit for the many important hobby activities in which it was engaged before its close in July 1943.

Another well-known club was the Universal Radio DX Club (not to be confused with the Universal DX Club, which was absorbed by the NNRC in 1938). The URDXC was headed by Charles C. Norton. Upon its founding in 1933 it began issuing a DX tip sheet every 10 days. Dues were 85 cents a year. By the late 1930s its weekly bulletin, *The Universalite*, was well known. It contained broadcast-band tips and station changes, shortwave information, a special report on DXing in Japan from a member there, and members' letters. The URDXC continued publishing into the 1960s, with Norton still at the helm. (Norton died in 1991 in Vallejo, California.)

The first major shortwave-only club was the International Short Wave Club, headquartered in East Liverpool, Ohio. It was founded by Arthur J. Green, Charles E. Schroeder, and J. R. McAllister, and commenced operation on October 4, 1929. Annual dues were $1. The bulletin, nameless at first but soon called *International Short Wave Radio*, was a 20–60 page 5" × 7" professionally printed publication containing interesting DX items, station lists, station photos, and advertising. At the outset, coverage was mainly utilities, but it soon moved into shortwave broadcasting, which became its main concern as increasing numbers of shortwave broadcast stations took to the air. In 1946 ISWC headquarters moved to London, from whence the club operated until 1967 under the tutelage of Arthur E. Bear at the well-known address of 100 Adams Gardens Estate. Over the years the ISWC was known for its anti–jamming campaign through which the club urged listeners not to report to countries that jammed other stations.

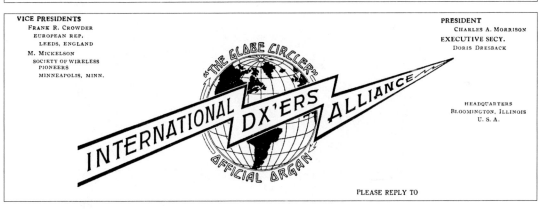

Impressive letterheads from the Universal DX Club, the International DXers Alliance, and the Radio Signal Survey league, all from the 1930s.

Another noteworthy club was the Quixote Radio Club. Formed in 1933, it issued a weekly bulletin, *The Short Wave Reporter*. Describing its antecedents, the club explained that it "was conceived in Habana—Cubita bella—where American programs, free of local interference, could be heard only by shortwave. Our interest remains ... primarily in distant reception of program value. Hence we prefer to style

# INTERNATIONAL SHORT WAVE CLUB

| $1.00 A YEAR | JANUARY, 1931 | 10c A COPY |

## BROADCASTING IN SIAM

ERHAPS the most interesting part of short wave reception is the ability of the listener to listen-in on strange voices, strange language, odd music and to tune in stations located in sections of the world where the customs, habits, religion, dress and manners of the inhabitants are vastly different from those of the listener. To many Americans, as well as others, the country of Siam is just a section of land south of China, but to American short wave listeners it is a land of tom-toms and Chinese fiddles, where our popular dance music is transposed into a new and different rhythm that even our greatest orchestras can not imitate. To many, listening-in on a Siamese station holds peculiar fascination that no others can bring.

Above is a group of Native Siamese musicians who posed for this photograph under the antenna towers of one of the broadcasting stations at Bangkok. The latest dispatches from Siam informs us that station HS1PJ is on 37.6 meters several days each week between 5 and 12 A. M., EST., and station HS2PJ is on 29.5 meters each Monday from 8 till 11 A. M., EST. They operate no stations near 49 meters.

(Courtesy of Donald F. Wright, San Pedro, Cal.)

## WINNERS OF SPECIAL BIRTHDAY PROGRAM AWARDS
### ANNOUNCED IN THIS ISSUE

The International Short Wave Club was the first major listeners club to concentrate on shortwave (*ISWC Bulletin*, January 1931).

ourselves 'mildly DXers.'"[2] Encouraging club activity by members was a concern then no less than it is today. Quixote members who submitted at least one report weekly received 20 issues of the bulletin for $1. Others received only ten issues.

Although the shortwave clubs, like their broadcast-band predecessors, appeared to be of limited size, there are some indications to the contrary. For example, the November 1, 1934, issue of *Short Wave Radio Reception News*, the biweekly publication of the Chicago Short Wave Radio Club, carried an insert announcing that, until the club had achieved its goal of adding *10,000 new members*, the membership fee would be reduced from $2 to $1 per year. There is nothing to suggest that the goal was announced in jest. In the International Short Wave Club's May 1942 issue of *International Short Wave Radio*, it was noted that the club had had at least 100 members in the Philippines during the period of the club's existence, and that there had been 200 members in Burma, and many in other parts of the Far East then under Japanese threat or occupation.

There were some less serious clubs as well, like the Before Breakfast Short Wave Club. It announced that "[t]here are no dues, meetings, minutes, or other parliamentary nuisances. It is merely a friendly, fraternal, and not too serious organization of early birds who believe in the old adage about catching the worm."[3] A membership certificate was sent upon receipt of two QSLs from shortwave stations 1,000 miles distant that were logged between 5:00 and 9:00 A.M.

Radio magazines also played a role in hobby organizing. In the very early days—1909 to be exact—Hugo Gernsback and his magazine, *Modern Electrics*, established the Wireless Association of America, which within one year claimed a membership of 10,000. There were no dues or other obligations; you just signed up. Despite this informality, the association's membership probably reflected accurately the overall level of interest in radio at the time.

Years later, when shortwave was well established, Gernsback again led a hobby organizing effort, this time through *Short Wave Craft*'s sponsorship of something called the Short Wave League. Although seemingly preoccupied with the issue of whether to abolish the amateur code requirement in the bands below five meters, the league held itself out as "a scientific membership organization for the promotion of the shortwave art." Members received a membership certificate, and could purchase stationery, maps, globes, and seals and the official Short Wave League button (enamel 35 cents, "solid gold" $2).

Another *Short Wave Craft* project was the Short Wave Scouts, the purpose of which was "to bring to [the magazine's] headquarters reliable information on the operation of the various shortwave stations of the world." A Short Wave Scouts silver trophy was awarded each month to the person who submitted the log containing the greatest number of shortwave stations verified during a 30-day period. The first silver trophy was awarded in January 1934. It was "designed by one of New York's

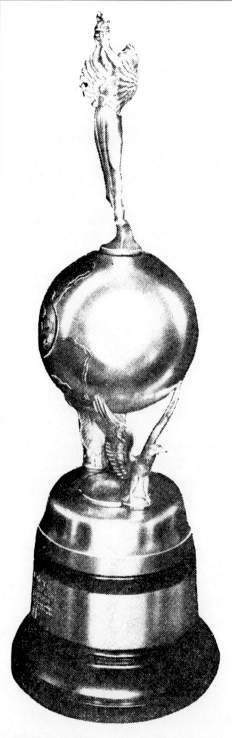

# FOURTH "TROPHY CUP" WINNER

Presented to

SHORT WAVE SCOUT

**Fred Bente**

Brooklyn, N. Y.

For his contribution toward the advancement of the art of Radio by

Magazine

● ON this page is illustrated the handsome trophy, which was designed by one of New Yorks leading silversmiths. It is made of metal throughout, except the base, which is made of handsome black Bakelite. The metal itself is quadruple silver-plated, in the usual manner of all trophies today.

It is a most imposing piece of work, and stands from tip to base 22½". The diameter of the base is 7¾". The diameter of the globe is 5¼". The work throughout is first-class, and no money has been spared in its execution. It will enhance any home, and will be admired by everyone who sees it.

The trophy will be awarded every month, and the winner will be announced in the following issue of SHORT WAVE CRAFT. The winner's name will be hand engraved on the trophy.

The purpose of this contest is to advance the art of radio by "logging" as many short-wave commercial phone stations, in a period not exceeding thirty days, as possible by any one contestant. The trophy will be awarded to that SHORT WAVE SCOUT who has logged the greatest number of short-wave stations during the month for which the award is made and at least fifty per cent must be "verified".

The Short Wave Scouts trophy (*Short Wave Craft*, June 1934).

leading silversmiths. It is made of metal throughout, except the base, which is made of handsome black Bakelite. The metal itself is quadruple, silver-plated, in the usual manner of all trophies today. It is a most imposing piece of work, and stands from tip to base 22-1/2"... . The work throughout is first-class, and no money has been spared in its execution. It will enhance any home, and will be admired by everyone who sees it."[4]

*All-Wave Radio* attempted to organize DXers through the Radio Signal Survey League, which was introduced in February 1937 and given its own column in the magazine most months. The purpose of the RSSL was to improve domestic and international transmission and reception conditions through a worldwide network of monitors who would conduct organized monitoring surveys for stations that requested them. There were five divisions: BCB, SWBC, amateur phone, amateur CW, and "noise survey," the latter intended to help alleviate man-made electrical interference in local areas. There was an RSSL section manager in each state, and local chapters were encouraged. Members reported their survey results on special forms that showed reception conditions in graphic format. The RSSL also offered listener supplies (survey forms, stationery, and RSSL metalette seals), and "DX Reception Citations," certificates attesting to one's verification totals.

Alas, a lot more was said than done in the RSSL. The level of survey participation was not what had been hoped for, and when *All-Wave Radio* was taken over by *Radio News* in August 1938, the RSSL faded into history. Still, the experiment was noteworthy as an organized, listener-oriented attempt not just to exchange DX tips but to actually improve international reception and thus make shortwave radio more attractive to nontechnical people.

Growth of the clubs meant that DXers and their reputations started to become known. Among the big names of the 1930s shortwave listening scene are many that have long since been forgotten, like Oliver Amlie, Ray LaRocque, Robert Skyten, Gil Harris, Paul Dilg, Emmett Riggle, Norm Kriebel, John J. Oskay, Harold Schrock, Earl R. Roberts, John DeMyer, Jimmy Hart, Ab Saylor, and Anthony C. Tarr. Others who come to mind a bit more easily are August Balbi, Ken Boord, Larry Lundberg, Art Hankins, Dave Thomas, Roy Waite, Grady Ferguson, Page Taylor, Matt Zahner, and Carroll Weyrich, and the man who is surely the dean of American shortwave DXers, Roger Legge. Many DXers, especially BCBers, adopted informal handles by which they became known. Howard Kemp was the "Brass City Night Owl," Ray Lewis the "Lotus City Globe Trotter," Lloyd Hahn the "Rooster," and Carroll Weyrich the "Snoozer," to name a few. And there were some even bigger names in shortwave circles. In October 1934 *RADEX* reported that Bing Crosby and movie actor Dick Arlen would stage a weeklong DX battle from their Hollywood homes. They would use identical McMurdo Silver receivers, and the one who logged fewer stations would write a check for $1,000 to a children's charity.[5]

There were many local and regional club gatherings. At first these were informal events, often held in people's homes until the numbers forced them into hotels. Some clubs had annual meetings, the NNRC affairs being the most elaborate. The first annual NNRC banquet in 1931 drew 250 people. A 1935 NNRC dance, with entertainment, drew over 1,000 people, with many having to be turned away because of fire regulations. The club started holding annual summer conventions in Lansdale, Pennsylvania, in 1936. Their masquerade parties, held in the newspaper's auditorium, were also a big hit. Early NNRC gatherings were often attended by famous radio stars like Kate Smith, Morton Downey, Rudy Vallee, and Fred Waring.[6]

Although there is some mention in an old NNRC bulletin (April 27, 1936) of an "R9 Listeners League of America" SWL fest that was to be held in Shenandoah, Pennsylvania, in June 1936, the first truly national shortwave DX gathering appears to have been the IDA-sponsored Golden Gate DX Festival, held July 8–11, 1939, in San Francisco, site of the Golden Gate International Exposition, a West Coast–oriented event held at the same time as the New York World's Fair. There were special broadcasts over GE's shortwave station W6XBE (later KGEI), which was situated on Treasure Island, a man-made island formed by dredging San Francisco Bay. There was also an IDA barbecue, plus displays and lectures. It was noted that "$15 or $20 should carry anyone thru the entire four days of the Festival and Exposition nicely, and that covers all expenses: registration, meals, hotel, sightseeing, etc. Many could do it for less than that by careful planning."[7] The IDA bulletin contained instructions for reaching the convention site by train, bus, and auto, and urged members to take the special "Globe Circler Tour," a seven-day railroad trip from Chicago to San Francisco by way of Oregon aboard the Northern Pacific Railway's North Coast Limited. The round-trip train fare, including sleeper coach, was $89.90–$98.90 per person, including some side trips and ferries. "Excellent meals, 50 cents, 75 cents, $1. Also 'off the tray items,' 5 cents to 25 cents." Those were the days.

The 1930s also saw the start of listener clubs, or clubs run by radio stations. One of the largest, and perhaps the first, was England's International Broadcasting Club, an arm of the International Broadcasting Company (IBC). IBC was the brainchild of Captain Leonard F. Plugge, M.P. Formed in 1930, it was basically an organization that purchased air time over various continental stations for the presentation of sponsored programs in English for Great Britain at a time when the BBC was vehemently opposed to commercial advertising on radio. IBC bought time from French station Radio Normandie, as well as stations in Luxembourg, Poland, Italy, and other countries. Most transmissions were on medium and long wave, but some were on shortwave (including EAQ, Madrid, on 10,000 kc.). IBC sponsors included Carter's Little Liver Pills, Pond's Face Powder, Cunard White Star, Milk of Magnesia, and Colgate Ribbon Dental Cream.

# JUNE, 1939

G. E. Station W6XBE on Treasure Island at San Francisco, will Broadcast DX Festival Programs for IDA, on July 11, at 6:30 P.M. (15.33), and on July 12, at 9:00 A.M. EST (9.53)

### In this Issue

GOLDEN GATE DX FESTIVAL—VIC-VAC SHORT-WAVE HONOR-ROLL—IDA 100 CLUB—NEW BRITISH BROAD-CAST FREQUENCIES—SHORT-WAVE NOTES AND LIST.

### ten cents

## INTERNATIONAL DX'ERS ALLIANCE

From the June 1939 issue of *The Globe Circler*, information on the Golden Gate DX Festival in San Francisco.

# INTERNATIONAL BROADCASTING CLUB.

11 HALLAM STREET
PORTLAND PLACE
LONDON W.1

PRESIDENT
CAPT. LEONARD F. PLUGGE, M.P.

TEL. LANGHAM 1221 (6 LINES)
TELG. INTERBROAD, LONDON.

Dear Sir, (or Madam)

We are very pleased to enrol you in the rapidly growing ranks of the International Broadcasting Club. As you probably know, this Club has been founded at the request of a great number of our listeners with a view to bringing into closer relationship all listeners to the International Broadcasting Company's transmissions, and also to create a greater feeling of goodwill and friendship among listeners to Stations situated beyond the Seas.

Your Membership Card is enclosed herewith. There is no entrance fee, no subscription nor any financial liability on Members, but in any correspondence with the Club, Members are kindly asked to enclose a stamp for a reply.

A very distinctive Members' badge has been prepared in various forms, details of which may be had on application.

Special Club broadcasts, competitions, town concerts and request programmes are regular features of the I.B.C. transmissions and we welcome all kinds of suggestions as well as requests for musical items from our Members. Please quote your Membership Number on all correspondence.

Enclosed is a specimen copy of the I.B.C. weekly programme sheet, to which we hope you will become a regular subscriber. This you should certainly do if you are in favour of the extension of our broadcast service to earlier hours in the morning and later hours at night. If the number of programme subscribers is sufficiently great this extension will be assured.

On the occasion of your becoming a new Member, may I extend to you a very warm welcome.

Yours very truly,

*Leonard Plugge*

President.

A letter that was sent to members of the International Broadcasting Club, an organization run by the International Broadcasting Company in London (1936).

The purpose of the International Broadcasting Club was to provide IBC with a vehicle for estimating the size, location, and makeup of its audience for the benefit of potential advertisers. Membership was free. Members received a numbered membership card, and could buy IBC jewelry bearing the IBC logo (which bore a strong resemblance to that of the BBC). There were ladies' brooches, scarf pins, and watch chains for 65 cents each, cuff links for $1.30. Members could have children's birthdays and special anniversaries announced for a shilling.

Plugge claimed 90,000–150,000 members at various times in 1933, although these figures are undocumented. Surveys showed that IBC programs competed favorably with the BBC, and advertising revenues grew considerably during the mid to late 1930s, making Plugge a wealthy man. The organization met an odd fate when in 1939 its prime outlet, Radio Normandie, was nationalized by the French government, seemingly the result of a business grudge between the station's owner and a former associate who had become an assistant to a French cabinet minister. Radio Normandie was taken over by the Germans during the war, and near the end of the war the French government prohibited private radio stations altogether. By this time Plugge was occupied with other business matters, and IBC activities lapsed.[8]

In those days there were many opportunities, large and small, for a serious listener to distinguish himself or herself (usually the former). Magazines were always offering a few dollars or a free subscription for the best operating tips, or "kinks," as they were called. *RADEX* offered a radio map or a copy of their magazine to the winner of the monthly puzzle contest. *Official Short Wave Listener* awarded a silver trophy for the best listening post photo.

*Short Wave Craft* ran a contest for the best article about a homemade shortwave receiver or converter in which the entrant had to not only write the article but also send in the set! First prize was $50. Cover contests were also popular. *Short Wave Craft* once offered over 100 prizes to readers submitting the best captions for a *Short Wave Craft* cover depicting an angry wife sitting up in bed shaking her finger at her spouse, who was in another bed with his headphones on. The winner of the grand prize, a Pilot 11-tube Super Dragon receiver, was "There 'Antenna' Justice." The second prize winner was "The Ethernal Triangle"; and the fourteenth prize winner, was "Radio Raises Spain but Wifey Raises Cain." I guess you had to be there.

There were also some serious competitions. DX contests developed initially among medium wavers. Probably the first was a 1922 contest organized by *Radio Broadcasting News* magazine and suggested by Frank H. Jones, the owner of well-known BCB station 6KW in Tuinucu, Cuba. It was called "Radio Golf" because it was a gentleman's game, with each person keeping his or her own score. The idea was to add up the distance in miles of each new station heard. The leader claimed a score of 82,470 miles.[9]

The *Philco Radio Atlas of the World* combined maps with time and frequency information (1935).

# LIKE ADVENTURE? TRY ASIA!

## Here's a fertile field for radio exploration!

### JAPAN

| Location | Station | Freq. | Time (Eastern Standard) |
|---|---|---|---|
| Nazaki(Tokyo) JVH | | 14.60 | 4 to 8 A.M. & 8:30 to 9:30 P.M. |
| Nazaki(Tokyo) JVM | | 10.74 | 1:30 to 7 A.M. & 7 to 11 P.M. |
| Nazaki(Tokyo) JVN | | 10.66 | 3 to 8 A.M. |

A good example of how short-wave broadcasting is slowly but surely improving, enabling the listener to hear programs from the other side of the world, is found in the broadcasts from Japan. A year ago short-wave broadcasts from Tokyo were intercepted but rarely by listeners here in America. But now, several of the Tokyo stations are heard more regularly. In fact, special broadcasts are being sent out for listeners in America.

Photo Courtesy Radio News

Young Nippon listens-in. These little Japanese are children of Rear Admiral Yamamoto. They are listening to their father's voice as he broadcasts by short-wave from London.

And the programs from Tokyo are like nothing you ever heard before! Many a Philco owner, under favorable conditions, finds a particular delight in listening to quaint Japanese music.

### INDIA

| Location | Station | Freq. | Time (Eastern Standard) |
|---|---|---|---|
| Bombay | VUY-VUB | 9.57 | Wed. & Sat. 11 A.M. to 12:30 P.M. |
| Calcutta | VUC | 6.11 | Daily 9:30 A.M. to Noon, Sat. 11:45 P.M. to 3 A.M. |

India, unfortunately, is one of the sections of the world from which short-wave entertainment cannot be obtained with any degree of regularity. For some unknown reason, the English have not given their Indian broadcasting stations anywhere near the power of those in England or Australia. The result is that reception of either the Bombay or the Calcutta stations is a real event in the life of any short-wave fan.

### SIAM and INDO-CHINA

| Location | Station | Freq. | Time (Eastern Standard) |
|---|---|---|---|
| | | **SIAM** | |
| Bangkok | HSP | 17.75 | 4:30 to 6:30 A.M. Irregular |
| | | **FRENCH INDO-CHINA** | |
| Saigon | FZS | 11.99 | Phones Paris mornings |
| | | **STRAITS SETTLEMENTS** | |
| Penang | ZHJ | 6.08 | Daily 6:40 to 8:40 A.M. |
| | | **MALAY STATES** | |
| Kuala Lumpur | ZGE | 6.13 | Sun., Tues., Fri. 6:40 to 8:40 P.M. |
| Singapore | ZHI | 6.01 | Mon., Wed., Thurs. 5:40 to 8:10 A.M. Sat. 10:40 P.M. to 1:10 A.M. |

Siam is another of the Asiatic countries from which reception is uncertain. However, the station at Bangkok has been logged by more than one persevering Philco owner. And the peculiar type of Oriental entertainment to which they have been treated, has more than amply repaid them for their early morning exploration of the dial. Saigon, in French Indo-China, has been heard a little more frequently, for the French use this station to communicate directly with Paris.

### OTHER COUNTRIES

| Location | Station | Freq. | Time (Eastern Standard) |
|---|---|---|---|
| | | **CHINA** | |
| Shanghai | XGW | 10.42 | Tests near 6:00 A.M. |
| Hongkong | ZCK | 8.75 | Daily 11:30 P.M. to 1:15 A.M. Mon. & Thurs. 3 to 7 A.M. |
| Macau | CQN | 6.02 | Mon. & Fri. 3 to 5 A.M. |
| | | **SIBERIA** | |
| Khabarovsk | RV15 | 4.25 | 1 to 9 A.M. |

The Orient is full of exciting adventure for those who have the true spirit of exploration within them—for those who like to travel unbeaten

Comrade Ikramov, lute player, who is attached to the Tashkent Radio Centre, in Tadjikistan, Central Asia. Many unusual broadcasts come from stations in the U. S. S. R.

aerial highways that lead to Siberia, China, the Malay States and other far-off lands. The average listener, however, should not expect to hear these stations because of the many factors involved.

In 1934 the IDA ran the Randolph Trophy contest for verifying the most medium-wave stations at least 2,000 miles distant during a six-month period. The grand prize went to a Hawaiian DXer who had 114 stations. Winners were awarded trophies. First prize was described as "a columnar trophy standing some 40 to 48 inches in height, and wrought in a combination of silver, gold, and copper. It will include a World Globe surmounted by a Figure of Victory."[10]

A big shortwave contest in the mid–1930s was the International Short Wave Club's Denton Trophy Contest, named after Clifford E. Denton, a well-known short-wave engineer of the day. The winner was the person who obtained the largest number of shortwave broadcast verifications from stations logged during a six-month period. First prize was a silver trophy, second prize a medal. Other winners received engraved scrolls.

Clubs issued awards, just as they do today. In August 1935 the IDA announced the "Doctor of Short Waves degree" (DSW), which required 100 shortwave verifications from at least 25 countries (besides the applicant's own), including three from each continent. Clubs, as well as *RADEX* magazine, had "singleton" contests wherein you registered a broadcast band verification that you believed no one else in North America had. Once entered, it could be eliminated from the list by someone else with the same verification.

The "radio map" was an interesting DX artifact of the 1930s. It was basically a map that also contained station information. The U.S. radio maps were broadcast band–oriented. An example was the 1933 RCA Cunningham/Radiotron map, an 18" × 24" color map of the United States showing each city or town where a station was located, along with the station's call letters, frequency, and power. The sidebars contained station listings by call letter and frequency. With the map came a "Radio Set Performance Yardstick," a paper ruler with markings at 300, 600, and 1,000 miles. By placing the yardstick on the map and measuring the distance from your location to the station, you could rate your receiver according to a scale on the ruler. Up to 300 miles was poor, 300–600 was fair, 600–1,000 was good, and over 1,000 was excellent. "If your radio set cannot bring in stations of 5,000 watts or over located in the 'Good Zone' area," it said, "let us make an inspection of your radio set, or bring your radio tubes in to us for test and examination. Replace worn out tubes with new powerful Cunningham Radio Tubes or RCA Radiotrons." On the back was a "Radio Tour," a few sentences about each state and some of its principal stations, and an RCA promotion.

A 1934 version of the map had a U.S. map and sidebars on one side, and a similarly designed world map with shortwave information on the back, plus a time conversion chart and some tips on shortwave listening, all for 10 cents.

There were many variations on this theme. In 1934 a receiver manufacturer, American-Bosch, issued a similar international map showing shortwave locations and listing broadcast stations and police transmitters. On the back was a promotion for American-Bosch "Round-the-World Radios." "Cram's Detailed Radio Map of the U.S. and Canada" measured 28" × 34" and showed the location of each station, along with a sidebar containing call letters, frequency, and station ownership.

As with the call books, the radio maps were sometimes made up as promotional items for electronics houses. Usually fairly large, they were sometimes folded over many times and placed in a small pocket-size cover.

An offshoot of the radio map was the radio atlas, a booklet combining maps, station lists, and information about the shortwave stations and their countries. Most prominent among the atlases was the 1935 *Philco Radio Atlas of the World*, consisting of 18 pages, 10" × 13" each. A second edition was published in 7" × 10" format. They both cost 50 cents. *Cram's International Radio Atlas* was the Cram map in booklet form, with some foreign maps and information added.

One reason maps were popular was that distance was a recognized measure of DXing prowess. Much was made of the ability to log stations 12,000 miles away, and receiver advertisements contained letters from satisfied customers attesting to the distance feats that were possible with particular receivers. In addition, DX contests sometimes had a mileage component. You might have to log a given number of stations in various distance categories, or the point value of a logging might be dependent on the station's distance. In the Denton Trophy Contest, for example, ties were broken based on total number of reception miles in the contestant's log.

*Chapter 9*

# VERIFICATIONS

THE STATION-LISTENER RELATIONSHIP produced some interesting radio memorabilia right from the start.

During the 1920–25 period, when stations were interested in knowing who was listening and what they thought of the programs, listener comments were commonly referred to as "applause." This was before the days of listener research, even before most commercials. Artists were seldom paid for performing on the air, and neither they nor the station knew who—if anyone—was listening. In 1922 such uncertainty prompted comedian Eddie Cantor to ask all those who were listening to send in a dime for charity. He was surprised at the shower of coins he received.

This led to the creation of the applause card, a fill in the blanks postcard that the listener sent to the station or artist, expressing appreciation for the broadcast— a kind of reverse QSL. Most applause cards were printed up and distributed by radio companies and other commercial firms, but some listeners designed their own.

In the very early days of broadcast-band experimentation, listeners were less concerned with obtaining written verifications than with just telling the station that it had been heard. Here are some letters from the files of New York experimental station 2XB, predecessor of American Telephone and Telegraph Company's broadcast station, WEAF, which will look familiar to today's DXer.[1]

Lakewood, N.J., March 16, 1920

At 10:15 P.M. on March 15, I was listening to the telephonic messages coming from your laboratory. I listened to all the talking until the end at 12 P.M. I heard you call Mr. Johnson at Schenectady, N.Y. Also reading from newspaper, subject on Democratic and Republican politics. You called Commander Taylor at Washington, requesting him to call you on the land line. You also stated you were using a 500 watt transmitter on 14 to 15 amperes. Mr. Warren read news of Civil warfare in Berlin. Called up Camden and requested an answer. You stated

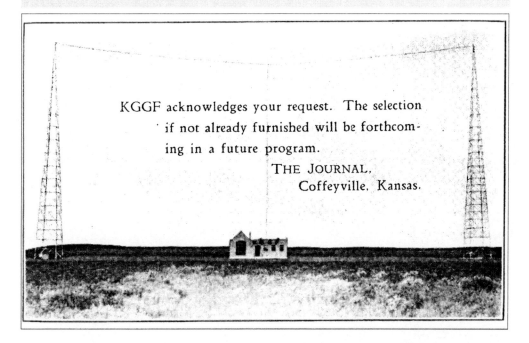

KGGF acknowledges your request. The selection
if not already furnished will be forthcom-
ing in a future program.

THE JOURNAL,
Coffeyville, Kansas.

Some stations were careful to acknowledge receipt of listener requests.

interference was great in your section, but I had absolutely no interference the whole evening. Voice was very clear. Later you called up
Mr. Bowman, Mr. Packman, Mr. J. Carter, Mr. Insell of 117 North
16th St., Mr. Lloyd, and Mr. C. Stevens. Mr. Ward was speaking. On
Wed. you will send part of time on 1700 meters. Hoping you the best
of success.

Brooklyn, N.Y., March 27, 1920

Conforming to your request of last night on the Wireless Telephone,
if anyone of long distance heard you, I cannot resist the temptation,
although I was only in Brooklyn, of congratulating you upon your
experiment. I enjoyed the music very much, especially "Hindustani."
I was somewhat surprised that one of you fellows could not read Italian on that record, but neither can I.

I was listening in on the Wireless of Mr. Hill of the Brooklyn Eastern District Y.M.C.A. who is a cripple, and would appreciate it very
much if you would call him out the next time you work after 10 o'clock
as you can be assured he will be with you.

Kindly acknowledge this letter and accept the best wishes of a
number of the boys here at the "Y" who are very interested in your
experiments.

Passaic, N.J., March 28, 1920

On Friday last I had the pleasure of listening in on my wireless to
your talking and musical experiments; and must say I thoroughly
enjoyed it.

# I LIKED IT!   THANK YOU!

**High Class**
**Radio**

George Lamay
Holyoke, Mass.

**High Class**
**Radio**
**Printing**

Alden Press
Holyoke, Mass.

 15

Date *March 8/25*

**Radio Broadcasting Station** *WOG*

This is to let you know that I am enjoying your splendid programs.   I especially enjoyed _____

_____

_____

Allow me to thank you and those who contribute to your entertainments for your efficient and highly enjoyable broadcasting.

Signed _____

Address _____ *400 North Main St*

_____

---

*Thank* **TO STATION**   *You!!* **TO ARTIST**

Clearness _____

Volume _____       DATE _____

Interference _____

Remarks: _____

MY RECEIVER IS—

NAME _____

Your selections of this date, were *very* enjoyable.

Requests: _____

_____

_____

_____

_____

NAME _____                   CITY _____

ADDRESS _____               STATE _____

Applause cards.

The talking was clearer than when heard over the ordinary telephone and the music sounded as though it was in the room. I could
hear every word plainly, especially the one of Harry Lauder's. And
the jazz pieces made my feet move in rhythm.

I would greatly appreciate your advising me, if possible, when these
tests are going to be made and how often; as I would like to listen
in, and enclose addressed envelope for your reply.

Colon, Panama, March 9th, 1920

I am pleased to report your telephone conversation as clear and under-
standable at Colon. This was on March 8th, 11 P.M. New York City
time. Tuning for Key West Press I heard you sending the following:

"Hello *Green Harbor*, Hello, this is 2XB talking, 1, 2, 3, 4, 3, 2, 1.
Let me know how this is. Is it clear? Anyone else hearing these signals please let me know. That's all now, good night.

I believe this is a record for your station and I am very pleased to
report such.

Stations valued reports, not only for their technical value but as a demonstration to potential advertisers of the range of their signal. It was reported that in the
foyer of station WDY, Roselle Park, New Jersey, "hung a large map of the United
States, with colored tacks indicating reports of reception. Eastern Canada and Cuba
were the up and down limits, and westward the station reached as far as Omaha.
This was not bad for 500 watts at 360 meters."[2]

The connection between radio transmissions, written reception reports, and
verifications dates back to the years around 1915, when postcard reports of amateur
radio transmissions from those who were listening in were encouraged, and generally welcomed, by the amateurs. The exchange of true verification cards, as we know
them, among hams, followed. The use of amateur QSLs had become widespread by
1920.

A verification, or QSL as it is commonly called (after the three-letter Morse
code abbreviation for "I acknowledge receipt") is a card or letter from a station that
says that it was in fact that station that the listener heard. Amateur radio operators
exchanged such cards after an on-the-air contact. Broadcast stations issued them
upon receipt of evidence, usually in the form of a narrative description in a letter,
of the programming that a listener reported. (See chapter 4 for additional examples
of QSLs). If the programming matched the station's records, it would warrant a
verification.

The most prized verifications were (and are) those containing full data, that is,
the date, time, and frequency of the listener's reception, and perhaps the power of
the transmitter as well. Not all stations were aware of such listener arcana, however, and many listeners had to (and still must) settle for something less, including

UNINDO AS AMERICAS

*Pela 2a. vez*

**as ondas sonoras
de prf 3 pelos
céos da America!**

✦ Coroando o exito extraordina-
rio da primeira irradiação directa
para os Estados Unidos, em 3 de
Janeiro de 1937 e accedendo ju-
bilosa ao pedido do Newark News
Radio Club, de Newark, New
Jersey — o maior club de radio-
ouvintes do mundo — a Radio
Diffusora São Paulo fará amanhã,
pela segunda vez, das 5 ás 6
horas, uma irradiação especial e directa dedicada aos Estados Unidos,
unindo, assim, atravéz do seu fa-
moso som de crystal e da musica
caracteristica do Brasil, num abra-
ço de confraternização, os dois
maiores paizes das Americas.

Speaker - **JAIR VASCONCELLOS**

**230**
attestados de rece-
pção, procedentes de
20 Estados America-
nos, coroaram de exi-
to a nossa primeira
irradiação para a
America do Norte!

*Radio Diffusora São Paulo*

**A ESTAÇÃO DO SOM DE CRYSTAL**

Stations often used long-distance reception as evidence of the power of their signal. Here, a medium-
wave station in Brazil boasts of the receipt of 230
reception reports from 20 states as evidence of the
strength of its signal in the north (1937).

no data, "thanks for your report" letters (which, however, all but the
strictest purists accept as a bona fide
verification of reception).

Considering the broadcaster's
need for program comments, it is not
surprising that QSLing took hold
among broadcast stations as well as
amateurs. The additional elements
of geographic and cultural distance
between broadcaster and listener
made QSLing a natural for shortwave stations. Presaging by over 50
years the interest that would eventually be shown in the historical
value of QSLs by today's Committee to Preserve Radio Verifications,
one *RADEX* reader in 1933 suggested that "verification collections
will some day be valued as a phase
of what other collectors call Amer-
icana, since radio is yet in a comparative infancy."[3]

The rules of the game were the
same in the 1930s as they are today,
as was the question of what it all
meant. "I send for every verification
that I can," reported one young
aficionado, "and when my pop sees
me writing out a dozen or so he
wants to know what's the sense of it
all. He says it does no good to have
a letter from a station saying that
they were broadcasting that time
and that they were glad that I heard
the program. I'm quite at a loss to
argue with him except to say that it
is an interesting hobby. He claims
that it is a waste of stamps."[4] As
medium-wave DXer Dick Cooper

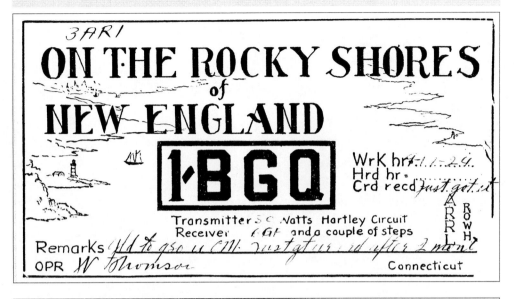

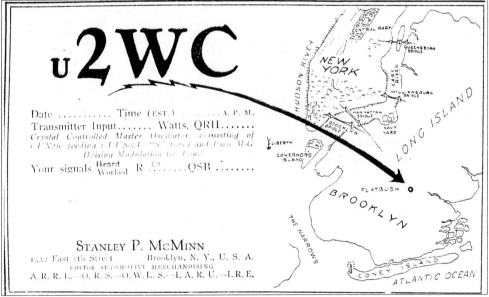

Early ham radio QSLs from stations 1BGQ in Connecticut (1924) and U2WC in Brooklyn (1927).

put it in his 1981 reminiscences, "[W]e really had an interesting hobby that was a lot of fun in the 1930s.... [But m]ost people think you're nuts. I wonder sometimes about that ... myself."[5]

Some listeners learned about QSLing by accident. Joe Lippincott, who listened to long-distance BCB stations in the 1920s and 1930s, didn't know for a long time what a "veri"—as verifications are sometimes called—was. He once heard a station in Virginia telling listeners to write in for a free apple. He got his apple, and a few days later a QSL. "The fools," said Joe. "Of course I heard them, or how

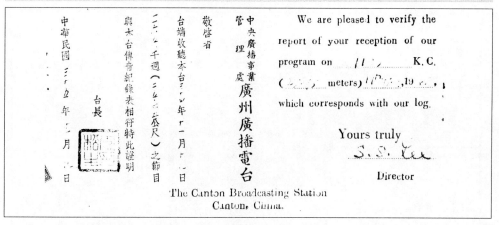

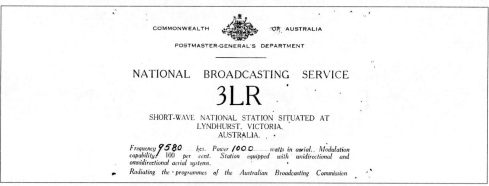

*Above and facing page:* QSLs came in many designs. XTPA was one of many Chinese shortwave stations (QSL, 1945). Radio Australia, distant cousin of NBC station 3LR, still broadcasts on 9580 kc. today (QSL, 1936). HC2JSB, Guayaquil, Ecuador, claimed to be the country's first commercial broadcaster (QSL, 1935). Sharq al-Adna was widely heard during the postwar years. The station is said to have started broadcasting from Palestine in 1942, and was most likely built by British intelligence. It moved to British-controlled Cyprus in 1948 (QSL, 1946). Verifications from Cuba were often artfully designed (QSL, 1936).

could I have written for an apple?" So he tore up the QSL. Soon he would know better.[6]

Reception reports were not of higher quality in "the good old days," as is sometimes thought today. An announcer who had set up various DX broadcasts at two BCB stations complained that most DXers were deficient in reporting signal quality, which was the station's main interest. He reported that in only 88 of 4,387 reports received was signal quality reported adequately. The rest were sketchy, often just a few words. As for shortwave, "I have a number of friends associated with foreign short wave broadcast stations," he reported, "and letters from them indicate that the number of slip-shod reports is astonishing. I find that even 'fake' reports are received by these stations in numbers that make the situation rather serious."[7] A former assistant secretary of the NNRC, who verified reports for a local medium-wave station, reported that 50 percent of the reports were illegible, contained no return postage, or were written on postcards.[8] The absence of return postage was a common complaint of the broadcasters.

The New Zealand DX Radio Association also released data indicating some faking of reception reports. In one case, 30 people reported a station that had been off the air for two months. In another, details of a fictitious broadcast that were published by the NZDXRA produced glowing reports from some "listeners." IDA President Charles Morrison editorialized on the problem as follows:

> Unfair or unsportsmanlike methods of obtaining verifications *do not pay*. A cheating DXer is invariably caught, and for what price—a few sheets of paper, or postal cards. These actions reflect seriously not only on the DXer, but on his comrades, the radio stations, and the entire sport. The vast majority of DXers are honest and would not think of

reporting a station unless they had some positive proof of identification. It therefore seems logical that the major radio clubs should unite to stop once and for all this menace to the wholesome atmosphere that has always been associated with DXing. We do not wish nor do we intend to condemn anyone unwarrantedly, nor is it our wish to stifle or censor any sincere reports. We shall continue to admire all exceptional achievements in DXing as we have in the past—but the day of the verification faker is over. To those who while not openly dishonest, nevertheless use unethical DXing methods, we beg of you to give them up *now*, and become a credit to the high standards adhered to by all *real* DXers.[9]

Some people sent reports on postcards, and many stations QSLed them as a matter of courtesy, even though it seemed impossible that one could provide convincing details of what one heard in such a small space, especially if one had to describe the programming generically, as was often the case under poor receiving conditions, rather than with more easily convincing details such as program title, artist's name, or song title. Bemoaning this practice, *All-Wave Radio* BCB editor Ray LaRocque observed, "If a DXer who receives a verification after sending only a postcard to a station does not feel that he has cheated the station, he must admit that he has at least taken advantage of their generosity."[10]

As suggested above, faulty reporting was not limited to BCB listeners. Shortwave station XEBT in Mexico reported receiving reports such as, "Last night we heard your station. It came in very clear and could be heard in every room in the house. We heard chime bells and siren. Please verify." The station replied with their usual QSL card, but with the word "verification" crossed out and "courtesy card" penned in.[11] Prospective members of the International DXers Alliance had to sign a pledge on the membership application that they would use "only honorable methods" in obtaining QSLs, and that they would do all they could to stamp out the use of any fraudulent QSLing methods and uphold the IDA policy of demanding the resignation of any member found wanting in this department. Such was the seriousness with which QSLing was viewed. Among long-distance listeners, false reporting was a hanging offense.

One reason for the existence of some defective reporting among broadcast-band DXers in the 1930s may have been the pressure resulting from the seeming possibility of verifying nearly every domestic broadcast-band station that was in existence at the time. For example, in 1935 Carleton Lord, DXing from Ohio, had verified 211 of the 230 stations operating on BCB graveyard frequencies (channels reserved for low-power, local broadcasters), and 77 of the 83 stations in the 3 West Coast states (including every one of the 28 stations running 100 watts or less). DXer Dick Cooper had verified all U.S. stations but 12. Ray Lewis had QSLed 775 stations; there were only 11 in the United States and a handful in Canada that he had not heard. The possibility of reaching the ultimate goal of hearing and verifying *all* stations may have prompted DXers to send out reports that were a little thin on details, or resolve in the listener's favor any doubts about a particular station's identity.

QSLs usually took the same form that they do today: cards or letters, with the latter often boasting eye-catching letterheads. Some were exceptional, such as the grand certificates issued by TI4NRH in Costa Rica and medium waver LR5, Radio Excelsior, Argentina. NNRCer Lloyd Hahn recalled what it was like to hear LR5 on their special test broadcast for the U.S. Department of Commerce in 1934.

> They broadcast on the same frequency [830 kc.] as KOA [Denver] and arrangements had been made for KOA to go off the air early, in order to clear the channel. I was all set and had the radio tuned to hair-trigger fineness on KOA for the last 15 minutes of their program. KOA was just giving the announcement of the impending DX from LR5 when, about five minutes before the hour for the latter to start, there was a very noticeable interference in the background. Lo! and behold, we were hearing LR5 before KOA had even left the air and, when KOA finally became silent, we could sit back and enjoy the entire program from LR5 like a local station. To say we were astounded is putting it very mildly. I'll never forget the opening number on that program. I can still hear the announcer saying, in very excellent English, "The first selection on our program will be, 'Hell's Bells,' by Art Kassel and his Castles in the Air."[12]

Unique were the great little QSLs that a group of Montana stations had embossed on card-size sheets of copper. Other stations also provided creative forms of verification. Some stations, particularly medium wavers, sent gifts to distant listeners: a pound of coffee from TGW in Guatemala; little bottles of orange blossom perfume or a carton of oranges from WJAX, Jacksonville, Florida; or a Black Hawk Tire and Rubber Company inner tube from another Des Moines, Iowa, enterprise, Bankers Life Company station WHO. Station WGPC, Albany, Georgia—"World's Greatest Pecan Center"—was known to send out five pounds of pecans. One listener received a live, 10 inch alligator from station WMFJ in Daytona Beach, Florida.[13]

Some stations did not verify as a matter of policy. The BBC policy of non-verification goes back to at least 1929, and was a product of the large number of stations that rebroadcast BBC news and programming. So many stations around the world carried BBC programs, said Bush House, that it was difficult to tell for certain which one you were listening to. Exceptions to the policy were made from time to time, however. For example, in the mid–1930s the BBC magazine, *World-Radio*, carried a column called "Which Station Was That?" The column included a coupon entitling the reader to submit a report (with the relevant particulars, *and* sixpence)

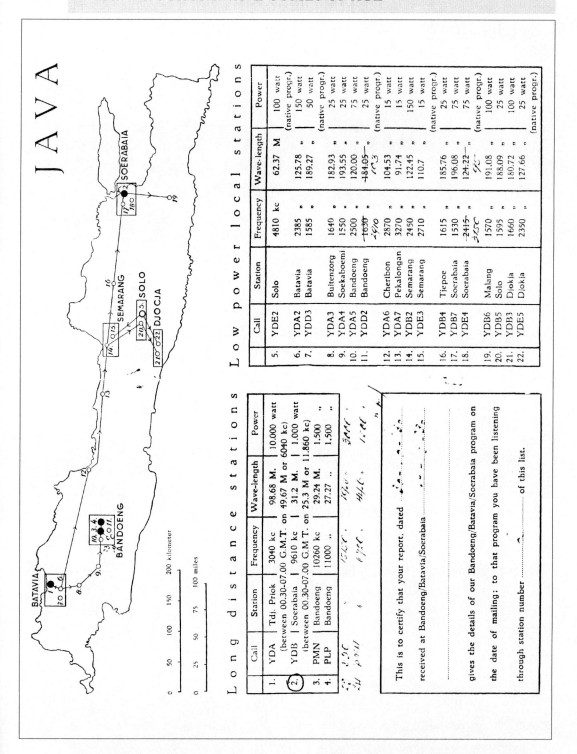

This verification is part of a folder containing information and pictures about the station NIROM, the Netherlands Indies Broadcasting Company in Indonesia, distant precursor of today's Radio Republik Indonesia (QSL, 1936).

Perhaps the most impressive verification of all time, a multicolored certificate (10" × 14") from medium-wave station LR5 in Argentina, issued on the event of a special test broadcast made on behalf of the U.S. Department of Commerce (QSL, 1936).

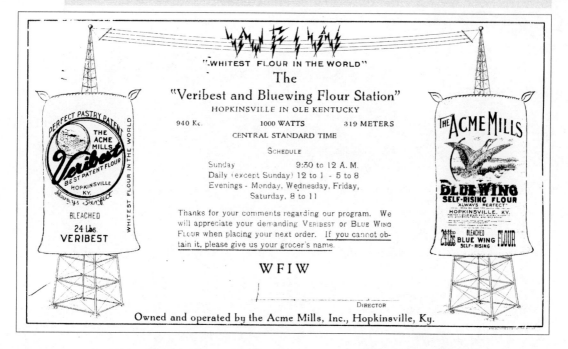

A unique card from station WFIW, operated by Acme Mills in Kentucky (QSL, 1931).

on a BBC medium-wave station to the "Which Station Was That Postal Query Service." The magazine responded with an official-looking form—not exactly a QSL, but pretty close—indicating which BBC station you had heard. Also, for a short period in the mid–1940s the engineering department of the BBC New York office issued its own official, full-data QSL cards to listeners who submitted reports.

There were also other stations that did not reply. In the broadcast-band arena, some stations felt that long-distance reception reports ran *contra* to the very goals of AM broadcast stations. The operator of Brooklyn station WBYN stated to a Maryland DXer in 1941:

> The standard policy of every broadcast station I have worked for or been in, in the past 10 years, has been to throw you fellows' reports in the circular file ... and not even trouble to look at them ... it being the secretary's duty to see that no one was bothered with them. Usually, the few hams in the station exhibited enough interest in them to habitually read them, and so the girls would sympathetically send them to the engineering department instead of tossing them out. Why? Well, in modern broadcast work the station does everything in its power to restrict the signal to some definite locality. Naturally there is some sky-wave reception, but it is of absolutely no interest to the station. Yet, while you are wasting your own and the station's time with QSL cards, the short-wave men who WANT your reports and comments, and particularly the ultra short-wave people who are the hardest workers, are STARVING for reports and data. Why don't

**KICK** 1340 KILOCYCLES

KICKAPOO PRAIRIE BROADCASTING CO., Inc.

FLOYD W. JONES, PRESIDENT • CHARLES C. SEIFERD, VICE-PRESIDENT AND GENERAL MANAGER

610 COLLEGE STREET ⟨ ⟨ ⟩ SPRINGFIELD 3, MISSOURI

April 1, 1950

To verify or not to verify, that is the question.
Whether 'tis nobler in your mind to suffer,
Wondering of your outrageous fortune in hearing our call,
Or for us to take arms against a sea of reports, and
By verifying, deplete them?
    To verify - to confirm --
Once more; and by confirmation say we end your
Headaches, and the thousand natural cursings
That a non-verifier is heir to - 'tis a confirmation
Devoutly to be wished for.
    To verify - to confirm --
To verify! Perchance to be indefinite!
    Aye! There's the rub!
For in a verification which is indefinite, what words may come
From an unsuspecting DXer as he reads the phrase, 'Thanks for your
Report - due to ad-lib announcing, we cannot verify-' must give us pause.
There's the station that makes a calamity of so much DX.
For who cannot say that listener Eugene Allen
Has won the hard fought battle on 1340 and correctly
Heard KICK? Who can delay in notifying this dial twister
Of his merit, brought on by his patience on our miserable channel,
When we were engaged in a special transmission on March 27, 1950.
Who could fail to verify your reception at 1:15-1:33 AM, PST,
As you fought and cursed the all nighters covering our signal?
But that our dread of the incapability of our
Gates Equipment, that the 176' height of our Lehigh Tower,
That our RCA speech equipment might fail - puzzles our engineers,
And your reports make us bear in mind that we need not fear these things.
For our good equipment does bring KICK to all,
And thus, the native hue of the Kickapoo Prarie is
Scattered all over these United States and Canada.
And with great pleasure, and not pity, at this moment,
With due regard, we realize your radio currents were tuned to
Our call, K I C K! Your heard us then - so know you now,
Our station is Mutual - largest of the networks.
Be all our programs remembered!

(by)

Jack D. Rhea,
NNRC - NRC

73's,

Lee Baker,
Chief Engineer

A station that could not resist exploring the inner meaning of QSLing (QSL, 1950).

Broadcasting House, London
West Front

THE BRITISH BROADCASTING CORPORATION

thanks you for reporting on reception of the

Empire Broadcasting Station at Daventry.

Due to the many stations that relayed the BBC, standard BBC policy for many years was to acknowledge reception reports but not verify them. This is one of the acknowledgment cards that was sent (1935).

you get your [club] to perform a real service, and commence listening down under.[14]

*All-Wave Radio* kept track of shortwave stations that did not verify and, as today, DXers tried every trick in the book to beat the odds. After nine attempts to QSL shortwave station I2RO in Rome, Italy, Captain Hall sent a registered letter to Il Duce himself, in response to which the Italian consul general in New York requested the captain's presence. The consul informed Hall that, as a result of his letter, Mussolini had conducted a thorough investigation of the conditions at 2RO. "Premier Mussolini thanks you so much for writing him," he said, "because he is interested in just these things. His policy is to investigate the smallest complaints." Hall informed the consul that many SWLs had blackballed 2RO because it was a poor verifier. Three months later he had a second audience wherein the consul informed him that things had been cleaned up at the station and that, among other things, they had hired an Englishman to answer correspondence. Hall's next report was answered in 21 days.[15]

And there were the usual mistakes, such as the saga of 500 watt CQN in Macao. It was Hall who first reported hearing it on a Sunday morning between 6 and 7 A.M.

> At first it faded, but the clarity of the signal was remarkable. There was absolutely no interference at all. Then, later the signal became steady. In all, it never became any stronger than R3. I sensed it was an Asiatic. Why? Because this is how I have logged all my Asiatics. To continue with what I heard. Then there appeared to be two men talking, one very faint and the other very loud. All the "louder voiced" man seemed to be saying was *Pe Co Pento* or *Pe, Co, Presto.* This was said over and over again, followed by a pause, and then he would continue. The fainter voiced man started talking in Portuguese and then in Chinese. Then truly oriental music followed. We had about forty minutes of this program. So CQN was pulled in, and here was another Asiatic snared....
> One has to do a certain amount of reasoning in order to identify the stations you hear.... With CQN, it was easy. Knowing of an Asiatic on 50 meters owned by Portugal and located in China, what more did I need when I picked up their signals?[16]

Other DXers also claimed hearing the station, until J. B. L. Hinds received a nonverification letter in response to his report. It turned out that the station didn't broadcast on Sundays. "All of us who thought we had the station on any Sunday were mistaken," he reported, "as that station never has broadcast on Sunday, and the station we did have was H1X, in [the Dominican Republic]."[17] All DXers know the feeling.

One thing that was different about QSLing was the cost. The 1934 postal rate

**WORLD-RADIO**
# Which Station Was That?
(POSTAL QUERY SERVICE)

No. M/452/1

*Name and Address*.... Mr Carroll H. Weyrich
4310, Evans Chapel Road, Baltimore, Maryland, U.S.A

### ANSWERS.

QUERY: B.B.C West Regional transmitter ( Washford) operating on
(1)
804 kilocycles and broadcasting London programme; a relay of a

(2) running commentary on the England-v. Australia Cricket Match
from Australia.

(3)

(4)

(5)

OBSERVATIONS :

DATE  May 5th 1937
J.G.A

**CONDITIONS OF POSTAL SERVICE :** A charge of sixpence is made for *each enquiry* ; this sum may be remitted by postal order or in postage stamps. Up to six queries may be submitted for an aggregate fee of 2s. 6d. Particulars, *accompanied by stamped addressed envelope*, should state date, time, approximate WL., call, or interval signal (if heard), language used, whether transmission was subject to fading or not, comparative signal strength, and any details of programme which may have been recognised. All queries should be numbered, legibly written, and accompanied by coupon published at foot of the "Which Station Was That ?" columns of *World Radio*.
**LETTERS** should be addressed to : Editor, *World-Radio*, Broadcasting House, W.1 ; and envelopes marked *Postal Query Service* in left hand top corner.
**NOTE :** If, owing to paucity of details submitted, or other adequate reason, transmission cannot be identified, a further query will be answered *free of charge*. In this case, the present form should be returned with the new application.

| FOR OFFICE USE ONLY |

BBC/N/20

An example of the type of letter that was issued by the BBC publication *World-Radio*, to help its readers identify stations they had heard (1937).

to the Americas was three cents an ounce (not a half ounce), five cents to the rest of the world. Of course, air mail to many areas became available only late in that decade. Registering a letter added 15 cents to the postage. An International Reply Coupon cost nine cents.[18] And you had to be careful how you addressed some reports. Letters addressed to "Russia" instead of "U.S.S.R." were returned.

One of the stranger contributions to the art of QSLing was the promotion in 1938–39 of something called SIRELA. Invented by a Professor Carlo Spatari, SIRELA was another word for "Spatari," a universal radio "language" that supposedly could be understood by stations everywhere and thus would be useful for writing reception reports. Professor Spatari had come to this country in 1905 when he was 17 years old, and was impressed that, despite his limited knowledge of English, he had little difficulty exchanging ideas with fellow musicians. SIRELA consisted of combinations of eight syllables based on the notes of the musical scale—DO RE MI FA SO LA "SI" "BO"—syllables that are phonetically the same in almost every language. The language was actually a code, each code word being composed of the note syllables, which were in turn "translated" into a phrase or sentence contained in a decoding book that was printed in the recipient's own language. Thus, for example, the ubiquitous program detail, "woman singing," was REBOMIRE.

It seems hard to believe, but it is reported that some DXers actually sent reports in the SIRELA "language" and received SIRELA QSLs. A station in the Dominican Republic and one in Ecuador, as well as the widely heard TG2 in Guatemala, supposedly had versions of their QSLs printed in SIRELA, and some also gave announcements in the language. While the whole thing is a little hard to take seriously, *Radio News* covered the subject in depth for four months.[19]

A lot of energy went into defining what did or did not qualify as a bona fide QSL, whether it was an actual verification or only an acknowledgment. This was partly because contests were often based on verified loggings, and the QSLs usually had to be submitted as proof. The decade of the 1930s was a period that provided some rather heated debates about QSLing. One such argument was over so-called "monitored veries." It started out fairly benignly in 1936 on the BCB side and came to a climax on shortwave.

By way of their general manager, two jointly owned and usually nonverifying local stations, WJRD in Tuscaloosa, Alabama, and WMFO in Decatur, Alabama, gave an Indianapolis DXer written permission to verify reports on their frequency tests on their behalf. The DXer pledged to personally monitor the tests, and he prepared a special two-color verification that he offered to DXers who submitted a correct report with return postage. It was an unusual arrangement, but it prompted few complaints.

As noted earlier, by the 1930s the BBC had adopted the policy of not verifying reports. In 1936 two well-known DXers started monitoring the BBC Daventry station at preannounced dates and times, and issuing QSLs for correct reports accompanied by five cents to cover costs, as in the earlier Alabama experiment. They did this, they said, to stimulate interest in the hobby. Reports had to be mailed within 24 hours and contain the names of at least two songs or an accurate description of a talk.

The process was well publicized in the hobby press, and the two public-spirited DXers not only were not criticized for their activities but were commended for doing a splendid job. Unfortunately, despite the organizers' apparent care in holding themselves out only as third-party monitors and not official BBC representatives, the QSLs implied something else. Headed "Daventry, England," and with the particular channel's call letters emblazoned in red, the card read: "Dear radio friend: Your report of reception of *[call letters]* on *[date]* has been carefully checked and found correct. Please accept this card as your verification of reception. Many thanks for your report. THE BRITISH BROADCASTING CORP. Checked by: *[signature of one DXer]* . Verified by: *[signature of the other]* ." It was postmarked "U.S.A.," but it looked authentic.

This prompted the BBC to demand an end to the practice. Soon a controversy arose, with much questioning of the motives of those involved. (Around the same time another DXer established a similar third-party arrangement for issuing verifications of reception for station ZBW, Hong Kong, which had ceased QSLing.) Although some 400 Daventry reports were verified in this way, with no indication that the process was other than completely honest, the whole thing was thought subject to abuse, and the organizers voluntarily ended it. At the heart of the matter, it looked too much like DXers buying QSLs from other DXers.

Of a similar genre were the "dime veries." In 1937 the Quixote Radio Club inaugurated a system whereby club headquarters accumulated reports for certain Latin American stations suffering from QSL lethargy, and forwarded them to the stations as a group. With your report you sent 13 cents: three cents to cover the cost of getting the report to the station, ten cents for the return postage.

The Quixote program started out with station HRN in Tegucigalpa, Honduras, but soon the QRC had 15 stations agreeing to honor reports submitted in this way, including some stations that were usually poor verifiers. Unlike the Daventry arrangement, these stations sent their own QSL directly to the reporter; the club was involved only in getting the report to the station. The service was available to QRC members and nonmembers alike.

The difficulty was that some of the stations adopted the practice of verifying *only* reports received in this way, ignoring others or returning them unverified with instructions to resubmit through the QRC. Some DXers were concerned that if the QRC program caught on, stations might insist that all reports be sent by way of such services and stop accepting direct reports altogether. Other DXers complained that, prior to commencement of the service, the "difficult" stations involved in the project *did* in fact verify some reports, and that those who had submitted proper reports to them and had them verified were being penalized by this homogenized reporting scheme. The QRC abandoned the project, probably because the service developed around the same time as the Daventry controversy.

The dime veries followed another unusual system that the Quixote Radio Club promoted among its members. It was called the connoisseur plan. Under the plan, a member could submit ten reports on any one or more of 30 stations, using QRC forms designed for this purpose. The QRC conferred on such members the title Connoisseur of Short-Wave Reception, and awarded them a linen-mounted National Geographic map. A log was sufficient if it included the name of a musical selection, part of an announcement, or the name of a product advertised. "Indeed," they said, "if English be not the language of the station, a lengthy report in English (which they do not understand) is not desirable. Rather than *what* was heard, the station really desires to know how well it was heard. Just enough to enable the station to identify its program, and no more, should be logged."[20] The QRC forwarded the various reports to the stations when a number sufficient to warrant a mailing was amassed. Members paid one-half cent per log. If a member wanted a particular log verified, he put a "V" in the margin and enclosed an extra six cents. He didn't have to write a formal report, and if the station didn't reply, the member's money was refunded.[21]

These novel approaches to QSLing eventually went the route of their BCB big brother, the EKKO stamp. Created by the EKKO Company of Chicago in the mid–1920s, these stamps were engraved, postage-size stamps carrying—for U.S. stations—a picture of an eagle (a beaver for Canadian stations), the letters "E-K-K-O" in the corners, and the call letters of the station. The stamps came in different colors. For $1.75 you could buy an EKKO stamp album that contained spaces assigned to the various stations, just like a postage stamp album. Other companies also sold radio stamp albums.

The album came with a supply of "Proof of Reception" cards, basically postcard-size reception reports. You sent the station one of these cards, or a regular reception report, enclosed a dime (some stations gave the stamps away), and the station sent you back its EKKO stamp, along with a QSL card or letter if they had one. Some people kept the stamps in the album, others affixed them to the veries.

Some stations had their own individualized verification stamps, a few used stamps from competing issuers (such as Bryant stamps, and the AFCO verification stamps sold for 5 cents each by NNRC vice president Arthur E. Foerster), and some did not use stamps at all. Later, the EKKO Company started selling the stamps directly to any listener who sent in the QSLs or a notarized list of stations verified.

The EKKO stamp fad ended when listeners started trading them. They

EKKO stamps were featured on this cover of *Radio News* that contained an article about "The New Radio Stamp Fad!" (February 1925).

Your reception O.K. If you desire an Ekko Stamp for verification, please forward 10¢.

FOLD

DIME HERE

FOLD

FOLD

BROADCASTER: PLEASE TUCK STAMP IN SLOT

MY NAME                          CITY                STATE

NUMBER                    STREET

**ON** _____ _____ **AT** ___:___ A.M., **I HEARD YOUR STATION** _____
MONTH   DAY              P.M.,                                    CALL LETTERS

**BROADCASTING THE FOLLOWING:** _____
ON THESE LINES FURNISH PARTICULAR

_____
IDENTIFYING INCIDENTS SUCH AS COMMENTS OF THE ANNOUNCER

_____
SEQUENCE OF NUMBERS, OR DEFINITE INFORMATION NOT APPEARING

_____
IN PUBLIC PRINT

PLEASE VERIFY THIS REPORT WITH YOUR STATION LOG. IF CORRECT PLEASE SEND ME YOUR EKKO VERIFICATION STAMP. THE ENCLOSED DIME IS TO COVER THE COST OF VERIFYING AND MAILING.

---

**My set is a** _____ **tube** _____
TYPE OF CIRCUIT

**Made by** _____
MANUFACTURER

**Our set is operated most between the hours of** _____ **and** _____

_____ **and** _____

∿∿∿∿∿

Our Preferences in Broadcasting Features are indicated in their respective order by numerals below:

**Orchestra**   ⎰ **Classical** ☐
               ⎱ **Jazz** ☐

**Songs**       ⎰ **Classical** ☐
               ⎱ **Popular** ☐

**Lectures** ☐  **Bands** ☐

**Sports** ☐   **Politics** ☐

_____ ☐   _____ ☐

_____ ☐   _____ ☐

*The Station will appreciate the above Information*

PRINTED IN U. S. A.
Chicago, Ill.
THE EKKO COMPANY, Daily News Plaza,
station.
an ekko stamp supplied by that
the broadcasting station to procure
convenience in communicating with
This card is supplied for your
**PROOF OF RECEPTION CARD**

remained an interesting radio collectible, but they lost their value as true verifications.[22] Verification stamps were resurrected in the late 1970s when international religious broadcaster Adventist World Radio began issuing verification stamps for their various shortwave and medium-wave transmitter locations and frequencies. The stamps come in various colors and show an antenna atop a globe, with a cross, a bible, and the letters AWR in the foreground, and the station location and frequency overprinted in black. They were originally intended to be affixed to a special QSL certificate issued during AWR Week in 1977.

The card that the EKKO Company suggested you send to the station to obtain an EKKO stamp.

*Part 3*

# THE WAR YEARS:
# 1940–1945

*Chapter 10*

# STATIONS AND VOICES OF WAR

THE ETHER WAS FULL OF COMPETING voices in 1940. Britain and Germany were locked in an all-out propaganda war. The British colonies of Australia, Canada, Newfoundland, South Africa, and India worked to develop improved shortwave signals, as did the French colony of Indochina. Europeans were particularly interested in increasing the strength of their broadcasts in order to reach American listeners; France adopted new wavelengths that for the first time allowed its broadcasts to be heard clearly in America.

As combat action picked up in the spring of the year, European broadcasts kept pace. Sweden offered evening transmissions, and Rome added Ethiopia to its network and scheduled broadcasts to coincide with American listening hours.

Soon, however, the German offensive began to overwhelm Allied shortwave broadcasts. Transmissions from Denmark and Norway were the first to be silenced, but not before Norway had made good use of them, as the *New York Times* noted in July 1940:

> During the Norwegian campaign short waves played important roles when directing ships from danger zones on the high seas of the north. Such special broadcasts, sent out in Norwegian and Danish were in addition to news broadcasts from London then instituted in Danish, Dutch and Norwegian. Orders to neutral vessels to head for neutral ports were carried by short waves.

Dutch announcer Edward Startz, whose broadcasts from Hilversum had been widely followed for more than a decade, disappeared from the airwaves on May 11, 1940, shortly after Holland was invaded by German paratroopers. The Brussels

Listeners were eager to hear war news directly from Europe (*Radio News and Short Wave Radio*, June 1935).

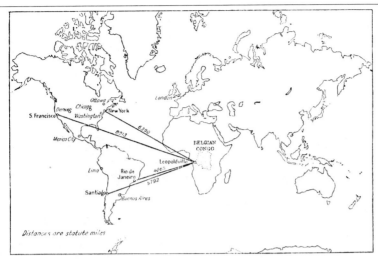

**B. B. S.**

*The B. B. S., New York office of the Belgian National Broadcasting Services, at the present time in London, gratefully acknowledges your report on the recent test programs of its Leopoldville station in the Belgian Congo, Africa.*

*We hope that very soon our voice is heard again, not only from England, the United States, and the Belgian Congo, but also from our liberated country of Belgium.*

*We thank you again for your courtesy which has been most helpful and is indeed very much appreciated.*

The BELGIAN BROADCASTING SERVICES is now operating from London, New York and Leopoldville. In Leopoldville (Belgian Congo, Africa) it has its own short wave station with a power of fifty kilowatts. The broadcasts from Leopoldville to the Americas are on 11.650 kilocycles, or 25.75 meters.

**During the occupation, Belgium broadcast to its countrymen via facilities in the then Belgian Congo (QSL, 1943).**

shortwave station went silent only a day or two later. Stations in the Congo and the Dutch Indies responded by throwing in their lot with the Allied side.

Stations in France worked frantically to keep up with their broadcasts as the Germans attacked Flanders, but all too soon the transmitters in Pontoise, Paris, and Bordeaux were silenced. Here, too, colonial stations proved valuable, as the French stations in Saigon and Martinique continued to broadcast.

"Generally speaking," declared the *New York Times*, "short-wave broadcasting at the moment boils down to a two-ring show staged by Britain and the Reich, with Soviet Russia and Italy working in on the sidelines.... Russia is using more power and more wave lengths at present to explain its recent moves toward the Balkans." The report further noted that women were filling in for male announcers on persevering British channels, "which have not missed a beat since the war began."[1]

The BBC heavily promoted its wartime broadcasts, sending out brochures that included schedules and detailed descriptions of its programming. One such brochure read, in part:

> Have you heard history in the making? You can hear it now—tonight and every night—coming to you instantaneously from the very centre of the struggle. It brings you the voices of the men and women of Britain, speaking to you while the sirens wail in the streets and the gunfire roars in the London sky.

*Above and facing page:* Verifications from the Third Reich (QSLs, 1935, 1936, 1939).

For six hours every night the voice of Britain speaks to Canada and U.S.A. in the North American Service of the British Broadcasting Corporation. Between 5:42 P.M. and 11:35 P.M. Eastern Standard Time, turn the tuning dial of your radio to 9.58, 6.11, or 11.75 megacycles to hear the authentic, human voice of the last stronghold of liberty in Europe.

You will hear the voices of famous Englishmen—writers and speakers whose names are household words wherever the English tongue is spoken—giving you, simply and sincerely, their observation and comment on what Britain is thinking and doing: the human side of history in the making....

You will hear up-to-the-minute news reports, news commentaries by leading journalists, eye-witness accounts of the day's events, and actuality broadcasts and recordings from the scene of action.

You will hear too the music and entertainment of a Britain that can be gay as well as resolute—troop concerns and vaudeville by stars of the London stage, dance music informally presented, and colorful feature programmes prepared by the Canadian Broadcasting Corporation's unit in England.

To Americans at least, the considerable Axis broadcasting efforts had little impact. "It is the consensus of most ... experts," said the *New York Times*, "that about the only people in this country who are directly affected by Axis shortwave propaganda are those who already have an Axis-ward inclination—the Bundists, the Anglophobes, our homegrown Nazi Fascists. Altogether their number is not great but their potentiality for trouble is."[2]

Germany Calling

via the D. J. Shortwave Stations

The Princeton Listening Center (see below) estimated that the number of persons who listened regularly to European shortwave and took it seriously was less than 1 percent.

[A] large number of people ... lose interest as soon as the novelty wears off, or as soon as they become convinced that foreign broadcasts, especially news programs, have little to offer which is not supplied by domestic radio stations. The turnover among short-wave listeners is considerable. Listening tends to be sporadic and haphazard. As sets get older, reception poorer, and novelty loses its charm, listening decreases and is soon given up entirely....

A few turns of the dial, a few attempts to get specific stations ... and [a person's] curiosity is soon satisfied....

**EIAR ENTE ITALIANO AVDIZIONI RADIOFONICHE**

**2 RO - 5 VIA MONTELLO - ROME**

Dear Sir,

We take great pleasure in verifying
your report concerning the following
program from our short-wave station
2RO 3.........; on August 19th.................1936
at 22:45 C.E.T. (Central European Time)
Yours sincerely,

*Eiar*

**EIAR was the wartime shortwave broadcaster in fascist Italy (QSL, 1936).**

[I]t was difficult for them to obtain information about shortwave programs, with the result that they ... gradually [gave] up the attempt and lost interest in the programs.[3]

## Official Monitoring

It was during the war years that, for the first time, activities on the shortwave bands were being carefully watched, both officially and unofficially, on both sides of the conflict. Germany was one of the first to set up a unit to monitor overseas broadcasts.

In the late summer of 1939 the BBC Monitoring Service came into existence. It operated first from the estate of the duc d' Orléans, Wood Norton, in Evesham (his family had been banished from France in 1886 as the pretender to the French throne, and so subsequently they lived in England), and in 1943 moved to a site at the Oratory School for Boys in Caversham, England. At the height of its wartime activities, BBCMS, as it came to be known, was listening to 1.25 million words a day in 32 languages, digesting them and making them available to key government leaders. It also had the distinction of monitoring many of Goebbels's "private" radio communications.[4] Even to the present day, BBC Monitoring continues to be the source of analyses of broadcasts from all over the world and up-to-the-minute information on station activity.

On this side of the Atlantic, with funding from the Rockefeller Foundation, the Princeton University School of Public and International Affairs set up the Princeton Listening Center (PLC) in November 1939. Its purpose was to study international wartime broadcasting from Berlin, London, Rome, Paris, and Moscow. Unlike the existing NBC and CBS listening centers, the Princeton Listening Center was completely independent.[5] It developed great analytical skills from recording and evaluating some 10 million words of broadcast propaganda. The PLC concluded at one point that about 150,000 Americans listened to the German shortwave station every day. The center prepared biweekly digests of what was broadcast, and distributed these to government officials, newspaper editors, radio commentators, and professors.

In November 1939, *Radio and Television* published a primer on the news correspondents who could be heard over various shortwave stations, under the headline, "Hear the Heart-Beat of WAR!" The listing ran as follows:

| Beamed to U.S. | Beamed to U.S. |
|---|---|
| BERLIN | PARIS |
| DJL—19.85 meters | TPA4—25.60 meters |
| DJB—19.74 meters | MOSCOW |
| DJD—25.49 meters | RNE—25. meters |
| DJZ—25.42 meters | |
| ROME | LONDON |
| 2RO3—31.13 meters | GSD—11.75 meters |
| 2RO4—25.40 meters | GSC—9.58 meters |
| 2RO8—16.83 meters | GSB—9.51 meters |
| 1RF—30.52 meters | GSG—17.79 meters |

### PARIS

NBC—Paul J. Archinard, representative; William Bird, Pierre Van Passen and Howard Claney, commentators; Walter Kerr, Taylor Henry, Kenneth Downs, John Elliott, William McGaffin, Robert Thompson, Henry Cassidy, Edwin Hartrick, Ralph Heinsen, Charles Foltz, Jr., Richard McMillan, John Lloyd, John S. Martin, Lawrence Hills and Joseph C. Fox, newspaper correspondents.

CBS—Thomas Grandin and Eric Sevareid.

MBS—Waverly Root.

### LONDON

NBC—Fred Bate, representative; John Gunther, Hugh Gibson, commentators; J. C. Stark. Wallace Carroll, Webb Miller, Ralph Barnes, William Hillman, Vernon Bartlett and David Wills, newspaper correspondents.

CBS—Edward R. Murrow, European director; Major George Fielding Eliot, American military expert; Bill Henry, newspaper correspondent; H. V. Kaltenborn, Paul Sullivan and other correspondents during crisis.

MBS—John Steele.

A postcard depiction of the FCC monitoring station in Nebraska (postcard, undated).

### BERLIN

NBC—Max Jordan, representative; H. R. Baukhage, commentator; Louis Lochner, Pierre Huss, Joseph W. Griggs, Jr., Melvin Whiteleather, Wallace R. Deuel, John McCutchean Raleigh and Richard Hottelet, newspaper correspondents.

CBS—William L. Shirer, chief of Continental staff; Ernest Pope.

MBS—Sigrid Schultz.

### DANZIG

NBC—William Bird, commentator.

### ROME

NBC—Richard Massock, newspaper correspondent.

CBS—Cecil Brown, newspaper correspondent.

### TOKIO

NBC—Newton Edgers, newspaper correspondent.

### SHANGHAI

NBC—Carroll Alcott, newspaper correspondent.

### GENEVA

NBC—Warren Irvin, newspaper correspondent.

(NOTE: Not all broadcasters listed here are making regularly

scheduled broadcasts. All three major networks also have news commentators whose broadcasts originate at points in the United States.)

The PLC closed its operations in March 1941 when the FCC, in cooperation
with the Defense Communications Board, established its own two-section radio
monitoring capability. One section consisted of the FCC Monitoring Service, radio
traffic police whose mission was to scrutinize illegal or suspicious transmitters. The
FCC Monitoring Service operated from 11 primary monitoring stations and some
80 substations equipped with powerful direction-finding equipment, some of it
located inside otherwise innocent-looking sedans. Chief of the FCC Monitoring Service was George E. Sterling, a former ship's wireless operator and an old FCC hand,
who was as much at home tinkering with radios as being the chief G-man of the
airwaves.[6]

The other branch of the U.S. government's monitoring effort was the Foreign
Broadcast Monitoring Service,[7] soon to be renamed the Foreign Broadcast Intelligence Service. From its staff the Princeton Listening Center supplied Lloyd Free,
the first director of FBIS, as well as the first assistant director, Harold N. Graves,
Jr. (the former PLC director).[8] Free had extensive experience with international
radio. He had also been editor of *Public Opinion Quarterly*, and he was said to be
one of the best students of content analysis in the country.

Utilizing four of the FCC's receiving sites—at Silver Hill, Maryland, Santurce,
Puerto Rico, Kingsville, Texas, and Portland, Oregon—within a year FBIS had 300
personnel working around the clock keeping the government informed of what the
enemy, as well as other stations, were saying. Eavesdropping on domestic broadcasting in Axis countries was also within FBIS jurisdiction. To accomplish its goals,
FBIS monitors combed the bands methodically, recording, translating, and tran-
scribing information thought to be important—600,000–900,000 words a day—and
distributing secret summaries to government agencies with a need to know the information.[9]

Nations often used their radio facilities to announce major events, and FBIS
was usually there when they did. On December 9, 1941, the FBIS East Coast station picked up Italy's declaration of war against the United States. It was the first
of many breaking events captured by FBIS over the years: Hitler's escape from the
July 1944 assassination attempt, Germany's capitulation to the Allies, and Japan's
acceptance of surrender, and then later the Korean invasion, the death of Stalin, the
fall of Dien Bien Phu, and the launch of Sputnik.[10]

In 1944 FBIS was looking for monitors to scan the shortwave bands. The job
paid $2,188. But by the end of the following year FBIS had become a victim of a
vendetta by two powerful congressmen, Representative Eugene Cox of Georgia and
Representative Martin Dies of Texas, against FCC chairman James Lawrence Fly.

The budget of the FBIS was cut drastically, and its monitoring functions transferred, first to the State Department, then to the Defense Department, and finally to the newly established CIA, where it became known as the Foreign Broadcast Information Branch and then the Foreign Broadcast Information Service. It became well known to 1950s DXers as the source of the periodic, multivolume publication, *Broadcasting Stations of the World*, which was published into the 1970s.

## Military and Related Broadcasting

World War II also witnessed the creation of the biggest radio network ever: the Armed Forces Radio Service.[11] AFRS was conceived as a major morale builder for American troops overseas. Although its roots can be traced back even farther than 1941, it had its start that year in the public relations section of the War Department's morale branch. The head of the morale branch was Brigadier General Fredrick Osborn, former chairman of the Rockefeller Foundation. Osborn changed the name of the branch to Special Services, and, with the help of its Information Services section head, Colonel E. L. Munson, Jr., and academy award–winning movie director (and Special Services major) Frank Capra, recruited one Tom Lewis to plan and develop a global information service for U.S. troops overseas. Lewis was vice president in charge of radio production at a large advertising agency. He had direct radio experience, having developed his skills in writing, announcing, and producing at WGY in Schenectady, New York. He was highly regarded in Hollywood, and he knew how to get things done. Lewis was the father of the Armed Forces Radio Service (and also the husband of actress Loretta Young).

AFRS was established in May 1942, and Lewis moved quickly to assemble a stellar cast of well-known writers, producers, engineers, and entertainers. He did not invent the concept of radio broadcasting for American servicemen, however. Short-wave station KGEI in San Francisco (see below) was already carrying a special mail-bag program for U.S. troops. Other private stations were producing some special programming as well, and transmitting an array of domestic "denatured" (commercial free) U.S. programming. The Office of War Information and the coordinator of Inter-American Affairs had produced some troop programs for shortwave, as had the army's Bureau of Public Relations. In addition, Press Wireless, Los Angeles, operated station KROJ, the Armed Forces Radio, which broadcast to American forces abroad virtually around the clock on 6100, 9897.5, 15190, and 17760 kc.

A lot of AFRS energy went into program production. The result was such World War II centerpiece programs as "AEF Jukebox" featuring "GI Jill," the girl next door that all the guys dreamed about (and who was, unbeknownst to them, already happily married to Mort Werner, later program director at NBC); "Command Performance," a creation of the radio division of the War Department's Bureau of Public Relations with an endless supply of the most popular talent in America; and the star-studded comedy show, "Mail Call."

At first AFRS had high hopes for shortwave, but it soon discovered that the relative difficulty of tuning shortwave in the field, combined with the poor receivers commonly available to individual GIs, meant that shortwave could not be the main delivery vehicle for direct radio entertainment overseas. It could and would be used for breaking events, like news, sports, and special events, but the bulk of the rest of the programming was soon being distributed by way of transcriptions, wired sound systems, and, in particular, low-powered AFRS broadcast-band stations. The first such stations were set up on an informal basis in Alaska in 1941 to serve the troops being trained there. Once AFRS was established, the number of military medium-wave stations throughout the world grew from three on January 1, 1943, to 274 in 1946 (this did not include other delivery vehicles such as broadcasts of AFRS programs by local government and commercial stations).

The shortwave capability of AFRS was provided by OWI and CIAA, which, by the end of 1942, had assumed joint control over American shortwave broadcasting. AFRS entered into agreements with OWI and CIAA for air time. After an initial period of reliance on the shortwave medium, the role of AFRS shortwave became the same as was envisioned in the early days of American civilian shortwave broadcasting: to relay domestic programs overseas for retransmission by local AFRS medium-wave stations. Secondarily, it served soldiers in isolated areas where there were no AFRS BCB stations. Still, by early 1945 AFRS was transmitting over 1,000 hours of airtime per week on shortwave. Signals were loud and clear in the United States, and AFRS programming would remain a welcome reminder of home to shortwave listeners for many years until AFRS (later AFRTS, the "T" for Television) ended scheduled shortwave broadcasting in September 1988.

Other American stations supplemented the AFRS role in important ways by serving both U.S. troops and the populations of occupied countries. ABSIE (American Broadcasting Station in Europe) was the American forces station in England. It was operated by the Office of War Information in cooperation with the BBC, and it began operations on April 30, 1944, using both medium and short waves. It was modeled after the BBC. With elaborate production facilities, it carried news, entertainment, prisoner-of-war broadcasts, and programs beamed to the enemy. In addition, it gave daily instructions in French, Flemish, Dutch, Danish, and Norwegian to the peoples of occupied Europe, and transmitted coded messages to the resistance. Some of its programs were carried in parallel by the BBC. ABSIE frequencies included 6010, 6070, 6090, 6180, 7070, 9625, and 9640 kc. It was estimated that, at peak, 80 percent of the radio listeners in occupied Europe tuned in to ABSIE.[12] The station left the air on July 4, 1945.

A station that played a special role in wartime was General Electric's KGEI in San Francisco. Originally licensed as 20 kw. W6XBE, the station began broadcasting on February 18, 1939, from the World's Fair in San Francisco. Primarily intended to showcase GE engineering, KGEI carried mainly NBC programming from medium wavers KPO and KGO. It was the only shortwave broadcasting station on the West Coast at the time. The Japanese soon began jamming it, and this led to the installation of two higher-power transmitters.

By 1942, when the station was moved to Belmont, California, KGEI was on the air 17 hours daily in nine languages, and was a favorite of American troops in the Pacific. Sometimes KGEI programs were fed through military public address systems, allowing hundreds to enjoy the programs. The notion that young recruits could hear news, music, and voices from home was miraculous in those days. As the *New York Times* noted under the headline "KGEI Tells Them" (July 19, 1942): "Nothing else, neither good news nor bad, neither programs of jive nor of classical music, according to frank testimony dug from the mail bag of shortwave radio station KGEI ... stirs the soldiers, sailors and marines on duty in the far Pacific as does the simple, straightforward introductory sentence to KGEI programs, 'This is the United States of America.'"

KGEI station manager Buck Harris was fond of telling the story of Commander William B. Goggins of the U.S. cruiser *Marblehead*, which, having suffered heavy damage from the Japanese, reached the West Coast after a three-month, 13,000 mile journey.

> One day the commander, in wrinkled summer khaki, walked into the KGEI office and said:
> "The officers' mess made a pledge that the first one to reach San Francisco should come in to thank KGEI before he does another thing. I'm the first man here."
> With that he started to leave.
> "Where are you going now?" Mr. Harris asked him.
> "Upstairs to phone my wife I'm back," he replied.[13]

KGEI also provided valuable service to American troops by responding to requests from General MacArthur to counteract Japanese propaganda during the buildup to Bataan. The station remained on the air in various forms throughout the years until its closing on July 31, 1994.[14]

Boston's WRUL also had a special place in the U.S. war effort. When the Germans, after invading Norway, forced Norwegian shipowners to broadcast instructions ordering their vessels to return to Norwegian ports, WRUL transmitted counter-advisories, telling the ships' captains about the true situation at home and urging them to head for Allied or neutral ports, which they did. WRUL's anti–German broadcasts in Serbo-Croat by former Paris correspondent of the Belgrade

*Pravda*, Dr. Svetislav-Sveta Petrovich, were a powerful incentive for Yugoslavia to fight the Germans. U.S. turncoat broadcaster "Mr. O.K." (see below) complained repeatedly that WRUL was inciting resistance in Germany.

WRUL also gave comfort to people under seige, "morale relief," as Walter Lemmon called it.[15] "'You have no idea,' wrote a listener from London, 'the comfort it has been to hear you on my portable wireless which I have on the floor beside me. I write this by the light of a torch held under the blanket—so you are receiving appreciation right from the front line!'" A Czech listener wrote, "Your broadcast is a bright star in the heavens of American liberty, shining into the darkness of our oppressed life."[16] Listeners used bed springs as aerials, or hid the antenna wire behind picture molding. The BBC provided similar support for occupied countries, especially France.[17]

The war years also saw the start of a special British forces network, the Forces Broadcasting Service. Initially under the control of the British Army Welfare Service, its first major broadcasting effort, the Middle East Broadcasting Unit, was headquartered in Cairo, from which the well-known FBS program, "Cairo Calling," emanated. In those days, FBS operated through existing civilian and governmental facilities, including the Egyptian State Broadcasting Service, the Palestine Broadcasting Service, Radio Lebanon, and Radio Baghdad. In order to increase its air time, FBS started setting up its own stations, specifically, on shortwave, in Jerusalem (call signs JCKW and JCPA), Haifa (JCLA), Cairo (JCJC, originally an Army Signals Corps station), and Nairobi, Kenya. Among the most popular FBS programs were "The Forces Hour" and the request program, "Ask for Another." And FBS stations were good DX.

Network headquarters was relocated to Jerusalem in 1946. When the British left Palestine in 1948, FBS Jerusalem headquarters (and the Jerusalem station) effected a harrowing evacuation to Malta. One thousand tons of equipment and a quarter million records had to be dismantled and moved under the noses of two opposing armies. The Malta station operated as part of the Middle East Land Forces, and broadcasts were soon going forth from two 7.5 kw. shortwave transmitters there. The Haifa transmitter, which also used shortwave, was moved to Cyprus. In the 1950s FBS was also heard on shortwave from Benghazi, Libya.

Two other well-known British stations of the time were Radio SEAC (South East Asia Command) in Colombo, Ceylon, and the British Far East Broadcasting Service in Singapore. Radio SEAC began operations in October 1944 as FBS experimental station ZOJ, transmitting a few hours a day over a 7.5 kw. shortwave transmitter (increased to 100 kw. in April 1946). The station provided good signals over the area of the Southeast Asia Command—an area extending roughly from Pakistan to Japan and Indonesia—and reached Australia, New Zealand, and the United Kingdom as well. It was also widely heard in the United States.

The Forces Broadcasting Service entertained British troops in the Middle East and many places around the world on shortwave. Today it is known as BFBS (British Forces Broadcasting Service), and operates mostly on FM frequencies (QSL, 1945).

THE FORCES BROAD-
CASTING     SERVICE

RADIO SEAC

THANK YOU FOR YOUR RECEPTION REPORT
DATED...*13/6/47*......OF RECEPTION AT
...*BROOKLYN*...*N.Y.*...ON.*15.12*..MCS.
AND WAVELENGTH OF...*19.84*...METRES.

(Signed)...[signature]..

FURTHER REPORTS AND SUGGESTIONS      For Wing Commander A. E. Smith
ARE WELCOME. PLEASE SEND THEM TO:-       *Station Director*
RADIO  SEAC, COLOMBO, CEYLON
(See Over)

Widely heard around the world, Radio SEAC was part of the broadcasting system serving British troops and nationals in South Asia. Its goals were entertainment, news, and a link to home (QSL, 1947).

Radio SEAC's broadcasting goal was to provide entertainment, news, and a link with home, the latter evidenced by a regular Sunday night program beamed to the United Kingdom. The station received as many as 8,000 letters a month, mostly record requests, and adjusted its weekly programming based on the number of requests received. There were no full-time announcers; all of the 20–30 voices heard over the air belonged to people who also did other things, like scripting, producing, and program compiling. The station operated until early 1949, when its facilities were handed over to the then new Radio Ceylon. The special U.K. program continued for a time even after that.

The British Far East Broadcasting Service (BFEBS) grew out of a British wartime propaganda station in India that shared facilities with All India Radio. It was run by the British Ministry of Information's Far Eastern Bureau. In 1945 the bureau merged with the Foreign Office's Far East Publicity Division (FEP), which was located in the Kandy, Ceylon, headquarters of the Southeast Asia Command. When the latter moved to Singapore at the end of 1945, some FEP personnel went with it and resumed broadcasting on a small scale from that city. They called themselves the Far Eastern Service of the Southeast Asia Command. Power was increased a few months later, and the station soon moved into its own Thomson Road studios.

Although BFEBS emphasized the British way of life and carried some English programs, these were intended mainly for a non–British, foreign language–speaking audience. The staff was small and worked long hours under stressful conditions. The Southeast Asia Command eventually closed down, and on-air references to it were dropped, effective June 1, 1946, when BFEBS began announcing as the Voice of Britain. The staff increased with new arrivals from England and Australia, and the station grew both technically and programatically until January 1948, when an economic crisis in England caused a cutback. The BBC took over in August of that year, and the station became the well-known BBC Far Eastern Station.

Another interesting development on the British wartime shortwave scene had to do with the BBC's Woofferton transmitter. In 1942 a major expansion of the BBC high-power shortwave capability in the United Kingdom was being planned, with new stations authorized in Skelton (Cumbria), Rampisham, and Woofferton. The plan was designed to increase BBC shortwave capabilities from the then eight medium-power units in Daventry to 37 high-power transmitters. The Woofferton site was equipped with the latest RCA 50 kw. transmitters, along with 26 dipoles, and was one of the most modern installations in the Western hemisphere. It came on the air in October 1943.

What is little known in modern times, and barely documented in British records, is that in August 1944 the station was completely dismantled and reinstalled at Crowborough in what has been called a desperate attempt to counter German V2 rockets. The British had thought it possible to jam the 30–60 mc. radio signal that they believed was used to launch the V2s, thus hopefully diverting them from their course. It was believed that the new RCA transmitters might do the job. The experiment was unsuccessful, however, and the transmitters were eventually reinstalled at Woofferton. The site was used intermittently thereafter until it was put into the service of the Voice of America on a more or less continuing basis starting in 1948.[18]

Another interesting Mideast station was FXE, Radio Levant, Beirut, which transmitted on approximately 8000 kc. with a power of 3 (later 10) kw. It was set up by the Free French Forces when they and the British entered Syria in 1941 to eliminate pro–German activity there. The station was destroyed and then rebuilt. Its signal reached many countries, including the United States, where the English news could sometimes be heard at 8:00 P.M. GMT. The station had another transmitter, Radio Damascus, on 7090 kc.

## Clandestine Broadcasting

The international radio to which both FBIS and ordinary SWLs were listening during World War II was dominated by both unusual stations and unusual short-wave personalities. One of the most interesting developments was the growth of clandestine broadcasters: stations whose location, and sometimes identity, were at least nominally unknown.[19] There was clandestine broadcasting in the 1930s, but the 1940s were the growth years.

Most clandestine stations were "black" clandestines, that is, stations purporting to be operated by one group but actually run by someone else, usually a government. A number of black clandestines were operated by the propaganda department of the Reich, known as the Büro Concordia. Its operations grew following the success of one of its early French-speaking stations, La Voix de la Paix (the Voice of Peace). The station operated simultaneously on 6040, 6270, and 7210 kc. Its programs expressed opposition to the French government and emphasized Germany's strength and the necessity of a peace policy in France. Among the Büro Concordia stations that followed La Paix were the Christian Peace Movement Station, Radio Humanité (French), and Station Corse-Libre (Corsican). Büro Concordia soon began concentrating on broadcasts to Great Britain, using station names like the Workers' Challenge (advocating worker strikes and sabotage) and Radio Caledonia (urging Scottish rebellion). The assistant head of the Büro Concordia was William Joyce, the British fascist who was better known as Lord Haw Haw (see below).

The most important of the Concordia stations was the New British Broadcasting Station. Announcing that it was operated from England by discontented British subjects, it was actually run by the German propaganda ministry and intended for what was in fact a nearly nonexistent British peace movement. It purported to broadcast uncensored news, which was invariably pro–Nazi. The station operated on 7305 and 11960 kc. Programs were 30 minutes long, opening with "Loch Lomond" and closing with "God Save the King." Signals in the United States were strong. The station was active until March 1945.

Another interesting German endeavor was Radio Debunk, the "Voice of All Free America." It was heard in the United States on varying frequencies, including 6275 and 7200 kc., around 8:30 P.M. EST, opening with "Star and Stripes Forever." It purported to use a mobile transmitter in the Midwest, but it actually operated from Bremen. The folksy presentations of "Ed and Joe Scanlon" were always anti–American.

The Germans also beamed black clandestines to other countries, including Italy ("Radio of the Italian Fascist Republic"), Russia ("Lenin's Old Guard" and "For Russia"), and even India ("Free India Radio"). The last may have been the same as the "Voice of Free India," reported to be heard by DXers at 11:30 A.M. EST on 15225 kc. It claimed to be broadcasting from "right under the noses of the English in India," and carried anti–Allied commentary in English, with the sign off preceded by a seemingly coded message of numbers and letters and an anti–British poem.[20]

The British were the leaders in black clandestine broadcasting. Their efforts were under the control of the Department of Propaganda in Enemy Countries, known informally by its address, Electra House, or EH (it later became Special Operations One, or SO1.) Among the British-run black clandestines that claimed to be operating from Germany in 1940 was Deutscher Freiheitsender (German Freedom Station), heard broadcasting anti–Nazi speeches at 4:00–5:00 P.M. EST on 10,100 kc.

Another Deutscher Freiheitsender had been operated by the German Communist Party from 1937 to 1939. It claimed to be in Hamburg, but it was actually located in Spain. A listener in Pittsburgh reported: "I ... tuned in my set on 29.8 meters and was successful in receiving the last part of the transmission of this station.... An appeal was made to the German Social Democratic and Communist party to solicit their members ... to listen to the daily broadcasts on the above-mentioned wavelength between 10 and 11 P.M., European time, which corresponds to 4 to 5 P.M., Eastern standard time.... The signal strength was fairly audible but very steady, without indication of blanketing on either side of the frequency."[21]

One of the European freedom stations heard by North American DXers was Sender der Europäischen Revolution, or the European Revolutionary Station, which transmitted on 9650 kc. and opened at midnight EST. On the air from October 1940 to June 1942, it was operated nominally by the British, but actually run by German members of a Marxist organization, Neubeginn.

A seemingly anti–Nazi, anti–Jewish, and anticommunist station that operated from May 1941 to October 1943 on 9545 kc. was "Gustav Siegfried Eins." It was on the air at seven minutes before every hour during the afternoon and evening. As RADEX described it, "As yet it has not been determined whether the station is pro-anything."[22] Later it was learned that the station was operated by the British, whose purpose was to emphasize the divisions between Nazi party leaders and the German military through presentations by the station's principal personality, the nameless "Der Chef." Gustav Siegfried Eins was the first of many British black clandestines, and the one that set the pace for those that followed. Intriguing theories to the contrary, the name had no special meaning whatsoever, Gustav Siegfried Eins being simply a phonetic spelling-out of GS1. At the start of transmissions, GS1 would call another "GS," such as "Gustav Siegfried Achtzehn" (GS18). A coded number message of no real significance—presented in a very basic code that it was hoped the Germans would gain some satisfaction in cracking—was presented first, followed by an address by Der Chef. The station became a model for American black clandestine broadcasting efforts that would follow.[23]

A second major British operation was Radio Atlantik. It went on the air on February 5, 1943, and operated 24 hours a day on 6220, 7420, 9760, 9800, and 9930 kc. Its broadcasts were aimed at the German armed forces, particularly navy and U-boat crews, among whom there was said to be a high level of discontent. Half the programming was popular music, and the station went to a great deal of trouble to make sure that it had the most up-to-date library of German and American recordings: music that would appeal to its target audience. The rest of the offerings were news and commentary, with different programs for different groups of soldiers. Listener Bob Hoiermann in Ohio reported as follows: "In the latest Russian offensive into East Prussia, DKSA reported the exact number of towns and inhabited places, and the number of people captured by the Russians. When our bombers have bombed towns in Germany, I have heard DKSA give the exact names of streets, etc., that were bombed out in these towns, and perhaps the number of people killed in certain factories that we had bombed. That is certainly revealing information that I'm sure the Nazis wouldn't want to be known!"[24]

In fact, Radio Atlantik pioneered the trick of providing bogus but well-researched and highly realistic first-hand reports about air-raid damage on German cities. These reports were intended to encourage defeatism within Germany. DKSA kept careful files of family gossip from POW letters and diaries, and these formed the basis of greetings and congratulatory messages to particular German soldiers. To further evidence its authenticity, the Deutsche Kurzwellendsender Atlantik would sometimes carry Hitler's speeches live, picking them up from German network stations or by way of a special captured teleprinter that received German news service broadcasts. The station also broadcast false reports of the Normandy invasion. Radio Atlantik, along with its medium-wave sister, Soldatensender Calais (which came on the air nine months after the commencement of Radio Atlantik's shortwave transmissions and which specialized in broadcasts to the German army), were among Britain's most successful black clandestine operations, and were widely accepted as bona fide German operations by the U.S. and neutral press.[25]

Soldatensender Calais was sent out over the "Big Bertha" of Britain's medium-wave transmitters, a 600 kw. BBC sender at Crowborough known as Aspidistra. Later in the war the transmitter's remarkably fast frequency-switching capability was used to mislead the Germans. The transmitter would come on the frequency of a local German station after the latter had shut down suddenly due to British bombing raids. Aspidistra would relay the programming of another German network station for a time so that the transmission would appear unbroken, and then the British would proceed with misleading announcements and instructions that appeared to come from the German authorities. These included such things as directives for women and children to leave their homes and head for evacuation centers, resulting in columns of people taking to the roads and obstructing military transportation.[26]

One of the reasons British clandestine broadcasting was more successful than that of Germany was that the Germans were forbidden to make derogatory comments about the Reich or its leaders. British clandestines were much more prone to be critical of Britain and the Allies and supportive of certain Nazi activities in order to make themselves credible in other areas.

Among other British black clandestine broadcasts were those aimed at Italy ("Radio Livorno"), France ("Radio Gaulle," "La France Catholique," and "Radio Patrie"), Czechoslovakia ("Radio Bradlo, Voice of the Slovak People"), and Poland ("Radio Polska Swit"), along with other countries as well. Another British black clandestine aimed at France was Radio Inconnue. It transmitted on 9750 kc. at 1:00 A.M. EST, and signed off with the reminder, "Think and act French."

Soviet black clandestines were of several varieties. Communist party exile stations included those beamed to Hungary ("Kossuth Radio"), Italy ("Radio Milano Libertad"), and Romania ("Romania Libera"). Radio España Independiente, heard by DXers as late as the 1970s, claimed to belong to the exiled Spanish republican government. Stations aimed at German troops on the Russian front included "Voice of the Front," "Sendung der Soldaten Wahrheit," "Der Soldatensender," "Polarsender Wahrheit," and "Deutsche Volkssender." Other freedom stations included those beamed to France ("Radio France"), Czechoslovakia ("Radio of Czech Liberation" and "Radio of Slovak Liberation"), and Poland ("Radio Kosciuszko"). Radio Moscow also carried a program called Radio Free Germany. It was the voice of the Free Germany Committee, a group of German Communist Party exiles and communist sympathizers.

There were, of course, some indigenous anti–German stations. One was operated from a mobile truck by Ernst Niekisch. He was a militant German nationalist who opposed Hitler and favored alliance with the Soviet Union. His station operated in 1938. Hitler's occupation of Austria that year led to the establishment of another genuine clandestine, the Austrian Freiheitsender, which was directed mainly at Austrian troops that had been integrated into the German Army. The station operated from a grocery truck within Nazi-controlled territory. It was tracked down in May 1938, but two of the operators got away and started another mobile, anti–Nazi station in Czechoslovakia that operated until the Munich Agreement was signed later in the year.

The United States was far behind the British in clandestine radio in Europe. American efforts were more modest, and were often driven by the tactical advances of U.S. military forces rather than broader strategic purposes. Many American stations used the medium waves. One of the larger and most successful of the American shortwave broadcasts was a series intended to lower the morale of German U-boat sailors. It was hosted by a fictitious, German-accented American naval officer, Commander Robert Lee Norden. The programs were aired seven times daily, three days per week, and sent out from transmitters in the United States and North Africa.

The United States also operated several black clandestine shortwave stations in China. On April 28, 1945, as the closing months of the war approached, the first of three such stations started broadcasting to Japanese-occupied areas from Chungking. It claimed to be run by an anti–Japanese resistance organization in Canton and headed by Liang Ting Han. The station used a 7.5 kw. transmitter and remained on the air for four months. For two of those months it was joined by two similar American stations broadcasting to Wuhan and Nanking. Each of the three stations sent out three 15-minute programs daily, and used the frequencies of 6812, 7880, and 9420 kc., respectively.

## Other Stations

There was much other interesting shortwave activity during the war years. In 1940, after the German occupation, stations in Poland and Czechoslovakia were given new German "DX" call signs, such as DXO, DXP, and DXQ. Germany established an enormous, coordinated, worldwide shortwave broadcasting network within its conquered territories. From Norway to North Africa, it could broadcast the same program simultaneously over transmitters in many different countries. At times even Japan was linked with this network.

An important station that changed hands twice during the war was Radio Luxembourg. A powerful medium-wave voice of popular culture (and, among British listeners, a major competitor of the high-brow BBC), Radio Luxembourg also transmitted on 7270 kc. shortwave. It fell into German hands in June 1940 and remained part of the Reich network for four years until it was recaptured, intact, by the Americans.

Paris Mondial was the French shortwave station. Though the government officially seized control of this private enterprise in 1939, its basic character remained unchanged. Largely a diversion for its former owner—government minister and businessman Albert Sarraut—it featured things like chamber music, classical dramas, and eighteenth-century comedies, all in total disregard of its listeners' wishes.

The North American service was not heard particularly well, and the station became victimized by fifth-column staffers who moved in as the station's poorly paid talent moved out. Paris Mondial also suffered from the omnipresence of two French radio personalities, Andre Obrecht and Paul Ferdonnet, journalists who had gone over to the Germans and were masters at playing on French sensibilities and persuading their fellow countrymen that the war wasn't really necessary. These "Radio Traitors of Stuttgart" acquired a large following among Frenchmen in all strata of

The "Radio Duel of the Dictators" took place with high-powered transmitters on the shortwave
bands (*Short Wave and Television*, July 1938).

| Donnerstag, 19. Mai | E.S.T. pm. | Thursday, May 19 |
|---|---|---|
| Ansage DJD und DJB (deutsch, englisch) | 4.50 | Call DJD and DJB (German, English) |
| Deutsches Volkslied | | German Folk Song |
| Grüße an unsere Hörer | 4.55 | Greetings to our Listeners |
| Funkbrettl | 5.00 | Radio skit |
| Nachrichten und Wirtschaftsdienst (deutsch) | 5.45 | News and Economic Review in German |
| Schöne Melodien | 6.00 | Gay tones |
| Deutschlandecho | 7.15 | Today in Germany. Sound Pictures |
| „Weiß ich doch eine, die hat Dukaten!" Der Heiratsvermittler in „Die verkaufte Braut" von Smetana. Verbindende Verse: Herman Roemmer | 7.30 | "I know a maid who is rich" The matrimonial agent in "The auctioned bride" by Smetana Accompanying verses: Herman Roemmer |
| Nachrichten und Wirtschaftsdienst (englisch) | 8.15 | News and Economic Review in English |
| Die schöne Stimme Schallplatten | 8.30 | Beautiful voices Records |
| Aufgaben und Ziele der deutschen Chemie (englisch) | 8.45 | Tasks and aims of German chemistry (English) |
| Nachrichten (deutsch) | 9.00 | News in German |
| „In dem Schatten meiner Locken" Franzi Formacher singt Lieder von Hugo Wolf | 9.15 | "Nestle in my locks" Franzi Formacher will sing songs by Hugo Wolf |
| Achtung, Gaunerstreiche! Eine bunte Folge moderner Methoden, Dumme übers Ohr zu hauen (Unseren Hörern zur Warnung!) | 9.30 | "There will be dirty work at the cross-roads!" A bright series depicting modern methods of deception (A warning to our listeners) |
| Nachrichten (englisch) | 10.30 | News in English |
| Grüße an unsere Hörer | 10.45 | Greetings to our Listeners |
| Absage DJD und DJB (deutsch, englisch) | | Sign off DJD, DJB (German, English) |

Program schedule of the German shortwave station (May 19, 1938).

society. The station changed after the Germans invaded Norway, but dissembled as the military threat against France became more serious. When the Vichy government came to power in France, Paris Mondial became "The Voice of France," and was well heard on 9520, 11845, and 15240 kc. It also relayed certain programs from Germany, during which time it was just called station "Y."

FZI, Radio Brazzaville, French Equatorial Africa, was set up in 1940 and supported General de Gaulle and the Free French Forces (Radio Dakar, on the other hand, followed the Vichy line). Radio Brazzaville had humble beginnings. It was started by two brothers, Captain François Desjardins and Lieutenant Pierre Desjardins. They had followed de Gaulle to Africa and, with a resourceful engineer named Defroyenne, managed to commence local operations after boosting to 350 watts a 50 watt amateur station that was located in a warehouse.[27] The station would eventually utilize 50 kw. and employ 65 Europeans and 100 Africans. It operated in 20 languages, and brought hope and consolation to millions of Frenchmen at home. Its English program was heard well in the United States, and closed with the "Star Spangled Banner." In October 1944 the station promised listeners that the Brazzaville staff "would be speaking from Paris" before many months.[28] Radio Brazzaville remained a popular favorite of shortwave listeners for many years after the war.

Radio Oranje was a program transmitted by the BBC and produced by Dutch refugees who were devoted to maintaining contact with the home populace (and the underground) in Holland. It went on the air in July 1940 on long, medium and short waves. Originally there were two programs, Radio Oranje and a more militant "De Branderis" (the lighthouse), the two combining under the Radio Oranje name in 1942. Early broadcasts stressed morale building, while later programs emphasized invasion instructions and postwar planning. At one point the station appealed to the Dutch to stock up enough food to see them through the Allied invasion period. The Germans later reported that "foodshops were stormed and housewives bought all their monthly rations as had been recommended by the London radio (Radio Orange)."[29] Resistance songs by the cabaret group Watergeus were also featured. The station closed down on June 2, 1945. Many of the Radio Oranje staff were eventually involved in the founding of Radio Netherlands.

Numerous regular stations were put off the air as a result of military action. In 1942 the International Short Wave Club reported:

> The Japanese invasion of several Far East countries have closed down a number of stations, much to our regret. We doubt, too, if the Singapore stations are on the air on schedule. Here is the list: In the Philippines were KZIB on 6.05 mc., KZRC on 6.10 mc., KZRF on 6.14 mc., KZND on 8.79 mc., KZRM on 9.57 mc., and KZRH on 9.64 mc. In Indo-China was Saigon on 6.18 and 11.78 mc. In Hong Kong was ZBW-3 on 9.63 mc. In Thailand was HSP-5 on 11.71 mc.

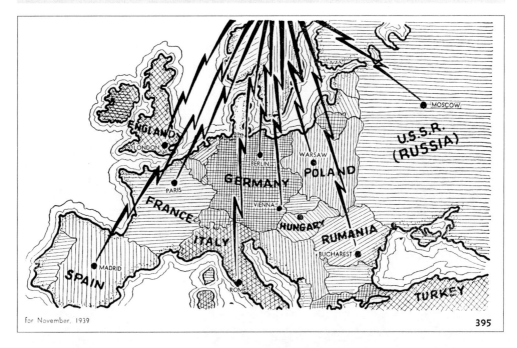

for November, 1939

395

A map of foreign news centers for various shortwave stations (*Radio and Television*, November 1939).

and HS6PJ on 19.02 mc. These last two still operate irregularly. In the Straits Settlement are ZHJ on 6.09 mc., ZHP on 9.69 mc., ZHP-2 on 6.17 mc., ZHP-3 on 7.25 mc., and ZHP-4 on 11.73 mc. This last station was operating 4:30 to 10:15 A.M., according to Simpson of Australia.[30]

Other stations came on the air, including PIRN, the Japanese station in Manila, heard until 9:00 A.M. EST on 6140 kc. and until 9:00 P.M. EST on 15320. And in late 1939 came this call from another station at 7:50 A.M. EST on 6130 and 11780 kc.: "This is a special broadcast for the United States. We do not expect that many listeners in that country will hear this transmission, but we would appreciate reports to be addressed to P.O. Box 412, Saigon."[31]

Tom Williamson reported the following:

[The year] 1941 gave several interesting stations: Radio Brazzaville, "The Voice of Free France," and on the opposite side, TPZ, Radio Alger, with its signature tune march, "Turkish Patrol," and call, "Avec le Marechal, famille, travail, patrie," in support of the Vichy government and Marshall Petain. Indonesia was still Dutch in those days, and PMA at Bandoeng [Bandung] was well received most days on the 18 mhz. band with the call, "Hier ist der NIROM de Batavia" and English language programs. The best entertainment, however, came from Cuba. A mighty signal nightly was heard from Havana, COK, with Latin dance rhythms and competitions with English

The National Company reminded readers that their high-grade shortwave receivers were in use at Radio Brazzaville, French Equatorial Africa, radio refuge of the Free French (*Radio News*, July 1944).

**THE BRITISH MALAYA BROADCASTING CORPORATION LTD.**

S I N G A P O R E
STRAITS SETTLEMENTS

*WE ARE PLEASED TO CONFIRM YOUR RECEPTION*

*of ZHP - 30.96 meters (9.69 m/c) on 22nd April 1939.*

The British Malaya Broadcasting Service operated from Singapore from 1938 (QSL, 1939).

announcements. More political loggings were non–Communist XGOY at Chungking, XGRS, Shanghai, with pro–German broadcasts, the Deutsche-Freiheit Sender (Free German Station), Radio Azad-Hind (the Voice of Free India), and Radio Metropole, supposed to be in France. A tragic note was added by the Singapore station, Radio Shonan, and Saigon, both operating under capture by Broadcasting Corporation of Japan.[32]

## Shortwave Traitors[33]

The war years saw the birth of a new brand of technological expatriates: nationals of Allied countries who would broadcast to their fellow countrymen on behalf of the Germans and other enemy powers. Most famous of the Europeans was William Joyce, widely known as Lord Haw Haw. There were actually two Lord Haw Haws, with Joyce taking over from the first, Norman Baillie-Stewart, about six months after the character's April 1939 debut.

Joyce was a British citizen by parentage but actually was born in New York City. After years as a minor fascist troublemaker in England, he moved to Germany where, with his upper-class accent and sophisticated manners, he was put in charge of the radio war against England, much of which he fought personally from behind the microphone. He came across as an agreeable sort, attacking first the British, then expanding his reach to America. Although he had an extensive audience in England, he misjudged the mood of his fellow countrymen as the military threats against Britain became more real. The British government finally had him executed in 1946.

America had more than its share of radio traitors, all of whom could be heard by listeners in the United States. Misfits mostly, the public outrage over their activities far exceeded their actual influence upon listeners. One of their number, Iowa's Fred Kaltenback, became known derisively as Lord Hee Haw. Senior among Goebbels's apologists, he was converted to nazism in 1936 while working on his Ph.D. in Germany. He played various on-air roles over the Zeesen station, such as host of the Thursday and Saturday feature, "Letters from Iowa," and the honest American character "Fred" in conversations between "Fritz and Fred, the Friendly Quarrelers." So committed was he to national socialism that he occasionally found himself in disagreement with less strident members of the nazi broadcasting hierarchy. He was captured by the Soviets in 1945 and died in their custody in October 1946.

Among the other American-born nazi apologists was roving reporter "E. D. Ward," actually Edward L. Delaney of Glenview, Illinois. A thespian of modest accomplishment, toward the end of the war Delaney fled to Czechoslovakia, after which he returned to the United States where an indictment against him was eventually dismissed. He served as a talk show host in Arizona in 1951, and a minor anti-communist activist thereafter until his death in an automobile accident in 1972.

Another of Goebbels's turncoat personalities was Robert H. Best, known as "Mr. Guess Who." A journalist driven by his limited career advancement, Best could be so rabid over the air that the nazis once preceded a series of his programs with the announcement that his views were not necessarily identical to their own. The intensity of his opinions was matched by that of a federal court that, following a jury verdict of guilty, sentenced him to life imprisonment. He died in prison in 1952.

A less dramatic personality was Donald Day, whose dispatches to the *Chicago Tribune* were said to have been at least as much fiction as fact. Day came to nazi propagandizing late in the war, and was driven principally by his hatred of the Soviet Union. He was confined and interrogated after the war, but the army wasn't interested in him and he escaped prosecution.

Chicago's Douglas Chandler always manifested a distaste for American society and mass culture. An occasional writer in the United States, he was once referred to as a walking nervous breakdown. Chandler was known over the air as Paul Revere, partly because of his envy of British organizational efforts to encourage the United States to participate in the war, and partly because the anniversary of the famous ride was only a few days before his first broadcast. He was not an easy person to like, often complaining about the inadequacy of amenities in the "U.S.A. Zone," as Zeesen's American service was known. He offended nearly everyone there. In 1947 he was sentenced to life imprisonment and a $10,000 fine. President Kennedy commuted his sentence in 1963.

Then there was highbrow nazi culture salesman and former Hunter College assistant professor Otto Koischwitz, known as "Mr. O.K." A man of considerable intellect and intensity, and a colorful and popular teacher, Koischwitz's drift into nazism was probably caused by the stagnation of his career, Hunter College having refused him a full professorship. He zealously embraced national socialism. On the air he played various characters, including the "Fritz" of Fritz and Fred, "Dr. Anders," counselor to an American girl who had supposedly come to Germany to live with her grandmother, and host of several programs designed for the better educated. Later he became a roving reporter. Despite press reports that he had committed suicide, he actually died in 1944 from heart failure and lung disease.

When it came to anti–American propaganda, the Germans believed in gender equality: there were many women among their stars. The best known (and best paid) was Mildred Gillars, widely known as Axis Sally. A theater student from Portland, Maine, who was mostly unsuccessful in her chosen field, Gillars eventually went to study in Dresden, where one thing led to another and she found herself broadcasting anti–American propaganda over the German radio. She and Otto Koischwitz became romantically involved while doing various joint propaganda programs —many involving American POWs—for the Reichsrundfunk. "Hello, gang," she would say. "Throw down those little old guns and toddle off home. There's no getting the Germans down." She was found living in cellars of bombed out buildings in 1948 Berlin, and was sent home to be tried for treason. Found guilty, she was sentenced to 10–30 years in prison. She was paroled in 1961 and died in 1988.

Another woman in service to the Reich was Constance Drexel, an early feminist and professional journalist who saw in Hitler's supposedly reformist ideas an agenda not unlike her own. Her on-air specialization was Third Reich cultural accomplishments. At war's end she was arrested by the Americans, but her indictment was eventually dismissed for lack of sufficient evidence.

Jane Anderson, known as the Georgia Peach, came to the microphone through her devotion to Generalissimo Francisco Franco. An alluring woman in her early years, she suffered greatly during a crippling period of imprisonment at the hands of Spanish Loyalists. While with the German radio she specialized in interviews and talk shows. Her career ended in 1942 in an odd way as a result of a broadcast she made describing the supposedly luxurious state of German restaurants. The

Allies rebroadcast the program to Germany, whereupon many ordinary (and increasingly poor) Germans became outraged at what they perceived as the excesses of the rich and famous. She was fired. Her involvement with the nazis having been fairly brief, the Justice Department declined to prosecute her.

Finally there was Gertrude "Gertie" Hahn whose program featured pro-nazi letters from her boyfriend, "Joe," supposed Berlin correspondent for the *Pittsburgh Tribune*. Her nazi sympathies notwithstanding, Gertie could not have been all bad because she continually importuned Americans to buy shortwave radios, even giving free on-air plugs to various manufacturers.

The two most famous American radio turncoats spoke not from Germany but from Italy and Japan. What, one might ask, was Ezra Pound, eccentric American poet expatriate and member of the international literati whose friends included Robert Frost and Ernest Hemingway doing in the studios of EIAR in 1940 broadcasting anti–American propaganda during 10-minute segments of the "American Hour"? The answer can be inferred from his last official residence in the United States: St. Elizabeth's Hospital for the mentally ill in Washington, DC, to which he was committed in 1946. As one observer put it, "it required 'an entire university course' to explain what was going on in the head of Ezra Pound."[34]

Pound had adopted Italy as his working home in 1925 at age 40. An increasingly irrational personality, he believed in a system of economics called social credit, which held society's central evil to be the control and centralization of money, credit, and finance in the hands of financial manipulators. The Italians thought his ideas foolish and recognized that, while he was well regarded as a poet, he had no following in politics or economics. This "pleasant enough madman" spent many hours before the microphones of Radio Rome, upholding and defending Il Duce's policies and practices and spewing forth a virulent strain of anti–Semitism on the shortwaves. "Europe calling, Pound speaking," began his broadcasts, for which he was paid the equivalent of $17 each.

Pound was indicted for treason in 1943 and turned himself in a year later as the Allies pushed through Italy. In 1946 he was found insane, and was committed to St. Elizabeth's, remaining there until released in 1958, whereupon he returned to Italy to live out his years. He died in 1972.

There is still uncertainty surrounding the story of Tokyo Rose.[35] There were many English-speaking female voices on the shortwave bands of the Pacific in the 1940s. Some of these announcers taunted individual units and soldiers, accurately predicted bombing raids, promised hot receptions at planned landings, and talked to soldiers about unfaithful wives. Others were just disk jockeys. Apparently, none actually identified themselves as Tokyo Rose, a generic name that U.S. troops used when referring to these English-speaking female personalities, many of whom broadcast from places other than Tokyo.

Iva Toguri was a California-born U.S. citizen who spoke little Japanese. The latest telling of her story suggests that she became trapped in Japan at the time of Pearl Harbor while on her first visit to the country. She was there to aid a sick aunt, and she was 25 years old. She took a part-time typing job at NHK, subsequently becoming, with some reluctance, a female disk jockey on NHK's English language "Zero Hour" program, which was produced by prisoners of war who had, also with reluctance, been pressed into propaganda service. Her programs were mainly of a fairly innocuous, entertainment variety, and, with her rather poor speaking voice, she was not one of the sirens of the airwaves. She apparently broadcast no anti–American propaganda; indeed, her pro–American views were well known at NHK.

Eva's problems were partially self-created when, at war's end and under some pressure, she found herself admitting to being Tokyo Rose without fully understanding what the name had come to mean in American parlance, and without appreciating the legal consequences of what she was saying. A jury eventually found her not guilty of seven counts of an eight-count indictment, but she was sentenced to ten years in jail and a $10,000 fine on the eighth count. It was a punishment of unusual severity. She served a total of more than eight years in prison, the only one of many Americans to be punished for playing Japanese wartime propaganda roles. President Ford pardoned her in 1977.

## Chapter 11

# LISTENING IN WARTIME

SHORTWAVE HOBBY ACTIVITY DECLINED at the end of the 1930s, and continued at a slow pace as the war's demands on the home front increased. The radio literature concentrated on military topics and the electronic service business. Equipment and station information were in short supply, as were DXers themselves. Many were in the military, and those who weren't were working long hours in the war effort.

Instability in staffing forced many clubs to slow their activities or close their doors altogether. In May 1942 the International Short Wave Club announced that, with the reduction in club advertising revenue caused by the preoccupation of radio manufacturers with government rather than civilian production, ISWC would go on an irregular publication schedule.

Stations also operated with smaller staffs, and this impacted their ability to broadcast special programs and QSL reports. In 1942 it was estimated that about 20 percent of the technicians of U.S. broadcasting stations were in the service.

The NNRC, which had been publishing weekly during the DX season, went to a twice monthly schedule in January 1942 and then once a month in June of that same year. Dues were dropped from $2 to $1. Clubs made special arrangements for members in the service. The NNRC waived membership fees for servicemen during the war, and some members made special contributions to pay for those who couldn't. The National Radio Club bulletin had a section called "Yanks in the Ranks." A serviceman's fund was set up, with 25-cent contributions defraying the cost of club membership for those in the armed forces.

The NNRC summer conventions were dropped after 1941. The club continued to publish DX news, although contributions from members were down considerably. The shortwave section was dropped in September 1942 when editor Earl R.

Roberts joined the military. It resumed in March 1943 in reduced size, and under new shortwave editor James J. Hart. In order to create interest in both shortwave and broadcast-band DXing, one member suggested a club contest for the largest number of verifications received during a given period. However, the board of directors turned the idea down. They felt that members in the service would feel slighted, that veries were too hard to come by during the war years, and that too many members were working long hours in war plants and would be too tired at the end of the day to participate.

Much of the NNRC bulletin was taken up with news of members in the service. The club published their addresses, and members on the home front were urged to write to them in order to keep up their morale. NNRC members were also repeatedly urged to buy defense stamps and bonds. Bulletin contributions from members picked up in 1944, and in 1945 the club returned to a twice-monthly publication schedule during the months of October through April. Annual dues were restored to $2 in December. Over the next few years the bulletin expanded rapidly.

At home, stations signed off a little earlier and verifications came through on wartime paper. Noted one observer, "I once got a verie on which was written a short note: 'We're conserving paper in support of the war effort.' There were government restrictions on the manufacture of paper."[1] The FCC ordered an end to request programs, so the NNRC Courtesy Programs Committee temporarily suspended the arranging of NNRC specials.

A desire to keep up with the belligerents overseas led to renewed interest in shortwave at home. Newspapers, many of which had dropped their radio sections altogether so as not to promote a competing medium, resumed radio coverage, and also did some opinion reporting based on foreign broadcasts. Among SWLs, particularly those who listened to the ham bands, the use of SWL cards grew. These cards looked similar to ham QSLs but were used by SWLs to report *hearing* ham contacts. Typically, the card showed a "call," like "SWL-W1" or "W3-SWL," the "W1" and "W3" corresponding to the ham radio districts (the specialized WRO/WPE/WDX listener "calls" of later years were still a long way off). SWL card swapping, where shortwave listeners exchanged cards among themselves, came into vogue. There was even a club for SWL card swappers, the Grand National SWL Club. It started in 1939 with dues of $1 per year.

Whatever the difficulties of shortwave listening in the United States, it became a dangerous pastime in some places overseas. In 1935 two men in Germany were sentenced to four years in prison and five-year loss of citizenship for having discussed politics while listening to a broadcast from Moscow. Five friends who listened received lesser terms. The seven were charged with "plotting high treason." In one year in Germany 1,496 persons were reported arrested for illegal listening, and 1,231 convicted.[2]

39 Golf Road       U. S. A.       Upper Darby, Pa.

MEMBER SHORT WAVE LEAGUE

SWL            SWL

Radio __W 1 N G__ Ur Sigs Hrd Hr __9:5:34__ At __11:28 P__ M. EST.

Qsa __5__ R __9__ Mod __good__ Qrh __4 MC__ Qrm __0__ Qrn __0__

Remarks __SO / W 8 J T H__

Bar Rdg __30.13__ Temp __68__ Wx __clear__

Rcvr~~XXXXXXX~~ Midwest - Majestic __Comet Pro Crystal Controlled__

Pse Qsl                  73                  J. A. BATEMAN

---

**STATE COLLEGE, PA., U. S. A.**

IN CENTRAL PENNSYLVANIA

GREETINGS FROM THE HOME OF PENN STATE

SHAKE! PSE QSL OM

QRC 392 Quixote Radio Club

S W 8 L

INTERNATIONAL DX'ERS ALLIANCE

Hrd at __11:___ EST

19.3___

UR Station _____

QSA (Quality) __5__ R ___

QRM ___ Without P-11

QRN ___

QSB ____

QSI ( Intelligibility) ___

RCVR: McMurdo Silver M-IV with Peak P-11 Preselector

Ant. Used

Inv. L _____ ft.

___ leadin off _____ end.

___ Doublet _____ ft. ____ (directional) _____

For Identification _____

_____ (over)

Best DX and 73's    R. B. OXRIEDER, 122 E. Hamilton Ave.

---

**RUTLAND, VERMONT, U. S. A.**

ISWC                 QRC

MONITOR STATION

**W4E1**

RADIO SIGNAL SURVEY LEAGUE

Reporting Signals of Station __W2-SWL__ as QSA __5__ R __9__

On __MAIL__ Meters, while __CALLING FOR MY CARD AND SENDING YOURS__ at __8:20P__ M-EST on __Oct. 9__ 193__8__

Interference ___ Static ___ Fading ___

Receiver: Hallicrafter SKY CHALLENGER II

73                 FRED ATHERTON, 23 Royce Street.

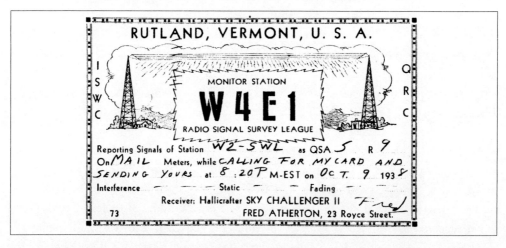

*Above and next two pages:* Many shortwave listeners utilized special SWL cards, principally for reporting the reception of ham signals, but also for swapping among themselves.

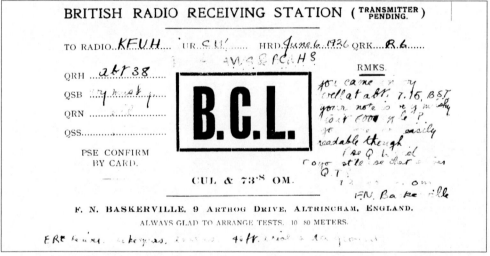

The German government tried to popularize inexpensive radios that could not receive signals from foreign countries.[3] In later years in Germany it was a criminal offense to tune in to antifascist stations, and some Germans were reportedly sent to concentration camps for doing so.[4] The situation was also dangerous in Japan. In 1937 the Japanese detained a Dane working for the Standard Oil Company of Yokahama because his American wife had brought back from the United States a "fine radio set" that the authorities suspected was being used as a transmitter.[5] There were many similar stories.

## SWLs vs. Hams

When the war started, amateur radio was enjoying sustained growth. Unlike today, with shortwave listening a hobby largely distinct from amateur radio, SWLs in the 1940s were thought of as a decidedly junior group whose proper goal was to join the ranks of the hams. "Some day we will get our diplomas, and will be working right alongside you Hams," wrote an SWL.[6] "I know that all my SWL friends are studying hard to get their tickets (Ham licenses)…. [A] lot of Hams answer our SWL cards. But *others do not*—and I would like to know why they are in this hobby of *Radio*? A lot of the Hams won't give us a break. They look upon us as a lot of *punks*! But they should remember that once they started from the bottom!" Wrote another: "In most cases, the SWL who sent you that card is a young fellow trying to get a start in amateur radio, just as you were once trying to do."[7]

One ham answered that the large number of reports he received from SWLs on his voice signal, versus the small number when he was operating in code ("CW" as it is called), showed that SWLs weren't really interested in learning the code that was necessary to obtain a license. Another was more explicit: he was "disgusted with the too frequent appearance of the familiar squawk of the Short Wave Listener, that the hams are not answering his SWL cards…. If the would-be ham is *so* interested in radio, why is he not studying theory or practising code? Radio jobs today are not filled by one who can make out an SWL card, but by men who are technically fit; who know theory; and have experience. I say, 'Enough of this.' Down with the SWL cards and make way for more study in the handbooks!"[8]

The dichotomy between hams and SWLs was sometimes stark. In the March–April 1941 issue of *RADEX*, Admiral Byrd said he would take up with the executive committee of his expedition the open question of whether QSL cards of the KC4 (Antarctica) amateur stations should be sent to reporting SWLs. The magazine reminded its SWL readers to "save their dope" on their loggings, in case the answer was favorable.

The SWLs felt they had a place, however. Said one: "[I]n time of National Emergency, it is the duty of every true American to do his or her utmost to cooperate with Government officials. Norway, Belgium, France and the others fell because of the 'Fifth Columnists.' Their favorite means of communication was by *Radio*. Here in America, there are many spies; and it is here that the *Shortwave Listeners* can help to defeat the purposes of these agents. The majority of Shortwave Listeners are equipped with good antenna systems, and with powerful, modern receivers. Every city or town has many Listeners who devote their spare time to shortwave listening. If these Listeners keep a lookout for subversive activities on these wave-bands, and immediately [notify] the police authorities or the district office of the FCC of any suspicious communications, the usefulness of Radio contacts would be greatly diminished. In this way, the *Shortwave Listener* would not only be helping to maintain safety and Democracy, but also to insure the lives and happiness of our loved ones."[9]

One club reminded its members as follows: "The enemies of America are depending on we short wave fans to carry their lies to our people, to create disunity and break up our morale. It is through we short wave fans that they hope to accomplish what they can not accomplish with guns and planes. So, whatever you hear that is not confirmed by our own forces, keep to yourself."[10]

The NNRC announced that the FCC had solicited the club's cooperation in collecting information on stations and frequencies and other data regarding shortwave broadcasting overseas, particularly in enemy countries. Members were urged to spend time at their receivers and submit their information to the club, which would in turn send it to the authorities. The bad news, however, was that the FCC's Foreign Broadcast Intelligence Service started compiling information on what DXers were hearing, and published a semimonthly bulletin, *Short Wave Schedule and Reception Notes*. About 25 hobbyists contributed to the effort. The publication resembled the shortwave sections of the club bulletins, and, while its distribution was restricted and its contents confidential, the clubs expressed their concern that continued publication after the war would pose a threat to the viability of the clubs themselves. FBIS assured them that they were a wartime agency whose appropriation would expire 60 days after the end of hostilities. In fact, the FBIS publication ceased in 1946.

Whatever the conflict between hams and SWLs, the latter had the last word during the war. Amateur stations were closed down soon after Pearl Harbor (save for limited War Emergency Radio Service activity on 112–116 mc.). However, there were no limits on the possession or use of shortwave receivers.

## Receivers

Once hostilities began, radio equipment manufacturers increased their wartime production to the maximum, with almost all units going to the war effort. Some were new designs, others were just slightly modified versions of regular commercial units. The initial shortage of radio equipment was so severe that the government had to buy used supplies from amateur radio operators. Manufacturers' advertising emphasized their contributions to the war effort and often referred to the various awards by which the government recognized companies for their work on behalf of the national defense.

In addition to the problem of wartime needs and the reduced availability of equipment for civilians, shortwave was losing some of its luster. It had not lived up to expectations as either an information or an entertainment medium, and this led to a decline in demand for both the consumer-type all wave sets and the hi-fi genre of shortwave receiver, both of which virtually disappeared during the early 1940s. Medium wave was clearly the band of choice, with shortwave left to the specialists, the SWLs, and amateurs whose interest in it was more than casual.

The exception was Zenith. Streamlining the name "Z-Nith" (an offshoot of ham call 9ZN, the station operated by the original company owners Ralph Mathews and Karl Hassel), Zenith started out in 1918 as Chicago Radio Labs. Commander Eugene F. McDonald, Jr., joined the firm in 1921 and was the main figure in Zenith's success. The company had a broad line of receivers, including many in the all wave category. However, it is best known among shortwave enthusiasts for the Trans-Oceanic series, which began with the introduction of the Zenith Trans-Ocean Clipper in January 1942.

The Clipper and its four progeny, which were produced from 1946 through the early 1950s, were large, wooden-cased portables covering the medium and shortwave spectrum in six push button–selected bands. The controls, besides on-off, volume, and airplane or slide-rule tuning, consisted mainly of slide switches for adjusting the audio. Most of the units contained a telescoping "Waverod" antenna and a removable "Wavemagnet" antenna (with window-gripping suction cups). Most of them also came with a foldout station log. The Trans-Oceanics were heavy (especially with batteries included), and, while they were not inexpensive, they brought shortwave to many new people.

The Trans-Oceanic *was* the home shortwave receiver of the war years and the postwar period. During the mid 1950s, a few RCA and Hallicrafters receivers of similar design provided some competition. The five early Trans-Oceanics were followed by four more modern versions, ending with the final Trans-Oceanic, the Model R7000, which was released in 1979.

Aside from the Trans-Oceanics, the communications receiver was the principal survivor after the all wave, hi-fi decline, and the big three of National, Hammarlund, and Hallicrafters were the chief manufacturers.

Among the National general coverage receivers built during the early 1940s were a few in the HRO series. Although the HRO would come into its own among hobbyists only after the war—when National would offer many variations of this classic receiver—the fighting in Europe caused Allied governments to order large numbers of HROs and other National receivers for the war effort. The United States did likewise when it entered the war, and during those times the number of employees at National jumped from several hundred to 2,500. The company went public in the late 1940s.

Hammarlund was also busy. Nearly all electronic equipment made in the United States during the war utilized Hammarlund-designed variable capacitors. At peak, ten different manufacturers were producing one million Hammarlund variable capacitors a month. Hammarlund also made many military variations of the Super Pro receiver line. In 1943 the company ran a series of ads highlighting the Super-Pro Series 200 receiver in service on the fighting fronts of Guadalcanal, Africa, Russia, Italy, and China. "We're proud that our equipment came through with our fighting

Readers were reminded that Hammarlund receivers were on duty in far away places (*Radio News*, July 1943).

men in the successful battles of Africa," said one; and "Hammarlund radio receivers are right in there pitching for nothing less than unconditional surrender of the rest of the Axis," opined another.

After the war the company weighed in with new receivers. In 1945 the HQ-120 was reintroduced as the HQ-129 for a price of $129. Though there were no additions to the Super-Pro line during the war years, the 18-tube SP-400, tuning up to 30 mc., appeared in 1946 (for $346).

In July 1940, Hallicrafters introduced perhaps the most famous of all its receivers, the standard-bearer of the day, the SX-28 Super Skyrider.[11] It was one of the best receivers available at the time, and it enjoyed widespread use in nearly off-the-shelf form by the military and by U.S. government monitoring posts. During the years 1940–46, some 50,000 SX-28's were manufactured.

The SX-28 was a favorite of the FCC's Radio Intelligence Division. It had 15 tubes and tuned up to 43 mc., with very good signal-to-noise ratio and good selectivity (but only fair quality fidelity). It had large handwheel controls for main tuning and bandspread. The main tuning control was direct gear driven, eliminating all backlash. The radio weighed 75 pounds and sold for $159, less speaker.

After Pearl Harbor, most Hallicrafters production was devoted to the military, with $150 million in government contracts. As with Hammarlund, Hallicrafters advertising promoted the company's role in the war effort. The company also awarded $100 per month to servicemen who submitted the best letters about their experience with Hallicrafters equipment in wartime (and $1 for "every serious letter received"). Still available on the home front was the Hallicrafters-produced Echophone line of low-priced ($19–49) communications receivers. After the war, Hallicrafters reentered the commercial receiver business with a variety of units, including three of its most famous: the modestly priced S-38 line ($39), introduced in June 1946; the somewhat more sophisticated S-40; and the much more expensive SX-42 ($275), a 15-tube set that was one of the first of the new postwar receivers.

An interesting chapter in wartime shortwave receiver development was the E. H. Scott "morale receiver." This was a multiband broadcast and shortwave receiver used for shipboard entertainment. The usual installation consisted of several receivers, each tuned to a different station, with all the audio signals fed to a series of individual amplifier-speaker units around the ship from which any one of the several channels could be selected. The important difference in these receivers was that they eliminated the minor emissions of the receiver's local oscillator, which most superhet receivers produced. The Germans had discovered how to detect these emissions from as far away as 100 miles, and thus pinpoint the location of distant vessels. Scott was the only company that had devised ways of reducing these oscillations to undetectable levels, and thus was able to sell a large number of "silent" receivers to the armed services without serious competition.

Many armchair commanders also used Hallicrafters receivers (*Radio News*, August 1942).

# Hallicrafters letter contest!

| |
|---|
| **$200⁰⁰ in Prizes EVERY MONTH** |
| **$100⁰⁰ 1st Prize** |
| **$ 50⁰⁰ 2nd Prize** |
| **$ 25⁰⁰ 3rd Prize** |
| **$ 15⁰⁰ 4th Prize** |
| **$ 10⁰⁰ 5th Prize** |
| **PLUS!** |
| **$1⁰⁰ for every letter received!** |

Here we go again. Another great Hallicrafters letter contest for service men. Write and tell us your first hand experience with *all* types of radio communications built by Hallicrafters, receivers and transmitters and the famous mobile radio station the SCR-299.

### Rules for the Contest

Hallicrafters will give $200.00 for the best letters received during each of the months of December, 1944, January, and February, 1945. (Deadline: Your letter must be received by midnight, the last day of each month.)

For every serious letter received, Hallicrafters will send $1.00 so even if you do not win a big prize your time will not be in vain. Your letter will become the property of Hallicrafters and they will have the right to reproduce it in a Hallicrafters advertisement. Write as many letters as you wish. V-mail letters will do. Just give us your own experiences in your own words.

Open to service men around the world. Wherever you are, whenever you see this ad, drop us a line. Monthly winners will be notified immediately upon judging and payment will be made as soon as possible.

Service men all over the world are learning that the name "Hallicrafters" stands for quality in radio equipment. There's a great and exciting future ahead for short wave enthusiasts. In peace time Hallicrafters will continue to build "the radio man's radio" and that means the best that can be made. There will be a set for you in our postwar line.

# hallicrafters RADIO

**Servicemen were rewarded for writing to Hallicrafters and telling them about their experiences with Hallicrafters receivers (*Radio News*, December 1944).**

Hallicrafters produced a different, less sophisticated morale builder receiver during the war under the names Echophone EC-6 and Hallicrafters RE-1 Sky Courier. These seven-tube sets, widely distributed among the troops, could operate on batteries, withstand extremes of temperature and humidity, take the tough conditions of the battlefield, and still get the GI's favorite programs.

Although wartime promises of major receiver technology advancements immediately after the war were not met (most mid–1940s sets were basically repackaged prewar equipment), many new receivers eventually came to market in the postwar years, and the field grew even bigger during the 1950s and 1960s. The big three continued to dominate the field, along with some new companies, like Collins, Heath, and Drake. Some of the smaller prewar companies, such as Howard, Patterson, and Breting, disappeared from the scene.

## Prisoner-of-War Messages

One of the more interesting aspects of home-front shortwave listening during the war was the monitoring of prisoner-of-war messages broadcast by stations in Germany, Italy, Japan, Singapore, Manchuria, and Batavia.

"The transmission for North America from Shonan (Singapore) on 9.555 megs. is being heard very well each morning in the Eastern United States," reported *Radio News* under the headline, "News of Prisoners Interned in Malaya." "News from the capitals of the world is given until approximately 6:20, by a man; then the woman reads messages from American prisoners of war interned in Malaya, for about 10 minutes. At 6:30 the man returns with a war commentary for 15 minutes, then until 7 o'clock more messages from war prisoners are read by the woman announcer."[12] The next month it was reported that "Following the 10 P.M. (EWT) [Eastern War Time] news broadcast from Berlin over DXL25 (7.28), DXJ (7.24), and DXP (6.03), messages from American prisoners of war interned in Germany are read by a woman announcer every evening except Sunday. Over these same stations on the 11:00 P.M. (EWT) newscast, news of American pilots wounded in action is generally relayed by the Berlin radio service."[13] And from Japan came the following report: "Radio Tokyo relays messages from American prisoners of war interned in Germany during the German hour each Saturday…. Messages from American prisoners of war interned in Japan are heard now 2–2:30 P.M. over JZI, 9.535, and JVW, 7.257, as well as JVW3, 11.725. Messages from Japan are also heard, 12–12:30 A.M. and 2:30–3 A.M. over JVU3, 11.897, JZJ, 11.70, JZI, 9.535 ("Humanity Hour" and "The Postman Calls" heard 2:30–3 A.M.)."[14] Prisoner news was also broadcast over Radio Australia.

Some of the prisoner broadcasts consisted of lists of POW names and addresses, and others included messages to friends and loved ones. A typical message might give the name and address of the soldier's mother, and read something like, "Dear Mom. Am prisoner of war in Germany. Not hurt or wounded. Am treated well and am in the best of health. Love, Tony."[15] Some family members, upon learning of these broadcasts, wrote to the radio clubs and asked their members to listen for any news about their particular loved ones.

The government, with its superior address information, operated a central clearinghouse for such messages, but many shortwave listeners made it a practice to monitor the messages and relay them to the prisoner's family direct, by card or letter. In July 1943 DXer Gus Magnuson reported that he had relayed 334 such messages, a number that grew to 3,368 by 1945.[16] Another monitor reported the following: "I've been in the radio game since 1916. At the present time I spend my spare time monitoring the Japs for the prisoner-of-war messages which I have relayed thus far to some 700 families. I have had some wonderful letters from the families of these boys. I 'phone for a radius of about 300 miles, which gives me a great thrill."[17] One of the Grand Old Men of DX, the late Arthur Cushen of Invercargill, New Zealand, reports having monitored news about a hometown friend over Rome radio. He personally delivered the news to the friend's mother four weeks after her son had been reported missing.[18]

Families often received news of the message from a number of different listeners, sometimes a large number of them. Most family members, not being knowledgeable about shortwave themselves, had not heard the actual message, and so they often responded warmly to listeners who relayed it to them. The files of the Committee to Preserve Radio Verifications contain a collection of such replies received by the late California DX veteran, August Balbi.

September 1942

I do want you to know that your postal card of the 4th in regard to my husband, Laurence M. Atwood, was deeply appreciated. No, I did not hear the broadcast, nor have I heard from him, though I had been advised by the Navy Department that he was a prisoner of war, taken by the Japanese from Wake Island. It is the kindness and thoughtfulness of people like you that makes the going a little easier. May I again thank you for your message and your thoughtfulness.

Sincerely,

(Mrs.) Loreace Atwood.

June 1943

Many thanks for your card, telling me of the message from my son, Donald. The message was repeated in the evening and my husband

and I heard it over a local radio station. Everyone has been so kind in writing me of the message, and I greatly appreciate it as it is the first word that we have had from him since war started.

Sincerely,

Mrs. Wm. J. Buckalew

May 1942

I write to thank you for your kindness in letting me know about the broadcast of my husband from Tokyo. We have been separated for one year and two months and I feel very sorry to think I didn't hear his voice. However, I am glad to know he is alive and hope I can send food soon.

Sincerely,

Helen A. Musto

June 1942

It was very good of you to write to me about my husband's radio message from Manchukuo. I have cabled to Dr. Simpson's mother in Scotland, telling her the cheering news. This is the first message I have had from my husband since Japan entered the war. It is a great relief to me to know that he is well and may soon be in East Africa. With many thanks for your kindness,

Yours sincerely,

Florence E. Simpson

July 1942

It surely did give us a lot of pleasure to hear of his broadcast, that he was well on the way home. We pray that the Good Lord will protect them on their way. Mere words are not enough to express the thanks I wish to convey to you for your kindness in thinking about others. We pray that God will bless and protect you and yours. Again thanking you, I am,

Yours very truly,

Thomas W. Early

# CONCLUSION

THE MID–1940S MARKED THE END of the beginning of shortwave broadcasting. Over 20 years had passed since the KDKA shortwave relays of 1923, and war had reshaped the world. The sun had not yet set on the British Empire, nor on the overseas possessions (and sought-after DX targets) of France, Portugal, and the other colonial powers. There was but one super power, America. Europe and Japan were exhausted, the communists had not yet taken control in China, and there was no thought of a Third World. When an out of the way place was heard on shortwave, it was real DX, not, as would become commonplace in later years, a high-power transmitter serving a small country's national pride.

Among the shortwave stations operating on shortwave in 1945 and heard around the world were such now-forgotten DX targets as the VOA, Algeria; ZNS, Nassau, Bahamas; KRHO, Honolulu; ZBW, Hong Kong; Radio Guadeloupe; Radio Andorra; Radio Congo Belge; ZQI, Kingston, Jamaica; and Radio Eireann.

In 1945 many shortwave stations, as well as other aspects of the shortwave listening scene that today's senior listeners remember, were still far in the future. Religious broadcasters 4VEH, Cap Haitien, Haiti, and TGNA, Guatemala City, would come on the air in 1950, followed by ELWA, Monrovia, Liberia, in 1955. Radio Free Europe would not commence broadcasting until July 4, 1950. Also in the future were the VOA transmitters in Tangiers, the Philippines, and Ceylon, and the VOA's floating shortwave station on the U.S. Coast Guard Carrier Courier. Although very high power was already in use on medium wave, most international shortwave stations, including the BBC, Canada, and the Vatican, operated with less than 100 kw.

With the decline of Heath Aircraft Company, its owner, Howard Anthony, came up with the idea of marketing electronic gear in kit form. The first Heathkits appeared in 1947, and Heath would go on to become the nation's biggest electronic kit manufacturer. That year also saw publication of the first edition of what is still considered by many as the international listener's bible, the *World Radio Handbook*. It was two more years before Hank Bennett wrote his first column for the NNRC. He would go on to be the *NNRC Bulletin* shortwave section editor, and a household name among shortwave enthusiasts for many years.

The now commonplace tape recorder did not come into general use until around 1950. In 1952 Gilfer Associates opened its doors as the first shortwave mail-order house. The Hammarlund HQ-180 appeared in 1959. Digital readout and solid-state technology could not even be imagined in 1945, nor could the idea that Japan would one day be the source of many high-quality shortwave receivers.

Radio would soon face the major battle of its life. Television, a medium that had been the subject of extensive experimentation for many years, made its consumer debut in early 1939. Though its full development had to await the war's end, companies like RCA, GE, Westinghouse, Stewart-Warner, Zenith, and DuMont started coming out with their first home television sets. By February 1, 1939, there were 22 TV stations in operation nationwide.

At the end of the 1920s, General Electric's manager of broadcasting, Martin Rice, made a prediction that would, if anything, prove an understatement.

> The day is at hand when reports of historic events, in which the peoples of several nations are interested, will be radiated from local radio stations. It is conceivable that in moments of international crises, leading statesmen will appeal to all nations through the medium of radio. International sporting events, of which there is an increasing number, will be found on the dials in many countries. The youth of tomorrow may learn his French from France and his German from Germany. Europe's best in music will reach the remotest hamlets in the United States and our best artists will gain a hearing throughout the world.[1]

In the mid–1930s, International DXers Alliance president Charles A. Morrison had written a four-part series in *Radio News* about the future of shortwave.[2] In addition to the need for better equipment, better development of the medium's commercial potential, and better frequency allocations, Morrison spoke of the desirable growth of "national radio voices." He said we were on the verge of a new "international unity." Shortwave would annihilate distances and bring with it peace among nations.

The development of shortwave in the 1930s and 1940s had indeed been breathtaking. For the first time, live radio broadcasting could take place with ease over great distances. The war years had proven that peace among nations would not be one of shortwave's natural byproducts. Whatever shortwave's future in the grander scheme of things, however, for the hobbyist, Hugo Gernsback's 1926 observation still rang true. "I can not imagine any greater thrill," he wrote, "than that which comes to me when I listen, as I often do, to a station thousands of miles away. It is the greatest triumph yet achieved by mind over matter."[3]

# NOTES

## Preface

1. Dick Cooper, "1981 NRC Convention Speeches," in National Radio Club, *The National Radio Club—50th Anniversary, 1933–1983*, p. 69.

## Chapter 1

1. Erik Barnouw, *A Tower in Babel*, p. 20. Brant Rock is located in the present town of Marshfield.
2. There are some other claimants for inventor of the superheterodyne. See Robert Champeix, "Who Invented the Superheterodyne?" *AWA Review* (Antique Wireless Association) 6 (1991): 97.
3. Gleason L. Archer, *History of Radio to 1926*, p. 105.
4. Bruce Kelley, "Rare Amateur QSL Cards," *Old Timer's Bulletin* (February 1993), p. 37.
5. For more discussion of other claimants to the title of "oldest" and "first," see Joseph E. Baudino and John M. Kittross, "Broadcasting's Oldest Stations: An Examination of Four Claimants," *Journal of Broadcasting* 21, 1 (Winter 1977): 61; Robert E. Summers, editorial, "A New First Station?" *Journal of Broadcasting* 3, 1, (winter 1958-59): 1; David L. Woods, "Semantics vs. the 'First' Broadcasting Station," *Journal of Broadcasting* 11, 3 (summer 1967): 199; and Mike Adams, "The Story of Charles Herrold—Broadcasting's Forgotten Father," *Antique Radio Classified* (October 1994), p. 4.

6. *Radio News* (August 1922), p. 314.
7. *Ibid.* (November 1922), p. 867.
8. *Ibid.* (June 1922), p. 1136; and William Peck Banning, *Commercial Broadcasting Pioneer: The WEAF Experiment, 1922–1926*, p. 132.
9. Detroit News, *WWJ—The Detroit News* (Detroit, MI: Evening News Association, 1922), p. 8.
10. Alfred N. Goldsmith and Austin C. Lescarboura, *This Thing Called Broadcasting*, p. 96.
11. *Radio News* (August 1922), p. 235.
12. *Ibid.* (December 1922), p. 1087.
13. For a description of the WJAZ case, see Marvin R. Bensman, "The Zenith-WJAZ Case and the Chaos of 1926–27," *Journal of Broadcasting* XIV, 4 (Fall 1970): 423–40. Early steps toward radio regulation, and the early activities of the Federal Radio Commission, are chronicled in Laurence F. Schmeckebier, *The Federal Radio Commission: Its History, Activities and Organization.*

## Chapter 2

1. "50 Years of Radio Broadcasting and DXing," *NNRC Bulletin* (December 1977), p. 1.
2. "Radio Threatening the Phonograph and Theater?" *Radio News* (June 1922), p. 1081. For the full story of the formation of the NAB, see David R. Mackey, "The National Association of Broadcasters—The First Twenty Years" Ph.D. dissertation, Northwestern University, 1956.

3. "Poles Smash Radio Set, Calling It Devil's Voice," *New York Times,* May 8, 1927, II, 6:2.

4. Carleton Lord, "1981 NRC Convention Speeches," in National Radio Club, *The National Radio Club—50th Anniversary, 1933–1983,* pp. 57–58.

5. Alfred N. Goldsmith and Austin C. Lescarboura, *This Thing Called Broadcasting,* p. 145.

6. R. W. Hallows, *Finding Foreign Stations—Long-Distance Wireless Secrets,* pp. 95–96.

7. "American Broadcasters Heard in England," *New York Times,* November 21, 1926, IX, 19:2.

8. "The Distance Fiend" by A. H. Folwell, appearing in *The New Yorker* and reprinted in *Radio Broadcast* (May 1925), p. 35.

9. Dick Cooper, "1981 NRC Convention Speeches," in National Radio Club, *The National Radio Club—50th Anniversary, 1933–1983,* p. 69.

10. William Peck Banning, *Commercial Broadcasting Pioneer: The WEAF Experiment, 1922–1926,* p. 90.

11. Carleton Lord, "I'm All Ears—A History of Broadcast Band DXing," in National Radio Club, *The National Radio Club—50th Anniversary, 1933–1983,* p. 142.

12. Charlotte Geer, "Another One," in *Radio Guide and Log* (Newark, NJ: *Newark Evening News,* 1927), p. 80. The occasional mention of "finally hearing the coast" in BCB circles refers to the ability of East Coast DXers to hear West Coast stations late at night as the movement of sunset from east to west brought with it the sign-off of stations in the same east–west pattern. This eventually left the bands free of all but the West Coast stations. The situation was later complicated by the presence of numerous "all nighters" that rarely left the air.

13. Orange Edwards McMeans, "The Great Audience Invisible," *Scribner's* (April 1923), p. 410.

14. Howard Vincent O'Brien, "It's Great to Be a Radio Maniac," *Collier's* (September 13, 1924), p. 15.

15. Goldsmith and Lescarboura, *This Thing Called Broadcasting,* p. 96.

16. ARRL, *Fifty Years of ARRL,* p. 36.

17. "Do We Need 'Silent Nights' for Radio Stations?" *Radio Broadcast* (October 1925), p. 754.

18. *RADEX* (midsummer 1931), p. 4.

19. This was undoubtedly the Art Blackbill who was present at the founding of the National Radio Club, and who served on its board of directors in 1938 and 1939.

20. S. Gordon Taylor, "Facts About DX Reception," *Radio News* (March 1933), pp. 519–20. The event was also reported in *RADEX* (March 1933), pp. 5–7.

21. For a more extensive description of the international tests, *see* Thomas H. White, "The International Radio Week Tests," *DX Monitor* (International Radio Club of America), November 22, 1975, p. 10. *See also* http://www.ipass.net/~whitetho/index.html

22 Clinton B. DeSoto, *200 Meters and Down,* p. 72.

23. Bill Taylor, "Vintage Vignettes," *FRENDX* (North American Shortwave Association, March 1981), p. 8.

24. Carleton Lord, "I'm All Ears—A History of Broadcast Band DXing," in National Radio Club, *The National Radio Club—50th Anniversary, 1933–1983,* p. 159.

25. Gordon Bussey, *Wireless: The Crucial Decade—History of the British Wireless Industry, 1924–34,* p. 11, quoting from *Wireless World,* February 4, 1925, p. 601.

26. Goldsmith and Lescarboura, *This Thing Called Broadcasting,* p. 307.

27. Marvin Hobbs, *E. H. Scott ... The Dean of DX,* is the correct and full title, pp. 11–12.

28. Carleton Lord, "1981 NRC Convention Speeches," in National Radio Club, *The National Radio Club—50th Anniversary, 1933–1983,* p. 58.

29. Herbert H. Steinkamp, "The Ultradyne for Real DX," *Radio Age* (October 1924), p. 18.

30. For an interesting group of photographs of the store of the Atlantic Radio Company, Boston, Mass., c. 1924, and related views, see the five-part series by Ron Boucher, "The Atlantic Radio Company," in *Antique Radio Classified,* May 1990, p. 6; August 1990, p. 6; December 1990, p. 4; May 1991, p. 6; and June 1992, p. 4.

31. *Radio News* (April 1928), p. 1097.

32. See Alan Douglas, *Radio Manufacturers of the 1920s,* vols. 1, 2, 3.

33. For an excellent review of the SW-3 and various aspects of reception using regen-

erative receivers, see Jim Hanlon, "The National SW3, or The Quintessential Regenerative Receiver," *Electric Radio* (August 1993), p. 10; and Roger Faulstik, "The SW3 and I ... and Other Stories," Part 1, *Electric Radio* (December 1993), p. 20; and Part 2, *Electric Radio* (January 1994), p. 20.

34. *Radio News* (April 1920), p. 535.

35. Tom Lewis, *Empire of the Air*, p. 153.

36. Douglas, *Radio Manufacturers of the 1920s*, 1:97.

37. Editorial in *Electrical World*, March 4, 1922, p. 419, quoted in Banning, *Commercial Broadcasting Pioneer*, p. 70.

38. There are many accounts of Sarnoff's role in the Titanic incident, the most thorough being in Kenneth Bilby's *The General* (New York: Harper and Row, 1986), pp. 29–36. Bilby reviews the facts of the event and the various accounts of it that were published over the years. He finds that Sarnoff himself was the first to promote a grossly exaggerated version of the story, which was then simply picked up and repeated. "[T]he later real accomplishments of Sarnoff's life were so profuse and so remarkable that any myth or legend seemed plausible" (p. 34).

39. For an overview of youth novels pertaining to radio, see Christopher Sterling, "Dime-Novel Radio," *Old Timer's Bulletin* (June 1992), p. 10. A series of articles describing the *Radio Boys* books in general, as well as each individual volume, may be found in Mike Adams, "Will the Real Radio Boys Please Stand Up?" *Antique Radio Classified*, September 1991, p. 8; December 1991, p. 20; May 1992, p. 16; and December 1992, p. 24.

40. Richard Arnold, "Early Radio and Scouting," *Antique Radio Classified* (February 1993), p. 18.

41. An excellent presentation about the spirited, long-forgotten debate over advertising in radio is Susan Smulyan, *Selling Radio: The Commercialization of American Broadcasting, 1920–1934*.

## Chapter 3

1. Keith Henney, "High Radio Adventure on Short Waves," *Radio Broadcast* (October 1925), pp. 789, 793–94.

2. For a brief history of KFKX, *see* Alice Brannigan, "KFKX: A Most Historic Broadcast Station," *Popular Communications* (October 1998), p. 14.

3. Gleason L. Archer, *History of Radio to 1926*, p. 329; "Eighteen Years of S.W. Broadcasting," *Short Wave and Television* (August 1938), p. 200; "Radio KFKX, Repeating Station at Hastings," *Radio Journal* (March 1924), p. 111; and "Re-Broadcasting, a New Era in Radio," *Radio News* (March 1924), p. 1242.

4. "Dear KDKA: Listeners Write from Around the World," *Pittsburgh Oscillator* (Pittsburgh Antique Radio Society; March 1990), p. 7. For a comprehensive history of the early days of radio transmission in South Africa, see Eric Rosenthal, *You Have Been Listening....*

5. Archer, *History of Radio to 1926*, p. 264.

6. Editorial, "The Short-Wave Era," *Radio News* (September 1928), p. 201.

7. "Why Short Waves Should Not Be Opened to Broadcasting," *Radio Broadcast* (February 1927), pp. 356–57.

8. "Eighteen Years of SW Broadcasting," *Short Wave and Television* (August 1938), p. 200.

9. "The New Pilot Universal Super-Wasp," *Radio Design*, 3, no. 4 (1931): 4–5.

10. *Radio and Television* (October 1938), p. 325.

11. "'Radio Row' Goes Short Wave," *Short Wave Radio* (July 1934), p. 9. See also "H. L. Schneck—A Legend of Cortland Street," *Antique Radio Classified* (July 1990), p. 6, and Francis H. Yonker, "Radio Row—Cortlandt Street 1930–1970," *Antique Radio Classified* (September 1998), p. 4. The correct spelling was "Cortlandt," according to a letter in "Letters—More on Cortlandt Street," *Antique Radio Classified* (November 1991), p. 13.

12. *Radio Craft* (May 1933), p. 647.

13. Douglas A. Boyd, "The Pre-History of the Voice of America," *Public Telecommunications Review* (December 1974), p. 42.

14. Fred Alan Fejes, "Imperialism, Media, and the Good Neighbor" (University of Illinois, 1982), pp. 133–36.

15. *All-Wave Radio* (October 1936), p. 441.

16. H. P. Davis, "The Early History of Broadcasting in the United States," in *The Radio Industry: The Story of Its Development*, p. 218.

17. *Short Wave Radio* (August 1934), p. 9.

## Chapter 4

1. Reminiscences of 1935, Tom Williamson, Peterborough, Ontario, Canada, 1985.
2. "British Short-Wave Broadcasts Unsatisfactory on 24 Meters," *New York Times*, December 4, 1927, XI, 14:7.
3. "A Race in the Ether," *New York Times*, May 26, 1935, XI, 11:7.
4. *Ibid.*
5. *RADEX* (October 1933), p. 18.
6. For a discussion of Axis broadcasting efforts, see Harold Ettlinger, *The Axis on the Air*.
7. "Unity of Germans Aim of Nazi Radio," *New York Times*, April 5, 1937, 12:1.
8. Editorial, *New York Times*, April 11, 1937, IV, 8:3. For a description of German wartime programming through the eyes of a "shortwave monitor war correspondent," see Henry B. Kranz, "War on the Short Wave," *Nation*, February 3, 1940, p. 123.
9. "Short-Wave Trails," *New York Times*, April 28, 1935, IX, 13:7.
10. "Radio's Short Waves," *New York Times*, February 27, 1938, X, 10:7.
11. "SOS from Madrid," *New York Times*, March 28, 1937, XI, 12:1.
12. *RADEX* (January 1934), p. 19.
13. *Ibid.* (December 1933), p. 29.
14. "Short-Wave Trails," *New York Times*, May 6, 1934, IX, 9:8.
15. *RADEX* (February 1934), p. 18.
16. *Ibid.* (May–June 1940), pp. 13–16.
17. For a closer look at the development of radio in Latin America, see James Schwoch, *The American Radio Industry and Its Latin American Activities, 1900–1939*.
18. *RADEX* (February 1935), p. 35.
19. "Short-Wave Trails," *New York Times*, April 28, 1935, IX, 13:7.
20. *RADEX* (April 1935), p. 9.
21. Lois Neely, *Come Up to This Mountain: The Miracle of Clarence W. Jones and HCJB* (Wheaton, IL: Tyndale House, 1980), p. 87. For another book about the founding and development of HCJB, see Frank S. Cook, *Seeds in the Wind* (Miami, FL: World Radio Missionary Fellowship, 1961).

22. *RADEX* (January 1934), p. 15. For an excellent review of Ecuadorian shortwave broadcasting, including the early Ecuadorian broadcasting families and their stations, see Richard McVicar, "It's in the Family: Ecuador on Shortwave," in *Proceedings 1992–93*, p. F27.1.
23. *RADEX* (September 1935), p. 11.
24. *Ibid.* (September 1933), p. 26.
25. For more on TI4NRH, see Don Moore, "The Unique Story of TI4NRH," *Monitoring Times* (March 1993), p. 18; and Adrian M. Peterson, "The Tiniest Radio Station in the World," *Popular Communications* (May 1990), p. 36. The Moore article includes observations from a visit to the site of TI4NRH.
26. "A Race in the Ether," *New York Times*, May 26, 1935, XI, 11:7.
27. "Short-Wave Trails," *New York Times*, June 2, 1935, IX, 8:8.
28. "China's Broadcasts Stir Wide Interest," *New York Times*, November 22, 1942, 35:1.
29. Harrison Forman, "The Voice of China," *Collier's*, June 17, 1944, p. 14.
30. James J. Halsema, "Early SWLing," *FRENDX* (North American Shortwave Association; August 1981), p. 11.
31. "Short-Wave Trails," *New York Times*, May 6, 1934, IX, 9:8.
32. *All-Wave Radio* (July 1937), p. 358.
33. "New Waves from Spain," *New York Times*, January 31, 1937, XI, 11:8.

## Chapter 5

1. Douglas A. Boyd, "The Pre-History of the Voice of America," *Public Telecommunications Review* (December 1974), p. 40.
2. Charles L. Rolo, *Radio Goes to War*, pp. 237–39.
3. Fred Alan Fejes, "Imperialism, Media, and the Good Neighbor," p. 147.
4. Harwood L. Childs and John B. Whitton, *Propaganda by Short Wave*, p. 35.
5. For a detailed treatment of the early days of U.S. shortwave broadcasting, see Michael Kent Sidel, "A Historical Analysis of American Short Wave Broadcasting, 1916–1942."
6. "European Music Crosses the Sea," *New York Times*, September 22, 1929, XII, 6:4.

7. "W3XAL on the Air," *New York Times,* September 14, 1930, IX, 10:2.

8. *Time,* July 17, 1939, p. 48.

9. "FCC Ruling Fought by Broadcasters," *New York Times,* June 6, 1939, 24:3; and "A Storm of Protest," *New York Times,* June 11, 1939, IX, 10:3.

10. Perry Ferrell, Jr., "Ultra-High," *All-Wave Radio* (March 1938), p. 136.

11. This discussion is informed in particular by chapter 2 in Lawrence C. Soley, *Radio Warfare,* and Robert William Pirsein, "The Voice of America: A History of the International Broadcasting Activities of the United States Government."

12. "Broadcasts of Good-Will," *New York Times,* November 29, 1936, XII, 12:1.

13. Fejes, "Imperialism, Media, and the Good Neighbor," p. 140.

14. Charles J. Rolo and R. Strausz-Hupe, "U. S. International Broadcasting—What We Are Doing, What We Must Do," *Harper's* (August 1941), p. 304.

15. Fejes, "Imperialism, Media, and the Good Neighbor," p. 147.

16. *Ibid.,* p. 134. Surely many of these requests were from people who were listening to a medium-wave rebroadcast, not direct shortwave.

17. "Offers a Subsidy on Latins' Views," *New York Times,* October 7, 1941, 13:1.

18. During the war, British intelligence paid for certain European exile programs over WRUL, supported several U.S. front groups that produced anti-Nazi programming over the station, and subsidized some WRUL commentators. It is unclear whether, or to what extent, station owner Walter Lemmon or the Rockefeller interests that supported the station knew of this connection. See Bradley F. Smith, *The Shadow Warriors* (New York: Basic Books, 1983), pp. 85–86; and Donald R. Browne, *International Radio Broadcasting: The Limits of the Limitless Medium* (New York: Praeger, 1982), pp. 151–52.

19. For an analysis of Voice of America programming during the war years, see Holly Cowan Shulman, *The Voice of America: Propaganda and Democracy, 1941–1945* (Madison: University of Wisconsin Press, 1990).

## Chapter 6

1. Unattributed and undated "History" of the NNRC, quoting one of Charlotte Geer's 1928 *Newark Evening News* radio columns. As noted in chapter 2, n. 12, the occasional mention of hearing the coast in BCB circles refers to the hearing of West Coast stations by easterners late at night as the movement of sunset from east to west brought with it the sign-off of stations in the same east–west pattern, eventually leaving reception from the West Coast relatively free of interference from other stations.

2. Reminiscences, Jack Jones, Jackson, MS, 1990.

3. Maynard Marquardt, "W9XAA—The Short Wave Voice of Labor," *Short Wave Craft* (February–March 1931), p. 348.

4. *RADEX* (November 1930), p. 16.

5. *Ibid.* (September 1935), pp. 51–52.

6. H. S. Bradley, "New Stations in Latin America," *Official Short Wave Listener* (June–July 1935), p. 107.

7. For some interesting browsing through pictures and information about vintage receivers, see Marty and Sue Bunis, *The Collector's Guide to Antique Radios*; Morgan E. McMahon, *Vintage Radio, 1887–1929*; and Morgan E. McMahon, *A Flick of the Switch, 1930–1950.*

8. For a year-by-year review of Philco's history and its line of radios, see Ron Ramirez, *Philco Radio, 1928–1942.*

9. Michael Kent Sidel, "A Historical Analysis of American Short Wave Broadcasting, 1916–1942," pp. 128–30.

10. For a comprehensive history of Zenith's early days, see John H. Bryant and Harold N. Cones, *Zenith Radio: The Early Years, 1919–1935.* With reference to the Trans-Oceanic, see John H. Bryant and Harold N. Cones, *The Zenith Trans-Oceanic—The Royalty of Radios.* For an interesting walk through the Zenith line from 1920 to 1946, see the *Zenith Radio Brochure Book,* a collection of reproductions of Zenith radio brochures and advertising for those years. It is available from Great Northern, P.O. Box 17338, Minneapolis, MN 55417.

11. *All-Wave Radio* (November 1935), p. 83.

12. *Ibid.* (November 1936), p. 524.

13. *Ibid.* (February 1936), p. 83.

14. For a history of the communications receiver, see Raymond S. Moore, *Communications Receivers, The Vacuum Tube Era: 1932–1981*, 4th ed. (Key Largo, FL: RSM Communications, 1997); and Elton Byington, "Communications Receiver History," *DX Ontario* (Ontario DX Association, April, May 1993), pp. 66, 69.

15. Moore, *Communications Receivers*, p. 5.

16. *Ibid.*, p. 4.

17. For an excellent review of the Hallicrafters line, and much interesting information about the company's start, see Max de Henseler, *The Hallicrafters Story, 1933–1975*; and Chuck Dachis, *Radios by Hallicrafters*. For more history of Hallicrafters and the most complete listing of Hallicrafters products that is available, see Chuck Dachis, *The Hallicrafters Company, 1932–1982: A Partial Product Listing Covering 50 Years of Production* (Austin, TX: Chuck Dachis, 1993).

In the 1950s, Bill Halligan sold the company and then bought it back. In 1966 it was acquired by a Northrop subsidiary, Wilcox Electric, where it became the company's communications equipment division. The last Hallicrafters shortwave receivers were the SX-122A and SX-133, introduced in 1969. Its last amateur offering, the FPM-300 transceiver, came on the market in 1972 and was available until the Hallicrafters division was sold to a Texas company in 1975. The Hallicrafters name disappeared soon thereafter. Bill Halligan passed away in July 1992.

18. B. Francis Dashiell, "An Analysis of the Super 'Skyrider,'" *RADEX* (February 1935), p. 3.

19. For a history of the National Company and some of its products, see John J. Nagle, "A Brief History of the National Company," *AWA Review* 1 (1986): 65. An interesting review of the annual National alumni dinners, with photos and vignettes about the company's early days, may be found in George Maier, "The National Company Alumni Dinner," *Electric Radio* (November 1992), p. 24.

James Millen left National in 1939 when the company expressed its intention to enter the home receiver market. He started his own company, the James Millen Manufacturing Company, which produced high-quality radio components and accessories. The National Company went through several changes over

the years, and, although it no longer manufactures shortwave equipment, it is still in business.

20. *RADEX* (April 1935), p. 13.

21. For a more complete review of the HRO, see Elton Byington, "HRO: Portrait of a Classic," in *Proceedings, 1992–93*, p. F31.1.

22. For a history of Hammarlund and some of its products, see Stuart Meyer, "Hammarlund Radio," *AWA Review* 2 (1987): 95. The company was sold several times during the 1960s and disappeared around 1973.

23. Marvin Hobbs, *E. H. Scott ... The Dean of DX*, p. 116.

24. *Ibid.*, pp. 111–12.

25. Hardy Trolander, "DXing With McMurdo Silver's Masterpieces," *FRENDX* (June 1981), p. 6.

26. For a brief, general comparison of the Scott, Silver-Marshall, and Lincoln receivers, see Norman S. Braithwaite, "E. H. Scott Receivers: 1931 Allwave Superheterodyne and the Competition," *Antique Radio Classified* (December 1993), p. 4.

27. Raymond S. Moore, *Hallicrafters Skyrider Diversity Receiver Fact Sheet* (Walpole, MA: RSM Communications, 1990), p. 10.

*Chapter 7*

1. Reminiscences of 1935, Tom Williamson, Peterborough, Ontario, Canada, 1985.

2. Daniel Stashower, "A Dreamer Who Made Us Fall in Love with the Future," *Smithsonian* (August 1990), p. 44. For other interesting reviews of the life and times of Hugo Gernsback, see Robert A. W. Lowndes, "Hugo Gernsback: A Man with Vision+," *Radio-Electronics* (August 1984), p. 73; "Hugo Gernsback, Founder," *Radio-Electronics* (October 1979), p. 62; and Paul O'Neil, "Barnum of the Space Age," *Life,* July 26, 1963, p. 62.

3. Stashower, "A Dreamer," p. 36.

4. *Radio News* (April 1928), p. 1175.

5. *Ibid.* (April 1933), p. 580.

6. *Ibid.* (October 1933), p. 198.

7. *Radio and Television News* (April 1955), p. 141.

8. The Flash Sheet had several "circuits," with a half-dozen DXers on each. In those pre-computer, pre–Xerox days, Ken would type up the Flash Sheet, using carbon paper to produce multiple copies, and start one copy around each

circuit. Each person on the circuit would keep it for a couple of days, make notes, and get it on its way to the next person.

9. *Short Wave Craft* (June–July 1930), p. 5.

10. *Ibid.* (December 1936), p. 467.

11. National Radio Club, *The National Radio Club—50th Anniversary, 1933–1983*, p. 147.

12. "Short-Wave Trails," *New York Times*, April 13, 1935, IX, 13:7.

13. Don Jensen, "The Legend and the Legacy," in *White's Radio Log* (North Branch, NJ: Worldwide Publications, 1985), p. 1.

## Chapter 8

1. Robert H. Weaver, "The Beginning of the National Radio Club," in National Radio Club, *The National Radio Club—50th Anniversary, 1933–1983*, p. 7.

2. *Short Wave Reporter* (Quixote Radio Club; October 1936), p. 2.

3. *Short Wave Radio* (July 1934), p. 42.

4. *Short Wave Craft* (January 1934), p. 529.

5. *RADEX* (October 1934), p. 32.

6. Unattributed and undated history of the NNRC.

7. IDA "Stop Press Sheet," June 1939.

8. For more on the IBC, see Donald R. Browne, "Radio Normandie and the IBC Challenge to the BBC Monopoly," *Historical Journal of Film, Radio, and Television* 5, no. 1 (1985): 3.

9. Carleton Lord, "I'm All Ears—A History of Broadcast Band DXing," in National Radio Club, *The National Radio Club—50th Anniversary, 1933–1983*, p. 143.

10. *The Globe Circler* (January 1935), p. 4.

## Chapter 9

1. William Peck Banning, *Commercial Broadcasting Pioneer: The WEAF Experiment, 1922–1926*, pp. 21–29.

2. Gleason L. Archer, *History of Radio to 1926*, p. 221.

3. *RADEX* (December 1933), p. 42.

4. *Ibid.* (April 1935), pp. 15–16.

5. Richard H. Cooper, "1981 NRC Convention Speeches," in National Radio Club,

*The National Radio Club—50th Anniversary, 1933–1983*, p. 65.

6. *NNRC Bulletin*, March 13, 1939, p. 9.

7. Morton W. Blender, "What About Reports?" *RADEX* (May 1937), p. 13.

8. Alfred W. Oppell, "Proper Reports Bring Verifications," *RADEX* (January 1934), p. 13.

9. *Radio News* (July 1934), p. 55.

10. *All-Wave Radio* (September 1936), p. 393.

11. *Ibid.* (January 1936), p. 20.

12. *NNRC Bulletin*, January 31, 1942, p. 6.

13. Cooper, "1981 NRC Convention Speeches," p. 63; and an excerpt from "DX News," March 28, 1938, printed in National Radio Club, *The National Radio Club—50th Anniversary, 1933–1983*, p. 111.

14. Letter from J. McDonough, W2GEI, operator, WBYN to Carroll Weyrich, Parkville, MD, July 9, 1941.

15. *Short Wave Radio* (March 1934), p. 32.

16. *Ibid.* (May 1934), pp. 6–7.

17. *Ibid.* (August 1934), p. 11.

18. *RADEX* (January 1934), p. 31.

19. E. Stanton Brown, "'SIRELA'—A Universal Radio Language," *Radio News*, November 1938, p. 34; January 1939, p. 31; February 1939, p. 38; and March 1939, p. 38.

20. *Short Wave Reporter* (Quixote Radio Club), March 1, 1936, p. 1.

21. *Ibid.* (October 1936), pp. 3–4.

22. For more on EKKO stamps, see Les Raynor, "Why Radio Stamps?" *Antique Radio Gazette* (Spring 1990), p. 12.

## Chapter 10

1. "The Changing Radio Map," *New York Times*, July 7, 1940, IX, 7:3.

2. "War of the Air Waves," *New York Times*, December 28, 1941, VII, 12.

3. Harwood L. Childs and John B. Whitton, *Propaganda by Short Wave*, pp. 306–7, 341.

4. Christopher Cross, "Listening to the World," *Radio News* (January 1946), p. 64.

5. For a discussion of these listening posts, see Gordon Gaskill, "Eavesdropping On the World," *American Magazine* (July 1941), p. 29.

6. For more on the U.S. government's radio monitoring efforts, see Cabell Phillips,

"G-Men of the Airwaves," *New York Times* magazine, September 14, 1941, p. 9.

7. Charles J. Rolo, *Radio Goes to War*, pp. 260–68; and Harold N. Graves. Jr., *War on the Short Wave* (New York: Foreign Policy Association, Headline Books, 1941), p. 64.

8. For an excellent review of the activities of the Princeton Listening Center, and findings based on its work, see Harwood L. Childs and John B. Whitton, *Propaganda by Short Wave*.

9. "War of the Air Waves," *New York Times*, December 28, 1941, VII, 12.

10. *FBIS in Retrospect* (Washington, DC: FBIS, 1971).

11. For a lengthy discussion of the origins and early days of AFRS, see Theodore Stuart DeLay, Jr., "An Historical Study of the Armed Forces Radio Service to 1946" (Ph.D. dissertation, University of Southern California, 1951). "[A] lighthearted [and highly informative] look at 50 years of military broadcasting" may be found in Trent Christman, *Brass Button Broadcasters*.

12. *Time*, July 16, 1945, p. 69.

13. "KGEI Tells Them," *New York Times*, July 19, 1942, VIII, 8:7.

14. For a brief history of KGEI, see Adrian M. Peterson, "Golden Gate Radio—Cannibalized in 1994?" *DX Ontario* (Ontario DX Association, October 1994), p. 62.

15. *Time*, November 3, 1941, p. 54.

16. Charles J. Rolo and R. Strausz-Hupe, "U.S. International Broadcasting—What We Are Doing, What We Must Do," *Harper's* (August 1941), pp. 303, 310.

17. John J. Michalczyk, "The Dice Are on the Carpet: The BBC and the French Resistance in World War II," in Nancy Lynch Street and Marilyn J. Matelski, *Messages from the Underground: Transnational Radio in Resistance and in Solidarity* (Westport, CT: Praeger, 1997).

18. James Wood, *History of International Broadcasting*, pp. 96–103.

19. Some of this discussion is based on chapter 2 in Lawrence C. Soley and John S. Nichols, *Clandestine Radio Broadcasting*; and Lawrence C. Soley, *Radio Warfare*.

20. *Radio News* (December 1944), p. 120.

21. "Secret Red Station Heard," *New York Times*, March 28, 1937, XI, 12:1.

22. *RADEX* (November 1941), p. 24.

23. For a detailed account of Gustav Siegfried Eins, see Sefton Delmer, *Black Boomerang*, pp. 30–80.

24. *Radio News* (January 1945), pp. 133–34.

25. For a detailed account of Radio Atlantik, see Delmer, *Black Boomerang*, pp. 81–141.

26. *Ibid.*, pp. 227–51.

27. Gordon Gaskill, "Voice of Victory," *American Magazine* (December 1942), p. 35.

28. *Radio News* (October 1944), p. 116.

29. *Ibid.*, p. 54.

30. *International Short Wave Radio* (International Short Wave Club, February 1942), p. 18.

31. *Radio News* (January 1940), p. 41.

32. T. B. Williamson, "Thirty-Three Years of DXing—DXing in the War," *FRENDX* (April 1971), p. SWC-1.

33. Some of this discussion is based on Horst J. P. Bergmeier and Rainer E. Lotz, *Hitler's Airwaves*, chapter 3; John Carver Edwards, *Berlin Calling*; and Rolo, *Radio Goes to War*, chapters 6, 8. Another interesting book on the subject is William G. Schofield, *Treason Trail* (New York: Rand McNally, 1964).

34. Humphrey Carpenter, *A Serious Character* (Boston, MA: Houghton Mifflin, 1988), p. 597. Another informative work on the politics of Ezra Pound is C. David Heymann, *Ezra Pound: The Last Rower* (New York: Viking, 1976). The texts of Ezra Pound's many shortwave speeches may be found in Leonard W. Doob, *Ezra Pound Speaking* (Westport, CT: Greenwood, 1978).

35. For the latest recounting of the story, see Russell Warren Howe, *The Hunt for Tokyo Rose*.

## Chapter 11

1. Richard H. Cooper, "1981 NRC Convention Speeches," in National Radio Club, *The National Radio Club—50th Anniversary, 1933–1983*, p. 68.

2. Charles J. Rolo and R. Strausz-Hupe, "U.S. International Broadcasting," *Harper's* (August 1941), p. 311.

3. "Tuned in Moscow, 7 Germans Get Jail," *New York Times*, November 1, 1935, 8:3.

4. "'Freedom Station' Hops, Skips and Jumps to Dodge a German Noise Barrage," *New York Times*, November 27, 1938, IX, 12:1.

5. "Japan Arrests Dane on Account of Radio," *New York Times,* February 9, 1937, 16:6.

6. *Radio and Television* (February 1939), p, 594.

7. *Ibid.* (June 1941), p. 128.

8. *Ibid.* (July 1941), p. 192.

9. *Ibid.*

10. *International Short Wave Radio* (May 1942), p. 12.

11. For the fascinating story of this Thunderbird of its day, see John Bryant, "The Hallicrafters SX-28: The Classic Shortwave Receiver," *Proceedings, 1992–93,* p. F30.1.

12. *Radio News* (June 1944), p. 128.

13. *Ibid.* (July 1944), p. 124.

14. *Ibid.* (February 1945), p. 86.

15. *NNRC Bulletin,* August 1, 1943, p. 2.

16. Carleton Lord, "I'm All Ears—A History of Broadcast Band DXing," in National Radio Club, *The National Radio Club—50th Anniversary, 1933–1983,* p. 157.

17. *Radio News* (October 1944), p. 54.

18. Arthur T. Cushen, "Secrets of Wartime Listening to Enemy Broadcasts," insert in Arthur T. Cushen, *Radio Listeners Guide,* p. 2.

## Conclusion

1. "European Music Crosses the Sea," *New York Times,* September 22, 1929, XII, 6:4.

2. Charles A. Morrison, "The Future of International Short-Wave Reception," *Radio News,* April 1935, p. 599; May 1935, p. 674; June 1935, p. 745; July 1935, p. 27.

3. *Radio News* (April 1926), p. 1395.

# READING LIST

The following references are listed for the benefit of the reader who is interested in further research on the history of various aspects of early radio and the radio listening hobby. They are diverse, and just a sample of the great many books that have been written on the history of broadcasting, shortwave, and early radio. Books no longer in print are often available through interlibrary loan. This list does not include all items that are mentioned in the notes.

## Books

American Radio Relay League. *Fifty Years of ARRL*. Newington, CT: American Radio Relay League, 1965.

Archer, Gleason L. *Big Business and Radio*. New York: American Historical Society, 1939.

____. *History of Radio to 1926*. New York: American Historical Society, 1938.

Banning, William Peck. *Commercial Broadcasting Pioneer: The WEAF Experiment, 1922–1926*. Cambridge, MA: Harvard University Press, 1946.

Barnouw, Erik. *A Tower in Babel: A History of Broadcasting in the United States, Volume I, to 1933*. New York: Oxford University Press, 1966.

____. *The Golden Web: A History of Broadcasting in the United States, Volume II, 1933–1953*. New York: Oxford University Press, 1968.

____. *The Image Empire: A History of Broadcasting in the United States, Volume III, From 1953*. New York: Oxford University Press, 1970.

Bergmeier, Horst J. P., and Rainer E. Lotz. *Hitler's Airwaves*. New Haven, CT: Yale University Press, 1997.

Briggs, Asa. *The Birth of Broadcasting: The History of Broadcasting in the United Kingdom, Volume 1*. London: Oxford University Press, 1961.

____. *The Golden Age of Wireless: The History of Broadcasting in the United Kingdom, Volume II*. London: Oxford University Press, 1965.

Bryant, John H., and Harold N. Cones. *Zenith Radio: The Early Years, 1919–1935*. Atglen, PA: Schiffer Publishing, 1997.

____. *The Zenith Trans-Oceanic—The Royalty of Radio*. Atglen, PA: Schiffer Publishing, 1995.

Bunis, Marty and Sue. *The Collector's Guide to Antique Radios*. Paducah, KY: Collector Books, 1997.

Bussey, Gordon. *Wireless: The Crucial Decade—History of the British Wireless Industry, 1924–34*. London: Peter Peregrinus, 1990.

Cain, John. *The BBC: 70 Years of Broadcasting*. London: BBC Information Services, 1992.

Childs, Harwood L., and John B. Whitton. *Propaganda by Short Wave*. Princeton, NJ: Princeton University Press, 1943.

Rosenthal, Eric. *You Have Been Listening....* Cape Town: Purnell and Sons, 1974.

Saerchinger, Cesar. *Hello America!* Boston, MA: Houghton Mifflin, 1938.

Schmeckebier, Laurence F. *The Federal Radio Commission: Its History, Activities and Organization.* (Service Monographs of the U.S. government, no. 65). Washington, DC: Brookings Institution, 1932.

Schwoch, James. *The American Radio Industry and Its Latin American Activities, 1900–1939.* Urbana: University of Illinois Press, 1990.

Settle, Irving. *A Pictorial History of Radio.* New York: Grosset and Dunlap, 1967.

Sidel, Michael Kent. "A Historical Analysis of American Short Wave Broadcasting, 1916–1942." Ph.D. dissertation, Northwestern University, 1976.

Smulyan, Susan. *Selling Radio: The Commercialization of American Broadcasting, 1920–1934.* Washington, DC: Smithsonian Institution, 1994.

Soley, Lawrence C. *Radio Warfare.* New York: Praeger, 1989.

Soley, Lawrence C., and John S. Nichols. *Clandestine Radio Broadcasting.* New York: Praeger, 1987.

Vipond, Mary. *The First Decade of Canadian Broadcasting, 1922–1932.* Montreal: McGill-Queen's University Press, 1992.

Walker, Andrew. *A Skyful of Freedom: 60 Years of the BBC World Service.* London: Broadside Books, 1992.

Wander, Tim. *2MT Writtle: The Birth of British Broadcasting.* Stowmarket, Suffolk, England: Capella, 1988.

Wood, James. *History of International Broadcasting.* London: Peter Peregrinus, 1992.

## Journals, Newspapers, and Periodicals

*Antique Radio Classified* is a monthly containing extensive advertising of antique radios and other early radio-related items, plus articles and other relevant information. For further information, contact Antique Radio Classified, P.O. Box 2, Carlisle, MA 01741.

The Antique Wireless Association is a national club for persons interested in early radio. It has a quarterly publication, *Old Timer's Bulletin*, and a series of periodic journals, *AWA Review*. For further information, contact the Secretary, Antique Wireless Association, Box E, Breesport, NY 14816.

The following is a list of other journals, newspapers, and periodicals that are mentioned in this work.

*All-Wave Radio*
*American Magazine*
*Antique Radio Gazette* (Antique Radio Club of America)
*Collier's*
*DX Monitor* (International Radio Club of America)
*DX Ontario* (Ontario DX Association)
*Electric Radio*
*FRENDX* (North American Shortwave Association)
*Globe Circler* (International DXers Alliance)
*Harper's*
*Historical Journal of Film, Radio, and Television*
*International Short Wave Radio* (International Short Wave Club)
*Journal of Broadcasting*
*Monitoring Times*
*New York Times*

*NNRC Bulletin* (Newark News Radio Club)
*Official Short Wave Listener*
*Popular Communications*
*Public Telecommunications Review*
*QST*
*RADEX*
*Radio Age*
*Radio and Television*
*Radio and Television News*
*Radio Broadcast*
*Radio Craft*
*Radio Design*
*Radio-Electronics*
*Radio News*
*Scribner's*
*Short Wave Craft*
*Short Wave Radio*
*Short Wave Reporter* (Quixote Radio Club)
*Short Wave and Television*

# INDEX

Bold indicates an illustration;
"n." indicates a reference number

Christman, Trent. *Brass Button Broadcasters.* Paducah, KY: Turner, 1992.

Cushen, Arthur. "Secrets of Wartime Listening to Enemy Broadcasts," in Arthur T. Cushen, *Radio Listeners Guide,* 2d ed. Invercargill, New Zealand: Arthur Cushen, 1990.

Dachis, Chuck. *Radios by Hallicrafters.* Atglen, PA: Schiffer, 1995.

de Henseler, Max. *The Hallicrafters Story, 1933–1975.* Charleston, WV: Antique Radio Club of America, 1991.

DeLay, Theodore Stuart, Jr. "An Historical Study of the Armed Forces Radio Service to 1946." Ph.D. dissertation, University of Southern California, 1951.

Delmer, Sefton. *Black Boomerang.* New York: Viking, 1962.

DeSoto, Clinton B. *200 Meters and Down.* West Hartford, CT: American Radio Relay League, 1936 (reprinted 1981).

Douglas, Alan. *Radio Manufacturers of the 1920s.* Vestal, NY: Vestal, 1988, 1989, 1991. Vol. 1, "A-C Dayton" to "J.B. Ferguson,"; vol. 2, "Freed-Eisemann" to "Priess"; vol. 3, "RCA" to "Zenith."

Douglas, George H. *The Early Days of Radio Broadcasting.* Jefferson, NC: McFarland, 1987.

Douglas, Susan J. *Inventing American Broadcasting, 1899–1922.* Baltimore, MD: Johns Hopkins University Press, 1987.

Edwards, John Carver. *Berlin Calling.* New York: Praeger, 1991.

Ettlinger, Harold. *The Axis on the Air.* New York: Bobbs-Merrill, 1943.

Fejes, Fred Allan. "Imperialism, Media, and the Good Neighbor: New Deal Foreign Policy and United States Shortwave Broadcasting to Latin America." Ph.D. dissertation, University of Illinois, 1982.

Fessenden, Helen M. *Fessenden—Builder of Tomorrows.* New York: Coward-McCann, 1940.

Fowler, Gene, and Bill Crawford. *Border Radio.* Austin, TX: Texas Monthly, 1987.

Goldsmith, Alfred N., and Austin C. Lescarboura. *This Thing Called Broadcasting.* New York: Henry Holt, 1930.

Hallows, R. W. *Finding Foreign Stations— Long-Distance Wireless Secrets.* London: George Newnes, c. 1932 (undated).

Hobbs, Marvin. *E. H. Scott … The Dean of DX—A History of Classic Radios.* Chicago: North Frontier, 1985.

Howe, Russell Warren. *The Hunt for Tokyo Rose.* Lanham, MD: Madison Books, 1990.

Jensen, Peter R. *In Marconi's Footsteps: Early Radio.* Kenthurst, NSW, Australia: Kangaroo, 1994.

Kneitel, Tom. *Radio Station Treasury, 1900–1948.* Commack, NY: CRB Research, 1986.

Lewis, Tom. *Empire of the Air.* New York: HarperCollins, 1991.

Lichty, Lawrence W., and Malachi C. Topping. *American Broadcasting: A Source Book on the History of Radio and Television.* New York: Hastings House, 1975.

Maclaurin, W. Rupert. *Invention and Innovation in the Radio Industry.* New York: American Historical Society, 1949.

McMahon, Morgan E. *A Flick of the Switch, 1930–1950.* North Highlands, CA: Vintage Radio, 1983.

_____. *Vintage Radio, 1887–1929.* Rolling Hills Estates, CA: Vintage Radio, 1981.

McNeil, Bill, and Morris Wolfe. *The Birth of Radio in Canada—Signing on.* Toronto: Doubleday Canada, 1982.

Mayes, Thorn L. *Wireless Communication in the United States.* East Greenwich, RI: New England Wireless and Steam Museum, 1989.

National Radio Club. *The National Radio Club—50th Anniversary, 1933–1983.* Cambridge, WI: National Radio Club, 1983.

Pirsein, Robert William. "The Voice of America: A History of the International Broadcasting Activities of the United States Government." Ph.D. dissertation, Northwestern University, 1970.

*Proceedings 1992–93.* Stillwater, OK: Fine Tuning Special Publications, 1992.

Radio Club of America. *Seventy-Fifth Anniversary Diamond Jubilee Yearbook, 1909–1984.* Westwood, NJ: Radio Club of America, 1984.

*Radio Craft "Jubilee Souvenir Number," March 1938.* Vestal, NY: Vestal, 1987 (reprint).

*The Radio Industry: The Story of Its Development.* Chicago and New York: A. W. Shaw, 1928.

Ramirez, Ron. *Philco Radio, 1928–1942.* Atglen, PA: Schiffer, 1993.

Rolo, Charles J. *Radio Goes to War.* New York: G.P. Putnam's Sons, 1942.